Speed Bump Himalayas

By Mark Giblin

To Mum and Dad,
Therese and Jonny

Foreword

By Sean Lock

Mark,

You asked me to write a foreword for your book about our trip to India in 1987 - or was it '86? Mere details. I said yes, without thinking what a foreword was. I never read them, or introductions. I just like to get on with the book. I do like that short paragraph at the beginning of books that tell you "The writer lives in Vermont and has a husband, one son and two dogs." I always think it's ironic how a writer who expects me to follow their endless musings on a trip to their grandmother's in 1962 and how they were frightened by a man in a shed can be so mean and blunt with details of their own life. If you want me to read your book tell me your favourite drink, whether you're scared of spiders or if you like speedway. I'd feel like I know you better.

I would suggest the same for you, but as the book is a sort of autobiography, there's no need.

Anyway, I don't know what to write because, like me, most people just get on with the book. Seems daft - like having cheese on toast before pizza, or mushroom soup ever.

So I'm just going to write down some words assuming no-one will read them. I might say something racist or sexist with the blissful security I have with my own thoughts. I might confess to an appalling habit that makes coke-ravaged bankers blush, or come up with a reactionary solution to the obesity crisis.

But I'm not stupid. There'll be one prick who'll read it, and before their thumbs have had time to warm up on Twitter, I'll be banished to reality shows on Channel Five (which isn't a great fall). Yes, I'm talking to you - there's always one: "Oh I must see what this book is about before I read it. I see it like a literary Sat Nav - gives me an idea of where I'm headed and what lies in store."

Wanker!

Just pick up the book and start reading it. What could possibly go wrong? I've read books that have had the first ten pages missing and have come to the conclusion that most books could easily start on page ten, twenty, or even further. Don't these writers realise how busy we all are these days, what with work, kids, Sky Sports and Facebook? You've got ten minutes at bedtime to get me interested and you blew it on a description of a plant in the hallway or the smell of coconuts.

I have to admit, I hate description in books. They never paint a picture for me - I just see a jumble of measurements, shapes and colours. Whenever a writer describes a face, I've no idea what the character really looks like. Stuff like "He had an aquiline nose, high cheeks and a curved brow, with open but deep set eyes." I see nothing in my head. I know he's not a troll, but it's like I'm playing Mr Potato Head - the Korean version. It'd be much better if they said "He looks a bit like Burt Reynolds in Smokey and the Bandit." I'd be "Yes, I know this guy." Or "She had a faint resemblance to Condoleezza Rice, but a Dutch version." It's interesting that in all the literary books I've read, no female character is described as having big tits, which is silly because the first thing you notice about someone with big tits is their big tits. It's not their hair, not their eyebrows, not the curve of the mouth - no, it's the tits. Men, women, children, even the Pope - even the celibate Holy Father of the Catholic Church. The first thing he'd notice when Sister Brenda brought him his cucumber eye bath after lunch is her massive knockers. He'd think "Father, you are testing me again, but I will not fail because I am the fucking Pope."

Anyway, the point I'm trying to make is that the human eye forces us to observe things, whether our aesthetic or imagined selves want it to. Or maybe women with big tits don't lead interesting enough lives to make it into novels. Maybe they're just forever in the background pulling pints.

But enough waffling; time for some forewording.

Just had a thought - if I do a really bad job of this foreword, it might put off the one freak that bothers to read it from continuing on with the book! So I will try harder.

This story is about a trip we took at what now appears to have been crossroads in our lives. It was briefly planned, on my part, as a reaction to other things going on in my life. I'd been at a drama school in London and had got myself thrown out after the first year (I wanted to leave but would have had to pay my grant back if I left, so I had to be ejected). I didn't want to be an actor - that was the main thing I'd learnt. I was also in an unsatisfying but intense relationship (for both of us) and thought that the best solution to the mess I'd made by the time I'd reached my mid-twenties, was to escape.

Travel had been a great way of avoiding the decisions that most young people faced - it was a solution that many of us who'd left school in the late seventies and early eighties considered. You left school in 1979, me in 1981 - just when Thatcher's Britain was taking shape. Our prospects didn't seem good, especially when you looked at our pitiful academic status. Collectively we might have scraped into a newly built Polytechnic in Lincolnshire. But only if we'd pooled together my one A-level, my brother Paul's HNC, and your five O-levels. Our travelling was also fuelled by books like On the Road, which I know will cause snorts of derision from many quarters, but it gave us a more exciting and romantic illusion than anything Woking could offer.

When I look back on our 'travelling' now, I see it very differently. We thought we were being brave, adventurous fools, unprepared to spend a life shackled to a desk or a lathe. But really we were being very indulgent. We just did whatever we wanted to do, wherever we could, for as long as we could get away with it. I'm not saying there's anything wrong with that - it was brilliant. I'd recommend it to everyone. Just don't delude yourself into thinking you're some kind of voyager on the "horizons of experience". We just didn't like work, or England. Well, the one Thatcher was creating.

Our trip to India had many repercussions for both of us, but the main one for me was that I realised I wasn't cut out for a life on the road. A bit like going to drama school taught me I wasn't an actor, that trip hammered home the fact that I wasn't a real traveller. I wasn't a cool guy who could drift around the globe, effortlessly soaking up experiences. I wasn't one of those hip, loose limbed, sun-fuelled voyagers that glide through street markets with a wry inner smile. I thought I was. I thought I was someone who thrived on embracing strange cultures, who observed chaos and beauty with the same calm delight.

But no. India in July knocked that out of me, with a big shitty stick.

I soon realised I was too neurotic, too attached to comfort and most of all - I was trained to work. I couldn't sit around just staring at stuff or drinking sweet tea whilst watching a grown man vainly trying to sell two corn on the cobs so he could feed his family.

I was brought up with a fierce work ethic by my parents. Both aspirant working class people, they programmed me to believe that staring at anything for more than a minute meant the your whole world would crumble beneath you. I remember the summer holidays when I was 14. Two weeks in, I was being harassed into getting a job. It was like: "You've had two weeks of idleness - that's enough, get busy or you'll end up masturbating or burning down libraries." I ended up walking the streets with a bucket of soapy water and a sponge offering to wash cars. My step-brother Peter who joined me was so determined to make some money to show for the hours we spent trawling the suburban streets of Woking that he started to wash cars in his sleep. One night he came into my room sleepwalking and said "We need to get washing cars." He was carrying his pillow like it was the bucket.

I'm not complaining about my upbringing - just pointing out that I wasn't reared to float around the planet like it was some cultural funfair. That work ethic stood me in good stead when I became a comedian.

The other repercussion of that trip is our great friendship. We were mates before, but not especially close. I'm sure that like me, in the first few weeks you were thinking "I like him, but he can be a right pain in the arse." I hope you did?

But the many ridiculous situations we stumbled into, and the trials and adventures we had sealed a bond that has lasted nearly thirty years.

It's a shame we live so far away from each other, but whenever we get together it doesn't take long for the subject of India to come up, and with a good bottle of whiskey we'll always end up rolling on the floor in hysterics.

Maybe one day we should do the trip again, and see if we can actually finish ourselves off this time? It'd be a much better way to go.

Good luck with the book Mark. I think it's great, and a big thank you for writing it all down.

Sean Lock
London, November 2016

1

On Thin Ice : Northern Pakistan, April 1986

The Passu Glacier, tucked away in the Karakoram mountain ranges of northern Pakistan, was an extremely scary place to be dangling above from one arm.

My right hand clung to a bulging rock as my left arm waved about uselessly in front of my whimpering face. No broken bones - the nerves and muscles just weren't firing, as if they'd had enough of me for the day. I'd been climbing the rocks, desperately trying to escape the glacier, when I'd slipped, just inches from the top. My right arm had saved me from the fall, grabbing onto the rock, which thankfully held firm, leaving my feet scrambling beneath me, kicking for a foothold.

The glacier was maybe six metres below - definite broken bones if I fell. That would leave me stuck, late afternoon, wedged between a rock face and a glacier, with absolutely no chance of rescue. I was on my own, and no one knew I was there. Not a bloody soul for miles around.

"Work, you bastard!" I screamed at my locked-up arm.

And then, an unexpected cry bubbled up from the terrified little boy trapped within the body of a twenty-two year old lunatic, bursting from my mouth into the surrounding silence, for no one to hear but myself.

"... MUUUUMMMMMM!!!"

But it did the trick. My left arm regained its connection with my brain and grabbed onto another rock, and I managed to pull myself up over a ridge.

I lay on my back, puffing, panting and gibbering, watching the weakening sun headed for the sharp edged peaks to the west. An orange glow was starting to appear on the white slopes of some of the more distant mountains. As much as I tried to push the thought away, I didn't rate my chances of seeing the morning if I had to spend the night there. It was stunningly beautiful, and I hated it.

A terrible feeling of the worst kind of doom - a doom of my own making - flooded through me. This was, without doubt, the most stupid thing I'd ever done.

I was on my way home to England from India and Nepal with my friend Gareth, who was bringing his bourgeoning nervous breakdown and an incredible amount of curly blonde hair along to keep things interesting. On entering Pakistan from the Punjab, rather than turning left and retracing our earlier route back towards Iran and Turkey, we turned right and headed north for the Karakoram mountain ranges. Gareth didn't last long. I'd noticed he'd not been saying much lately, but we'd been together for the best part of a year and speaking wasn't always necessary. We almost knew what the other was going to say, or at least we thought we did, which was enough, most of the time. In fact, he'd not really said a lot since he'd seen the full moon come up, go down, then pop again in Goa some months before, during a particularly heavy party night. Things had been building since then. The hash-induced paranoia that had followed him around for months completely took hold in the quiet mountain town of Karimabad. One night, he cracked, flapping around the tiny, candlelit room like a winged cuckoo on uneven legs, muttering about impending death.

I'd presumed he'd meant his own.

I was lying on my bed, laughing hysterically at a book we'd discovered in a colonial era bookshop in Islamabad about the adventures of Sir Harry Paget Flashman. I slapped the bed and guffawed as a terrified Flashman uncontrollably farted his way into battle 'like a sheep on windy-grass.' I'd only just discovered what windy-grass was, from a Thomas Hardy novel I'd recently ploughed through. If sheep ate a certain kind of grass they would swell with wind, causing unimaginable pain in their bubbling abdomens that could even drive them to sheepy suicide, if there happened to be a cliff nearby. A windy-grass fixer would travel from farm to farm with a small pipe that they would stick into the inflated sheep's tummy, to let the high pressure exhaust out. What a great job, I thought - bringing relief to troubled sheep.

It was during my laughing fit that Gareth's mind set sail for unchartered, stormy waters.

"Mark, MARK. I'm dying. I'm dying." He was pacing between the beds, puffing on an imaginary fag, which was odd, as he didn't smoke.

"I'm dying. I'm going to die."

"You will, if you keep smoking like that," I sniggered from my place of happy merriment, before realising that he wasn't joking.

I chased him around the dark little room, trying to calm him down. I probably wasn't that far behind him in the mad stakes myself, but my madness had manifested itself in a different way - I just thought everything was great, even when it clearly wasn't.

"I'll be finished with the Flashman book soon - that'll give you a laugh. You know that thing we read about windy-grass, well..."

"I don't need this. I. Don't. Need. This. *I don't need this!*"

He was muttering from the corner, squatting on his haunches, shivering as he puffed on what must have been at least his twentieth imaginary fag. The poor bugger looked so incredibly gaunt, as I'm sure I did. We'd hardly been eating for months - often just once a day, in a ludicrous attempt to stay away from England and keep travelling for as long as possible, which had been our goal since landing in Greece on a one-way ticket ten months previously. Only go home when you're half mad, half dead, or both, we used to say, back when we still spoke a lot, and weren't half mad or half dead.

"Looks like you'll be going home then!" I offered cheerily.

What a bastard.

The next morning, as the sun crept over the mountains, illuminating orchards of blossoming apricot and walnut trees spread across the Hunza River far below, Gareth staggered off down the steep hill to await the thirty hour bus back to Islamabad, and somehow travel from there back to England. It wasn't exactly an easy journey at the best of times, and Gareth was about to undertake it with virtually no money and a mind that was spinning like a disco ball, shattering his thoughts into disjointed shards of panic, which you could see raining down behind his eyes. I waved goodbye as his big green backpack weaved down the track, his mass of sun bleached curly hair bouncing with every skinny step. His mum was in for a shock when she looked into his raggedy eyes.

I stayed on in Karimabad, extremely happy to be in this untouched part of the world, completely alone. There were a few pangs of guilt for allowing my best mate to wander off, skint and mental, four thousand miles from home, in a potentially dangerous place - both geographically and politically. But not quite enough to chase after him to offer any help or reassurance. I did give him the Flashman book to take though.

I was completely free from any ties to my old world, which made me even more insanely happy, and I roamed around some of the world's grandest valleys grinning like I'd stumbled into a magical heaven. Little kids followed me through the villages that perched on the green hills in the shade of the immense Mount Rakaposhi. I clambered up the tracks and sat with an ancient goat herder, staring at the mountains for hours as the curly-horned goats boinged and bleated along the steep terraces. I hitched even further north, and after a week of happy mountain wanderings I ended up in a tiny place called Passu, almost at the very top of Pakistan.

China to the left of me, Afghanistan to my right, here I am…

I wanted to be in the most remote place possible. I'd heard talk of a glacier that you could walk right up to and touch.

That had tickled my stupid fancy.

Glacier day started well. I left my hut for a stroll down the Karakoram Highway for a few kilometres. The road was still busy as the morning rush hour of trucks poured across the border from China. These trucks, fantastically painted in the wildest of colours, like escaped cars from a debunked fairground ride, were driven hard and fast over the torturous mountain roads by bearded Afghanis with kohl-darkened eyes, who frequently slowed to a crawl when they saw me, whistling and gesticulating with what seemed like bawdy gestures as I plodded along the roadside.

I took a dusty path to where I thought I should be heading, and climbed a few rocky hills before the whole place opened up into a valley surrounded by some of the world's highest mountains. The Passu Glacier lay right in front of me, the maze of jagged white ice gently climbing towards the surrounding mountains, and it all seemed like it was there just for me. This is why people climb mountains, I thought. I could easily be on another planet.

I swung down from the rock I was perched on for my first ever step on a glacier. I whooped and hollered and sprung into a little icy jig. Once I'd stopped laughing, the only sound in my world was the crackle of the ice beneath my feet and the echo of the wind whistling around the peaks thousands of feet above me. Adrenalin bubbled through me, burying any sense of caution that might have arisen.

My five dollar boots - prize possessions from an Istanbul market many months before - had the opposite of grip. They had in-built slide. My

Turkish hadn't been good enough to read the label.

"Incredible! They look like a boot, but act like a skate!"

I upended onto my skinny traveller's bones countless times as I headed in, crunching and skidding over the ice. I was kitted out with useless boots, a pair of old jeans, a hippy jumper from Kathmandu that looked like a rainbow had assaulted a yak, and a cheap backpack which felt like a wrestler's knee was permanently forced into my back: as inappropriately decked out for glacier scrambling as any young clown could be. I may as well have been wearing a tutu and a pair of bowling shoes.

The gentle, undulating white ice soon gave way to complex, looping ice structures, which I clambered through, wide eyed and gullible, like some nork in a Boys' Own adventure book. Within an hour, my happy stumbling brought me to a series of giant cracks that splintered through the glacier. I could bring the word 'ravine' in here, but that sounds too grandiose. But the cracks were deep - worryingly so. Any real climber would now be strapping on their crampons, untethering their ice picks, roping up to some experienced buddies and arming a round of red flares, just in case.

I chose an alternative approach and launched into a series of wayward triple jumps and helicopter arm leaps up and over the yawning cracks, slamming into the ice, grabbing with my hands on the sharp surface, leaving thin trails of blood as my palms had their skin grated away. This at last brought some panic bubbles to the surface. Blood on ice on a glacier will do that - even to the biggest fool.

Panic and adrenalin were now thundering through my body, which resulted in me spinning around in circles in my rainbow jumper, jabbering to myself.

"Oh shit oh shit oh shit oh shit."

For want of a better plan, I still carried on, until I was hemmed in by an entire maze of ice, every direction now involving either a climb or a leap. Extremely unnerving creaking sounds rose up from below. I pictured myself slipping down one of the larger cracks, breaking a leg, and scrabbling around, helplessly trying to clamber up the sheer sides like a rat in a glass cage.

I would never be found. No other idiot would be strolling around on this glacier any time soon.

The sun was now overhead, and the glacier acted like a huge under chin reflector, bouncing the burning rays back up at me from all sides, unhindered by the thin mountain air. I was thirsty as hell, so I scooped up some of the cold, silty water that pooled around my Turkish boot skates.

Another mistake.

The freezing water hit my insides, and within moments I was down on all fours, my stomach cramping as I vomited violently onto the ice. I crouched, snivelling at my lousy predicament. The shadows from the ice sculptures were lengthening around me.

Late afternoon, and I could see no escape.

"You stupid bloody idiot, Mark!" I screamed, punching the ice, splashing vomity blue water everywhere. "You stupid, stupid idiot!"

I slowly climbed up a huge ice block in an effort to escape this incredible death-trap glacier, which by now I absolutely loathed. There was no obvious route back though the maze, but a glimpse of some rocks way over to my left offered some hope of firm ground, which I helicopter-arm jumped towards. Roughly six hours after my naively joyful first step onto the ice, my boots crunched down onto good, hard rock, but I was now hemmed in by rock walls on either side, and glacier to the rear.

I had to climb. Maybe six metres, but it felt like a hundred. I shook and babbled my way upwards, with zero confidence in my ability. At least I'd got that right, because on reaching the top, my footing gave out and put me in the dangling-over-the-glacier predicament, screaming a four thousand mile scream for my mum.

As I lay on my back, shaking after the haul back up onto the rocks, my momentary relief vanished as I scanned the surroundings. I now had to traverse this ridge that ran along the edge of the glacier, and find my way down to the start of the ice and back to the track. Walking along the ridge was easy, so long as I remained upright, but getting down was another matter. Everywhere was a sheer drop. Several times I dangled my legs over the edge, but I couldn't convince the rest of me to follow.

Eventually I found a possible path of descent down a line of shale that ended in the most unwelcoming body of water I'd ever seen.

A sheer-sided gravel pit was waiting for me at the bottom. The depth could have been anywhere from five feet to cold infinity. Terrified, I sat astride my pathetically fraying backpack, and launched myself down the shale. The ground whipped by, my hands and feet dug painfully deep to slow the pace, and I pulled a face like Batman inching groin first into the circular saw. I stopped just short of the lake. My weight was dissolving the ground beneath my feet, sending shale plip-plopping into the water as I began inching around the lake, scared and exhausted, my pack pressed to the sheer sides that rose up from the water. My legs wobbled uncontrollably at the very real possibility of slipping into the freezing cold water. I would've been under in seconds, pulled down by my wet rainbow jumper and my pack.

It took me five shaky minutes to creep around the lake, which was probably the worst part of the whole debacle, as the shale could only take my weight for seconds at a time, so I had to keep moving forward as my boots destroyed any chance of retracing my steps. I made it back to the same dusty, rocky track I had merrily waltzed up eight hours earlier that morning.

I could only manage three steps at a time before falling to the ground in exhaustion. I crawled back out onto the Karakoram Highway as the local women were returning from their work in the apricot and walnut orchards. They gathered around this colourful ball of terrified, sunburnt English boy, on his hands and knees in the dust on the mighty Silk Road, helped me up and shepherded me the two or three kilometres back to the hut where I'd been staying in the five-hut town of Passu.

I sat in the dark all night, swigging on endless bottles of water, my face burning from the sun, my body twitching with shock, reliving the day over and over, traumatised by my own stupidity. Rather than sitting in the hut, I could easily have been wedged down in the belly of the glacier with a broken leg. Imagine how that creaking would sound in the dark, as the millions of tons of ice surrounding me shifted and settled, lining themselves for the big push to convert me into a high altitude squashed-up version of myself. The stars, moving across the opening way above my head, would probably be the last thing I'd have seen. Or, I could be floating in the icy gravel pit, where at least there was a chance that some other wayward nutter would one day find my body.

I had to get away from these mountains.

2

Kuşadası Dreams

At first light I started hitching. The winking and roaming eyes of the truck drivers who picked me up did little to settle my rattled nerves, nor did the death wish speeds we reached on the crumbling roads that hair-pinned out of the mountains, hundreds of feet above the Indus River. I hardly stopped until I reached northern Iran, a couple of thousand miles later. I wanted as much distance between myself and that glacier as possible.

From Iran I crossed into Turkey, and finally felt like I was safe and on familiar ground.

Though I'd almost certainly fulfilled the requirements of our 'only go home when you're half-mad or half-dead' scenario, I still wasn't quite ready for England, so I found a job playing guitar and selling carpets to backpackers in a bar in Kusadasi, on the Aegean Coast of Turkey. Europe seemed like a place well worth avoiding for a while longer, as the Chernobyl nuclear disaster had just cast widespread fear across northern Europe. As far as anyone knew, the winds weren't blowing the radioactive clouds eastwards, and the blue water and Mediterranean sky remained clear in the warm Turkish spring.

I calmed down over the next few weeks, though I'd gained a whole new set of images that stormed their way into my nightmares. I'd wake sweating in the pitch black, thinking I was stuck under the glacier, staring up through the ice at the night sky.

But a steady supply of well earned Efes beer, good Turkish food and endless swims helped the glacier experience shrink enough that my waking thoughts weren't just about massive shifting tons of ice, squashed bones and my apparent death wish.

My daydreams would always magic carpet me back to India, where, up until the glacier incident, I'd had the best six months of my travelling life. The heat, the smells, the chaos, the cities, the deserts, beaches and mountains. India, I realised, had everything I wanted, and a whole lot more than I'd bargained for.

Varanasi: where shrouded bodies lined the streets, awaiting their turn at the funeral pyres perched on the broad steps that led down into the filthy brown water of the Ganges. I'd stared agog at the skinny young lads swinging long sticks, hitting the burning corpses with thumping whacks as bereaved families looked on. The faster the skull exploded, the faster the soul would be on its way to wherever souls go next. Burnt, black limbs rose from the flames as the ligaments tightened in the heat; little burnt waves goodbye. Or, for a cheeky exit, a raised leg, then - WHACK! You're off. Bloated dead pigs floated by, belly up, as dogs ran around dragging human entrails. People drank and bathed in the sacred Ganges water. It was all perfectly natural, in India. Naked Sadhus toked on huge hash pipes, black eyes shining behind thick, crazed hair that Medussa'd half way down their backs, some still caked in forest floor mud. Shrines were everywhere, incense and offerings of burning oil and candles. Chaos, noise and heat. Travelling around India was like relaxing in a heightened state. It suited me perfectly.

And I wanted more. In Nepal, our trekking pace had slowed to a hilarious crawl as we stumbled across huge marijuana plants towering over our gleeful heads. We gorged our stoned young selves on buffalo noodle soup and huge portions of cakes in Kathmandu, where everyone seemed to be smoking party sized hash chillums or rolling huge spliffs in warm, welcoming cafes.

We went to Chitwan National Park, not believing there actually were rhinoceroses in Nepal. We were wrong. One of them chased us through the trees, which we then had to scramble up, as the rhino snorted and tossed at the ground below, his ears spinning like gristly radars; vicious tree ants biting into our fingers.

We really should have paid for that guide. Especially when he told us that the river we were wading through every day was alive with crocodiles.

"No Mister. They are not logs!"

I guess not that many people break into wildlife parks. Especially ones advertising free roaming rhinos, crocodiles, elephants and tigers.

I knew I had to get back there. Back to Goa and the acid-fuelled full moon parties, with huge speaker stacks driven hard by DJs pumping out banging electronic music that I didn't understand in 1986, as painted cows sat watching on the sandy dance floor. Laughing Indians let off fireworks just when you'd least expect it - the rockets screaming head high through a sea of candlelit chai stalls, like comets zipping through the stars, inevitably taking out some completely unsuspecting zonked out hippy on their fizzing way. A naked Frenchman named Ricard walked around with a small monkey on his head, selling magic mushrooms. He'd recently crashed his motorbike into a pig, and received a vicious beating from the farmer as he lay grazed and sore on the road. His jaw was badly wired up, but he'd still continue to do the party rounds, keeping his customers happy and deranged.

India. There was literally nowhere else on the planet I wanted to be. That all became perfectly clear to me as I sat on the Turkish cushions strumming my guitar, boot-skates tapping the beat. Tap tap slide. Tap tap slide. But I'd need money. More money than I was capable of earning in Turkey. I'd have to brave the radioactive cloud.

A few weeks later, I arrived home completely unannounced. Mum nearly keeled over at the sight of me.

"Och Mark, you wee bugger, you frightened the life out of me! Stand back, let me see you... God almighty son, what the hell have you been up to now?"

I'd been up to plenty, but India and Nepal had something else in store for me, something that made the glacier incident seem like a short stroll in the Karakoram mountains.

3

Heading South

I wasn't born into a travelling family, but my parents had been on the move by the time I turned up. They couldn't be doing with the flack they'd generated over their Catholic/Protestant marriage, so they fled Glasgow in 1960 with a couple of superb Scottish accents and their baby girl, Amanda, south to Derbyshire, where Mum's mum had settled some years before. Dad's arms were decked out in blue-inked tattoos from his two sunburnt years in Hong Kong, where he learnt to box and throw his pink legs around endless football pitches. He'd ticked the box on his National Service enlistment form for a place called 'FARELF', thinking it was somewhere in the Highlands. Turns out 'Far Eastern Land Forces' is another way of saying 'Hong Kong.'

I don't think he drank too much out there. That hadn't started yet.

The trippy 1960s didn't make it to the tiny mining village of South Wingfield, where Mum and Dad spent the next decade in a small council house. Three more kids were born, all on winter nights, the snow from the Dales forcing the always-in-demand midwives back into their warm homes, leaving everyone to cope as best they could. I was the third born, popping out a frisky sixteen months after my brother Eric, and eighteen months before my sister Alison.

My first five years were spent with a death-like grip on my mum's apron strings, until the world backfired and I was sent off to school at the top of our street. I screamed incessantly as my mum prised herself free, tears streaming down her young face as she dragged Alison by the hand back through the school gates. I escaped four times that morning, running back up Parks Avenue at full throttle, emitting a thousand decibels from my wailing little head.

I relented slightly over the afternoon and settled down to the red building blocks at the back of the class, strategically placed by the teacher as far from the door as possible. This way she at least had a fighting chance if I made another bolt for it.

Then, I grew up a bit.

Our backyard was the first place to adventure from - if you could get past our two white rabbits, Pinky and Perky, who had somehow upgraded their jaw springs and honed their strike responses to enable them to clamp their buck-toothed weapons deep into your arm before you'd even noticed you'd been disemboweled by their slashing rear claws, powered by bulging, fast response thigh muscles. Dad was the only human they'd allow near. We'd stand on the kitchen table - safe behind Mum, the brick wall and the closed window - as Dad went into the pen to feed the fearsome little shits their brown pellets, which they'd wolf down and then plop out as slightly darker brown pellets from an exit just under their fluffy little bobbing tails, thereby proving that they were actually genuine rabbits.

Once past Pinky and Perky's pen, the next obstacle was a rusted up barbed wire fence that took some practice with bounce rate and exit speed, but once I'd learnt to lift my trailing leg on the descent, thereby avoiding a face-first downwards swing into the rusty tetanus tangle, that was it. Freedom. The cow fields and surrounding woods were there for the taking. The River Amber gurgled away behind a clump of trees that cooed with the warm sound of nesting wood pigeons. The river was still used to power the grinding wheel to make flour at the mill and, more importantly, provide enough moss, sticklebacks and mud for the village kids to remain happy. The slag-heap from the now silent coal mine was a constant source of dangerous fun, which we'd run up at full pelt, until our legs sunk beneath us, shouting "Quick sand! Quick sand! Help, I'm going underrrrrrrrrr!"

It stood like a black, cancerous lump beside Bluebells Wood, where we'd hunt out cuckoo spit, foxgloves and snapdragons in summer. Or, we'd get pushed by the bigger lads into ditches sky high with nettles and run home shrieking, our skin bubbling up in white dotted brail, each little dot a separate ouch.

The sewage works were another eye-popping place to explore. We'd sneak past the gate after the workers had cleared off for the day and take it in turns riding around on a slowly spinning pipe as it sprayed urine - our own urine! - over the filtrating coals.

I asked one of the bigger boys what it was all about, and his answer confused me for months.

"It cleans yer piss."

And at the top end of the village, just past a set of brutal farmyard geese that made patting Pinky and Perky seem like a safe move, along from the terrifying Ravens Wood where only the biggest kids would venture, was Wingfield Manor, a ruined fifteenth century manor house, and once the house-arrest home of Mary, Queen of Scots.

We'd ding the gatekeeper's bell, and his wife would stick her head out the door.

"Hey-up, me ducks."

"Hey-up. Can we come for play in manor, please?"

"Aye, course ye can. No accidents, mind. I don't wanna be fetching yer mams."

And we'd be in. Up the winding, worn stone steps of the big tower, popping out the top a few minutes later, clinging to thick stone walls with heaving chests and wobbly legs, peering over the ramparts at the green, woody countryside that spread below. All that was missing were the attacking armies, battering rams and the opportunity to pour boiling oil over soldiers' heads as they scaled the huge walls screaming for our blood. Then we'd race back down the spiral steps to the cold, spooky crypt and stand petrified at the dark arched entrance, daring one another to run past the big sarcophagus-like boxes, which obviously had crumbling dead bodies inside that would pull you in and keep you there, wrapped tight against their decomposed ribcage, where you'd stay until someone ran home to fetch yer mam.

Mary, Queen of Scots wasn't the only Scottish lady to feel trapped in South Wingfield. Mum never fitted in. The Saturday night highlight was bingo up the Miners' Welfare Club. She'd do her best to avoid coming along, but we'd beg and plead with her, because we thought it was absolutely brilliant. Social status for me was measured in how many bingo booklets a family would have spread out amongst the crisp packets and half pints of warm Double Diamond, the smoke from unfiltered Woodbines turning the air blue and the yellow curtains brown.

When bingo-calling Frank, the smooth dancing dandy with the Brylcreemed combover purred "Legs, eleven" into the dancehall microphone, the wolf whistle response shot round the club like a miners' Mexican wave, almost taking the roof off. Several restless moments would pass before the uproar would settle and the bingo could begin again.

My Papa - a gentle local man married to my mum's mum - leaned over, head positioned inches above his booklet to gain that crucial bingo edge, grinning and smirking, chewing on his smile and nudging us in the ribs as we slurped down our fizzy lemonade pop. He'd been waiting for legs eleven time all week.

My mum would die a little more every time. These weren't her people, and this wasn't her town. Maybe she didn't know herself what she wanted from life, but it definitely wasn't bingo on a Saturday night down the Miners' Welfare Club. She hadn't finished her travels just yet.

After calling the bingo, Frank would trot various ladies round the dance floor, his shoes skimming the surface like he'd wrapped a pair of shiny ravens round his nifty size eights, whilst we kids would run outside to sniff the beer barrels and empty bottles of sweet smelling Mackeson Stout and Light Ale, which were piling up near the back door. Then, on late summer nights, we'd leg it up the Wreck and flick each other with as much cow shit as had been plopped out the day before. Two day old shit was much better to chuck than a fresh pattie. The perfect crispy frisbee with a stinky wet underbelly.

The Wreck was a field, not a ship - Derbyshire being about as far as you can be from the seaside in England. This made the yearly holiday to a caravan park in Skegness almost insanely exciting. Even just watching other families from our avenue pack their roof-rack high and set off with a beep for the distant sand and cold waves was enough to send me demented.

Obviously, I couldn't have wished for anything more. But whilst we were busy invading the countryside, things weren't going well between Mum and Dad. There'd be shouting matches at night, followed by weeks of silence on his part. Mum packed her bags to leave once, though where she would've gone I can't imagine. But she would've left, if we'd let her. She couldn't get past her four bawling kids blocking the door, begging and crying for her to stay. So she stayed.

Around this time, Dad fell out with his beloved Catholic Church, due to their unyielding views on contraception, which opened up a hole in him that he never even came close to filling. We were hanging on by the skin of our teeth, both financially and emotionally, and another kid would have sent my parents over the edge. They were only in their late twenties, with four little-uns under seven, and very little money.

So as the decade clicked over, Mum demanded change. She'd spent ten years in South Wingfield with not a friend to turn to, and I don't suppose she could take it anymore. She also felt her kids would have more opportunity in life if we headed further south. She pushed Dad, a car salesman - "I've gawt a nice wee mini forrrrya, sir" - to take a job in Virginia Waters, not too far from London, selling lovely yellow and red Volvos to chaps that spoke like the ones we'd heard on the BBC. It was all very exciting, though I was not at all happy to be leaving my beloved Derbyshire behind.

Mum was.

Dad's new job came with a small house with white, pebble-dashed walls, tacked onto the side of a Volvo garage. We had a phone on the wall with a four-digit number, and a conservatory - a word we'd never even heard before - where I'd drool over my collection of birds' eggs, gathered from years of sticking my murderous little hands in hedgerows and bushes, climbing trees, or wading up rivers and swamps in search of kingfisher, wren and chaffinch eggs. The tiny garden had a shed where I'd store tubs of maggots in summer and huge boxes of conkers in autumn, which would turn to mush by the start of winter.

We loved it. It was like a posh Derbyshire. Rivers to fish in, woods to play and hide in, and super rich rock stars and celebrities living just up the road in mansion strewn Wentworth and Ascot. John Lennon, Diana Dors, Elton John, and - most excitingly for us - Bruce Forsyth.

I'd developed bad asthma, and would spend sleepless nights downstairs on the couch wheezing into hot cups of tea, with Mum telling me stories of Ancient Egypt and Tibet; places that she loved to read about, places that fascinated her. I promised her that when I grew up I'd visit Lhasa and bring her back a stick of rock.

Many days were spent at St Peter's Hospital in Chertsey, Surrey, trying to get my wheezy young chest under control. I didn't mind as it was time spent alone with Mum and her stories of the world, gleaned from the endless books she read. I was always being given new asthma drugs to try out by the doctors, one of which sent my heart into overdrive and my brain flipped its switches into a full hallucinogenic trip, where Mum oscillated between a three-inch gonk and a doorframe-filling giant. I laughed hysterically on the bed, screaming "Gold! Gold! Bring me Gold!"

Tripping at ten is probably not the ideal way to prepare for your teenage years, especially if you enjoyed it. And I definitely did.

For a while down in Virginia Water, things were going well for Mum and Dad. They had friends, went to parties, knew a French man. Mum started wearing kaftans and smoking herbal cigarettes. They went on holiday to Moscow; one of the first tourist groups allowed in since the Iron Curtain slammed shut. Mum came back with stories bursting with culture: onion-shaped architecture, the Bolshoi Ballet, symphonies dished out under the eye of their ever present Russian guides. Dad's stories were mostly vodka driven - how he was nearly arrested for pissing in the snow in Red Square, drunk and singing 'Fly Me To The Moon' to the near frozen guards.

I think a lot of men used to fancy Mum. She was slim and good looking, with a thick head of black hair. She had a warm, easy laugh. She listened to classical music; she knew about the world, and always showed interest in people. I thought she was beautiful, and would tell her to go in for the Miss World contest, or even Miss Universe, though the idea of an intergalactic beauty show really confused me. I presumed Captain Kirk would be the judge, as he was the only man I'd seen on TV actually kiss an alien woman. Her strong Scottish accent was warm and round, even though she grew up in Paisley, only a few miles across Glasgow from Dad. His accent was the opposite. Not even Mum knew what he was saying half the time through his big beard that was already turning grey in his early thirties. He was quite a handsome man, although he never really got the hang of his full set of false teeth, which he assured us he'd won at the fairground. He was a strong looking fella, with his *Scotland Forever, I Love Mum and Dad* and coiled serpent and dagger tattoos running up his arms to meet the lions' heads guarding his broad shoulders. He learned to manage his new social life by drinking way too much whiskey, and before long his gruff Glaswegian drunkenness turned most of their new friends away. Thanks to Dad's drinking, Mum's new life - the life that she'd so nearly grabbed hold of - spluttered and died. The phone on the wall stopped ringing. I used to feel so sad for her. I think she felt that her happiest times were gone for good.

When I was twelve we moved again. For me, it was time to go. Huge trucks were digging up my beloved woods and sandpits not far from the back of our pebble-dashed house, concreting over the streams and laying the foundations for what would become a loathsome stretch of the M3. I used to wee on the big yellow steering wheels when all the workers had gone home for the day.

4

Young Punks

Mum and Dad took a mortgage on a three bedroom semi that was built on a reclaimed swamp in New Haw, Surrey, only a few miles from the concrete, multi storey car park strewn planning disaster known as Woking.

Woking.

One of those words that drops from your mouth and lands in a lump at your feet, waiting for the stamp of a heel or the punt of a toe to kill it off.

Woking.

Twenty-nine miles south of London.

Woking in the 1970s was a great place to be, if you were a fan of concrete and trouble. For me, the only remotely exciting thing on the high street was the coloured pen selection in WH Smith, which left for dead any coloured pen selection I'd ever seen. I had no idea there could be so many shades of blue.

I was so nervous about joining Fullbrook School mid-term that I had a two week bout of asthma and stayed at home, drawing blue things. Blue whales in blue lagoons. Blue aliens in blue rooms. Blue policemen chasing blue robbers against a blue sky.

I had every reason to be nervous, as I'd already walked past the imposing school building at playtime. The playground, to my eyes, was a war zone of high velocity missiles in brown blazers smashing into each other, like one massive, self-propelled conker fight. A screaming boy had his arms forced through the bars that ran shoulder height around the playground wall, and attached to each spread leg was a line of bigger boys, pulling like a tug-o-war, lifting the poor lad perpendicular to the ground and yanking his legs almost out of their sockets, bending his arms up and back at the most horrible angles. They'd recreated the rack, which happened to be my favourite torture instrument at the time. It's a whole lot scarier when you see it in action.

I'd stubbornly held onto my Derbyshire accent, and I was terrified of being thrown in with these ballistic sadists. I'd read books about the Middle Ages and knew that being different is not particularly helpful if you're unfortunate enough to be delivered into the hands of torturers.

My mum walked me to school, after my wheezing had cleared up, and I slid into the playground just before nine, hoping to avoid the pre-bell slaughter. The first person I saw was a kid of a similar age, but to my horror, he only had one arm - the left one, which he was using to eat an orange. From the other blazer sleeve hung a false plastic hand, wrong in colour, like a muddy pink mannequin hand, with a metal rod running from the hinged thumb and disappearing up his sleeve. He walked towards me, arm swinging, chewing on his orange. I pictured the metal wire running up the plastic arm, through his shoulder and up into his brain, where it connected to the thumb control centre, which I presumed he could activate at will, and the thumb would flick up in a welcoming gesture, and his mouth would smile and say "Hello."

But he didn't. He activated the bit that made him spit his half-chewed orange straight into my face and scream:

"WHAT THE FUCK ARE YOU STARING AT?"

As he shouted, he punched me full in the face with a rock hard fist that almost lifted my curly head from its retaining assembly - a punch way beyond the force you'd expect from a twelve year old boy. I peered up from the playground floor, holding my freshly stunned, orange-splattered head. He leant over me, plastic hand dangling above my face, thumb still in its rest position.

"You're new here, aren't ya? We're gonna wall-bar ya next playtime. Shithead."

Not only could he punch like a man, he could swear like a bastard too. I hadn't even spoken yet.

Ten minutes later, in my first lesson, the greasy haired ratty bastard in a cardigan who was our student teacher sent me off to collect Bibles from a tiny cupboard at the end of what seemed to be a thousand miles of long, empty corridors. When I eventually made it back, I staggered through the door, balancing a green tower of New Testaments under my chin.

"Don't you dare drop those Bibles, boy!" he shouted, as the whole class stared at me in delight. I edged across the room, the pile teetering and wobbling - as was my head from the man punch less than half an hour before - and tripped, the Bibles covering the floor in Gideon green.

"I SAID, DON'T DROP THE BIBLES!!!!!" His ratty head bellowed at me. He pulled me to the front of my new class, who all sat grinning up at this great piece of Monday morning fun, drew a big chalk cross on my back, bent me over a desk and cracked me twice across the arse with his open hand, warning me that if he saw me again that day and the chalk had worn off, I'd be up for a caning.

I hid in the toilet block at playtime. And at dinner time. And afternoon playtime.

When I got home, I didn't mention anything about my day. Again, it was time to grow up a bit. As boys across the world do, I learnt how to fit in - mostly through studying playground survival tactics and weaponry. A hard leather briefcase with metal tipped corners, packed with heavy maths and physics books, was an ankle smashing missile in the right hands. They'd be scudded across the playground floor at high velocity, like a big square bowling ball, smack into the achilles tendon of some unsuspecting boy munching on his packet of Cheesy Wotsits. Down he'd go, clutching his scuffed heels, spots of blood already showing on his socks, face scrunching up in pain.

On freezing cold winter days, ears that were already pink with cold would be snuck up on from behind and flicked with such excruciating force - the arm punching out from the shoulder, the elbow extending, the wrist whipping the hand forward, the middle finger straining against the thumb with huge pressure and released at EXACTLY the right time, almost like a perfect, tiny, karate punch - sinking the speeding nail into the sinew just above the earlobe with a withering CRACK! You could spend an entire lunch break recovering from just the surprise alone, never mind the stinging, ringing ear which glowed like a towel-whipped, angry baboon's arse. And because you were then weakened, you'd be perfect prey for the roaming bands of dead leg mercenaries who attacked from broadside with swift knees driven SMACK! into the thigh muscle, sending you buckling to the floor in almost hilarious pain.

At fourteen I had my first real crush on a girl, though I never had the nerve to talk to her, and it wouldn't have helped if I had. She was Spanish. I'd see her at the Woking outdoor swimming pool, scampering around in her red bikini, all curvy and tanned, with long, curly dark hair tumbling down over her brown shoulders. I wanted to measure her all over with the piece of winning conker string that I still carried around. Admittedly, a difficult notion to force across the language barrier.

"Err, hello. You know conkers? No? Conkers - tree nuts on string. Smack smack. This is the string from my eighty-eighter. Big winner. Can I measure your thighs with it, please?"

She was older than me, and seemed absolutely carefree. For one whole summer I was smitten. I'm sure she never even noticed me. If she had, she would have seen a fairly skinny lad, face down on a towel, shoulders burnt pink from the sun, peeping up from behind his arms through a head of unwanted curls.

For me, she was now the highlight of Woking, easily taking the place of the blue felt tip pen collection. The rest of the town seemed bored and violent. Squaddies from the nearby Aldershot Army barracks would flock to town at the weekend for drinking sessions and what was horribly known as 'Paki bashing.' Recently settled Indian and Pakistani families had spread over whole streets. Football nutters from south London would come down to fight the squaddies. The Woking hard nuts, of which there were many, weren't fussy. They'd fight anyone that bumped their lager, looked them in the eye, or happened to be nearby when they were pissed, which was pretty much all of the time. So the chances of them turning on you were very high. Police and their frothing Alsatians patrolled the weekend night trains. It was like the schoolyard had spilled out into the pubs.

Then - BANG! Punk rock roared out of London and ignited the bored towns all over the country with noise and energy, releasing armies of spiky haired kids trained in playground warfare to fill up on cider and lager and go absolutely berserk. Woking shouted out loud and proud with The Jam; an angry Paul Weller spitting out 'In The City', and sending the remainder of my school days down the pan.

For the next few years, Woking wasn't such a bad place to be for those of us jumping around trying to be young punks. Not far from London and Guildford, which meant plenty of gigs, and the pubs would serve just about anyone who had either a crash helmet, teenage spots or a pair of breasts.

I started knocking around with a new bunch of boys at school, who had managed to steal the school drum kit over the period of a couple of weeks. First the connectors, then the cymbals. A week or so later they made off with the toms. Maybe they thought they were being discreet. But then they thought fuck it, broke in again and nicked the kick, snare and hi-hat, thereby reducing the school band rhythm section to a boy sitting on a stool wondering why he was there. That was, of course, until they nicked the stool as well.

The stolen kit was relocated to my new mate Gareth's bedroom, and a punk band grew around it: The Statix. I joined when they realised I could actually play the guitar, as opposed to wearing it round your neck, plugging it in and hitting it with an open fist. I brought my mate Nosher along, who could make his guitar sound like a loud quacking duck.

Thursday night was practise night. Cheap guitars through shitty amps, loose drum skins covered in masking tape and stencilled punky slogans - muffled with pillows as a cursory nod to the neighbours - and foul-mouthed lyrics howled through a crackling plastic mic that was also nicked from school and held together with tape and chewing gum. We sounded like two bands having a song fight in a cupboard, along with someone murdering an amplified duck with a really heavy plectrum.

"SHIT HEAD!" Boom boom boom.

"SHIT HEAD!" Quack quack quack.

"SHIT HEAD!" Bang bang bang.

"SHIT HEEEEEEEEEEEEEEEEEAAAD!"

Eventually, Gareth's mum would poke her head around the door, after the neighbours in the friendly little close had all come home from work.

"I think that's enough now, boys."

"URINATION BABY, DEGRADE MEEEEEEEEEEEEEEEEE!"

"Boys! That's enough for one night," she'd scream over the obscene din.

"Oh! OK Mrs Pugh! Thanks." And we'd all traipse downstairs, knuckles dragging on the fluffy carpet, to drink tea around the Roberts radio in the kitchen and talk about finding some gigs.

On one of those spectacular Thursday nights, a new teenage face appeared in the hall. He'd been visiting with his parents, who were friends of Gareth's family. His dad introduced him.

"Hello boys, this is Sean."

We trudged past the tall, surly looking oik, flicking our heads up one by one with a grunt for a greeting.

"Allroight?"

"Allroight."

"Allroight?

"Allroight."

"Allroight?"

"Allroight."

Sean must've liked what he'd heard upstairs, because next week he was back, perched on the bed as we resumed the band fight and honking of our punk songs. The bass guitar now had four strings - occasionally even in tune - and we'd found a microphone that actually looked like a microphone. I'd nicked a foot pedal from the guitar shop that did absolutely nothing.

Sean fitted in straight away. It didn't take us long to figure out what kind of character he was. He'd have us in hysterics with his antics and throwing-himself-round-the-room dancing. You'd be happy to have him by your side when things got too wild at parties or gigs. His big frame, cropped head and intense eyes looked pretty threatening, though he was never interested in the violent side of punk - he was just brilliant to be around. And we all began drinking way too much. Which was perfect for punk gigs.

When The Statix breathed their last - probably because we got banned from the three venues we'd managed to persuade to let us play in - Sean joined the new band that rose from its ashes, parping into a saxophone and looking menacingly wild in his crombie and freshly skinned head.

Once punk died off, and synthesisers and big haircuts dominated Top of the Pops - Phil Collins being the awful, balding exception - Woking was once again swamped by lager lads in purple cardigans looking for someone to bust their knuckles on. There's something really wrong about being chased by a gang of neat-looking drunk blokes with side-flicked haircuts, checkered cardigans, and a truly terrible taste in music. Some of the meanest bastards you could meet would be dancing to Kajagoogoo in the corner of the pub. It made no sense.

For myself and several friends, leaving Woking was the fairly obvious thing to do. Sean was away a lot working on big building sites, and we'd only see him now and then for heavy drinking sessions. For the rest of the gang, motorbikes had gone a long way to broadening our horizons, but even the most reckless of us had given up on those, once the crashes became more worrying. Mine was particularly horrific, landing me back once again in St Peter's Hospital with some awful holes in my body, a couple of impressive scars and four very swollen limbs.

Not long after my crash, just after eighteenth birthday, my brother Eric waved goodbye to us all and flew off to spend time on a Kibbutz in Israel. He was the first person we knew to ever actually go somewhere and not come back two weeks later. Mum cried all day. Six months later, the front door bell rang and I heard Mum scream. Half of my brother had returned. He'd shed the half he didn't need anymore somewhere in the desert around the Red Sea where he'd been living. He was burnt almost black by the sun, his mass of dark hair twice as big as his head. He actually looked like Jesus. Maybe that's what scared Mum. If your son has left home and Jesus comes ringing, it's probably not a good sign.

"Och Eric, is that you son? Och, come here," and she grabbed hold of him like she'd just been given her life back, and hugged her skinny oldest boy till his brand new traveller's bones cracked.

So Eric had ventured out and found the answer for most of the boys I knew: travel.

Our trips away gradually grew longer and more adventurous – from long weekends eating dope cakes in Amsterdam to months on cheap vodka on a Kibbutz in Israel, or a few months hacking around Egypt, Turkey and Greece. I returned from Israel full of stories and met up with Sean for an afternoon of drinking in the Cotteridge Hotel in Woking; a pub filled with hilarious misfits munching on crisp bags full of dried magic mushrooms, ex-punks still speeding from four years before, and rock-hard looking bikers eyeing the place off menacingly and never really saying very much.

"Sean, you've gotta go to a Kibbutz, they're brilliant. Swedish birds, gorgeous Israeli birds, forty pence for a bottle of vodka, only four hours work a day - and that's presuming they can drag you out of bed…"

Within days he'd cleared off, where he managed to get himself kicked off almost as many Kibbutzim as I'd had for over-boisterous behaviour.

During this time, Dad hadn't been at all well. It ramped up very quickly. He had to have his stomach removed from a cancer, his kidneys all but packed up and his blood was turning almost poisonous. A doctor told us it was like his body was turning on itself. He wasn't expected to survive. He looked like a seventy year old man, though he was only in his mid-forties. All the muscles from his body vanished, and never really grew back. Mum spent her days up at London's St Thomas' Hospital with him, watching him struggle from one disaster to the next. But somehow he survived his numerous operations; eventually proving the doctors wrong. He seemed like a changed man after his eventual release from hospital. Obviously he couldn't drink, as he weighed hardly anything. He was too weak to work, and walked around stooped for a while with a feed tube dangling out his nose, but slowly, he built his strength up. He was a good man to be around - pleased to be alive. Mum had nursed him well, and they actually seemed quite happy to be together.

With Dad on the mend, I felt that the time was right to do some proper travelling. In 1985, a trip to Greece for myself and a couple of mates turned into the fantastic impromptu overland journey to India and Nepal that for me almost ended in the belly of the Passu Glacier, and for my best mate Gareth, almost culminated in a stint in the local mental institution back in

Woking - once he'd finally managed to get his messed up head back home from that tiny village in northern Pakistan.

5

Simple Plans

The good news on returning home was that Dad had found a job selling cars again, the house had been decorated and made smart with a new sofa and chairs, and Mum had a whole stack of new records to plough through at high volume. Home had a good feeling about it, like life had restarted for them again. Dad was having the occasional drink, but he seemed in control. He was still skinny, the strong Glaswegian build having disappeared for good. His fading tattoos now seemed to wrap themselves around his bony arms and shoulders, but he was alive, earning and eating. Mum had found herself a dream job in the local library. I was so proud of her. I'd not seen her this happy since we lived in Virginia Water.

Within days of returning from my big India trip and the glacier freak out, it was time to get cracking. Woking always had this urgent, repelling effect on me - as did being back in western society generally, with its grey normality, daily routines and lurking career paths - none of which held any interest for me whatsoever. There was no way I'd be hanging around for long. My reading was all beatnik - Kerouac, hobo life, travelling tales, mountaineering adventures. I was coming out of my hippy Neil Young guitar-playing days and diving into twanging the blues.

My escape plan - hatched on a cushion in Turkey - was simple: save as much money as possible, fly to Delhi, hit the ground running, and carry on where I left off. This time, no plans for coming home. On to Thailand and the bits after that, before hitting Australia.

I moved back into my old bedroom at Mum and Dad's, hunkered down low and took an awful nightshift job in a Tesco warehouse - a huge ugly shed that had swallowed up a good part of the once proud Brooklands race track. Where single seater Jags had roared around the famously banked corners, now sallow, bored youths and older men thankful for a job plodded around on battery powered, low lying forklifts, piling nappies and cases of Fanta onto cold, rattling cages for a few quid an hour.

I made some friends amongst the strange, lurching, nocturnal humanoids that I shared the nightshift with. One fella, Craig, with huge feet and a motorbike so fast it could leave your spine behind if you weren't zipped up properly, would pull his forklift up to mine and ask me endless questions about India.

"Mark?"

"Yes, Craig?"

"You know in India…"

"Yes?"

"Did you see any lions?"

"Nope."

"Never?"

"Pretty sure I didn't."

"Tigers?"

"Nope."

"Hmmmmm."

Then he'd be off round the warehouse again in his forklift, digesting this piece of the India jigsaw puzzle, and how it might fit in with his own travel fantasy. Half an hour later, he'd be back.

"I think I'd like to see a tiger. What about lepers?"

"Everywhere."

"Really?"

"No. Not really."

"So you didn't see any lepers."

"Well, yeah we did, loads of them."

"But not everywhere?"

"No. Not everywhere."

"But some places you'd see them."

"Yep."

"Hmmmm."

This would go on, night after night, for hours.

"Did you ever worry about getting sick out there?"

"No. You get sick, and then you worry about it. Then it goes away, and you're happy again."

"So basically what you're saying is that everyone gets sick."

"Yes. Especially if you eat. Or drink."

"Well everyone does that. So everyone must get sick."

"Well spotted, Craig."

"Hmmmm." *Whrrrrrrrr.* Off he'd go.

We'd have dinner at two in the morning, with huge piles of custard and pudding, spooned up by the chirpy nightshift dinner ladies - always the quickest half hour of the night.

"Can I get batteries for my Walkman in India?"

"I can only presume so, Craig."

Craig still firmly believed that the first four Led Zeppelin albums contained all the music a man would ever need. The thought of not having these modern parchments of wisdom constantly available would be a serious setback to his plans.

One night I was in the washing powder aisle, hiding, as ever, from more work.

"Mark, I'm coming to India."

Not with me you're not, I thought. Not because I didn't like him - I did - but I wanted to be heading off on my own.

"Good man! You'll bloody love it."

"Yep, me and Gavin are going together."

Gav also worked the nightshift, rode an old woman's pushbike to work and had acquired a terrible nickname - 'Greebo'. Somehow, it suited him perfectly.

"Maybe we'll meet you somewhere?"

"That'd be great Craig."

No way pal. When I leave here you won't see me for dust. I'll be scooting round India like a pro, in places you'll never hear of, hanging with the other India heads, well away from you fresh-faced India virgins reeling from the shock of the place.

I've been there and back overland. I know the score. I'll be getting the best hash. Going to the best parties. Might cruise round on a Royal Enfield motorbike, thumping across the lower Himalayas from hill station to hill station. I'm gonna cross into Tibet on foot and hitch to Lhasa. I'm gonna sneak into Bhutan and trek up to Kula Kangri in the Eastern Himalayas, where I'm gonna sit in a hut for a month and twang the guitar from stoned morning to stoned night.

I'm gonna meet a gorgeous hippy girl and travel down the east coast, from Calcutta to Madras, and she'll make drawings in her diary from the erotic temple carvings of orgies and impossibly bendy sex. And we're gonna figure them

all out in a cabin bed under a stormy dawn sky, and cool off in the morning
sea, after which I'll write her a song about it so we'll never forget, and promise
to meet her again when we're older and non-the-wiser.

"Do you think you can get alkaline batteries?"

"I don't bloody know, Craig!"

"Oh." He looked crestfallen. "I really hope so."

The weeks and months plodded along, an endless nightshift of boredom, boxes and bonus slips. Every minute of every shift was logged, tallied, accounted for, measured, quantified and tracked by the humourless, mean-spirited swines that sat behind the sliding glass partition, growing fatter and fatter as they gulped down their endless cans of Coke, lazy thighs busting at their shiny, grey Tesco seams. I was desperate to get back to the madness of India. The beaches of Goa with the mad-eyed Westerners banging their brains out of whack on acid and mushrooms. The desert towns of Rajasthan, with the camels and dust and old palaces crumbling back into the sand. The fish curries of Kerala, dolloped out onto wide green banana leaves - all you can eat for a few rupees. The huge waves hammering the yellow beaches strewn with coconut palms and dead sea snakes, decapitated by the knife-wielding fishermen who dragged their boats out into the deadly surf everyday. The chaos which passed for the norm in most Indian towns full of temples and noisy, colourful religion, traffic and commerce all blending into one big sensory overload. I missed it. I wanted to be far away from home, far from England, and a million miles away from monotony and anything approaching a routine or a bonus slip.

The Tesco winter of 1986 was cold, and many a morning I trudged two miles home in the pre-dawn snow, thankful for the silence after being force fed eight hours of local radio heavily peppered with Simply Red and UB40. And that bastard Phil Collins, who was still somehow penning hits.

But the money was building up, and that's all that mattered. That, and one big night out a week to shake me up.

Pete and I, another mate from Tesco, were in Woking for one of these beer fuelled nights. He brought a friend along - Jeanie, and Jeanie brought a friend along: Maria. And there she was - the gorgeous Spanish girl from the pool, though she wasn't a teenage girl anymore. She was twenty-seven, I was twenty-three. It had been almost ten years since my swimming pool summer of infatuation. I could barely look her in the eye. She wore a tiny black miniskirt, high heels, fishnet stockings and a tight top that I daren't even peek at. Her curly black hair was down over her shoulders, and golden hoop earrings framed her lovely Spanish face. She squeezed up on the bench, patting the empty space beside her.

"Hello," she smiled up at me, "sit here. Are you going to make me laugh? I hope so."

Maria was not interested in normal conversation. She wanted to laugh and giggle, crinkle up her nose, drink, smoke, take acid, play confused, hide behind her curly hair and pretend the world wasn't happening. We did all this on our first night in the pub. She took my arm as we walked back to Pete's flat, jumping at the shadows, pressing herself against me. My brain was whirling, and not just from the acid she'd fed me. I prayed to God that she wouldn't turn into a three-inch-high gonk. She wasn't very tall, so there was a very real danger of that happening.

We danced around the flat for a while, before she whispered in my ear to follow her outside. In the garden she hung onto my arm as she wriggled first one leg free from its fishnet stocking, and then the other.

"My legs get so hot when I'm tripping. Do yours? Mark?"

I let out a noise like a small kettle boiling.

Her perfect thighs were shining, reflecting the kitchen light that filtered through the trees. I couldn't work out if I was a fourteen year old boy on the way home from the swimming pool, measuring string in hand, or if I was here now and this was actually happening. Maybe my fourteen year old brain had resurfaced and was beaming out its fantasy for me.

The first exotic woman I'd ever seen was now stepping out of her suspender belt just as I was stepping out of my mind.

When her overheated legs were freed from the stockings, she turned on her heels and disappeared back inside, leaving me wrapped around my own brain that was trying very hard to keep up with events. I was smitten. Again.

Later that week, on a long, boring nightshift, the local radio piped out a dedication along the lines of: "Mark and Pete at Tesco warehouse - Saturday night was great, let's go again this week. Maria and Jeanie." That got the forklifts beeping, and, just for a moment, the race cars roared around the historic Brooklands track once more.

Things slipped into place after a few more of these fantastic Saturday nights. I moved into Maria's council flat in Woking, a tiny flat with a huge Swatch watch clock hanging on the living room wall. I soon got the hang of life with her: don't mention politics, don't even mention books. Both made her nervous, and she had no interest in either. Don't bother with any theories or abstract notions – unless it's to do with tripping. Do play guitar, do tell funny stories, do make sure there's always pot around. A perfect afternoon for Maria would be a joint followed by a three-hour nail filing session in a bath overflowing with more bubbles than there are stars in the universe, with Gregory Isaacs' *Night Nurse* album thumping from the stereo downstairs. After which, I'd have to hop on my bike and ride to Brooklands for my ten hour nightshift, where time slowed to a Tesco crawl and the only respite was the bunch of cheery, fifty year old dinner ladies. My India plan remained solid though, as I explained to Maria from the start. Come July, which was only a few months away, I'd be off.

She just smiled a "We'll see about that" kind of smile.

Men plagued her. Everywhere she went, they would approach her, stunned by her sexiness. Since her early teens in Spain, men would become obsessed with her, follow her; pester her. She told me her aunty was the village witch, and had taught Maria a spell to deal with the unwanted swarthy suitors. I pressed her for details.

"So how did she do that? Bury a donkey upside down in the garden? Or is that to get rid of warts?"

"You think I'm silly Mark, but my aunty was a real witch. A good witch. You wouldn't understand."

"I would! I've read loads of Colin Wilson books."

Oops. Don't mention books, Mark.

"So did your aunty teach you any spells? I bet she did. Come on, tell me."

"I'm not talking about this anymore. I'm going for a bath. Coming?"

She certainly had a strange power over men. Going for a drink with her could be a real trial. Random characters would approach her, and wouldn't leave her alone, even if I asked them politely to fuck off. I watched a singer jump off stage at a gig in London and run through the crowd to throw himself at her.

"I know you. I've seen you in my dreams. You HAVE to come with me."

She just clung to my arm and completely ignored him, which was impressive, as he was kneeling at her feet like a crash-landed flamingo, looking up at her with an expression that seemed to say: 'bed me or behead me, but just don't ignore me.' She just put on her nail-filing face and looked away until he'd skulked back onto the stage with his microphone between his legs.

"Bloody hell Maria, that bloke stopped his gig for you."

"Oh Mark, he's just a silly boy. Come on now, buy me a vodka." And she'd perch on a barstool, her stockinged legs jittering away with nervous energy.

Maria did not want to meet my mum. I convinced her, finally, and she frocked up in a lovely white cotton dress that was only see through if you looked at it for more than a second, and bright red high heels that lifted the top of her head almost up to my shoulder.

"Your mum will hate me. She'll think I am an idiot. What can I talk to her about? If she talks about books I'll die. Don't let her mention books, Mark!" She knew Mum was working in the local library. Just the thought of a building dedicated to books gave Maria the horrors.

"Maria, she's not a headmistress. She's my mum."

I arrived with Maria on my arm. Mum did her best to pull the conversation into at least first gear, but Maria's brain - never the most nimble of organs - had dropped anchor, lying inert in its holding chamber like a trapped octopus awaiting release from this unwelcome, stressful stimulus. All she could manage was: "Yes, Mrs Giblin." Or, for variety, "No, Mrs Giblin."

When we left, maybe an hour later, Mum looked at me with an expression I'd never actually seen before. A real "What the hell are you doing, Mark?!" look.

Of course, she wasn't naive. She could see why I was obviously attracted to Maria. My smitten-ness. But I think I'd disappointed her. Even despite all the crazy things I'd brought into Mum's world, she'd never before looked disappointed in me.

It was around this time that I bumped into my old pal Sean again, the honking sax lad from the punk days. He was still a wild character - smart, very funny, a bent up paperback stuffed in his pocket, and he was always up for taking the night a step further. Why have six beers in the pub when you can have six beers plus half a bottle of tequila, and wear an old lady's dress? Why go to a party and chat when you can go there and pretend you're a deaf, drunk, highly expressive dancer that can't hear the beat, or know when the songs have finished? Why bother impersonating the Elephant Man for five minutes when you can do it for six hours? Buying four pints of snakebite in Elephant Man mode takes some doing, especially when it's last orders and there's eight lager lads behind you desperate to squeeze more lager in.

His trip to Israel had also taken him to Egypt, Greece and Turkey, and he'd ended up as a goat herder in France. I loved the idea of that. Very Kerouac. From there, he'd changed career paths for a stint at calling "Legs Eleven!" at the bingo hall in Woking.

He was sporting the remains of a once healthy quiff when we met up again at a canal side pub in Woking. It was early summer - perfect weather to sit drinking on the towpath and watch the massive jets leaving Heathrow, and turn to silhouettes against the evening sky. Concorde would be along at ten past seven on her supersonic way to New York, leaving England behind with a click of her heels and a dip of her wings - just as I intended to do very soon.

Sean was a year into an acting course in London, possibly in an endeavour to take life a little more seriously. But things weren't going well. He wasn't enjoying the whole experience, and he clashed with the teachers.

"I'm trying to get kicked off the course. If I just leave, I'll have to pay the grant back to the council. Bastards."

"I thought they would've kicked you off as soon as they saw you in a leotard. Sean, if anyone can get kicked out, you can."

"I'm getting closer," he grinned. "I'm drinking myself into expulsion."

"Well, I'm going back to India. Up to Kashmir for a look around - supposed to be beautiful up there - and head over to Nepal. You'd love it. Best place you'll ever travel. I swear, I had the best month of my life there. Wanna come? We'll have a right laugh. I can show you how to break into a wildlife park. We could get chased by a tiger AND save ourselves a couple of quid. Go down to Goa for a month. You wouldn't believe the nutters you meet there. Well, you will, cos you'll be one of them. Make sure you bring your leotard."

"Nah, I'm staying in London. Try get my equity card."

"What, you're gonna be an actor or something?"

"Dunno… Not sure yet."

I scoffed heartily into my beer.

"You're missing out, pal. You should come along." Having Sean along would have been fun, but I was more than happy to be clearing off solo.

The next few weeks shot by as time drew nearer to my leaving date. I quit my job to spend my last two weeks with Maria. Walking out of Tesco after my final nightshift has qualified as one of life's definite highlights. Especially seeing as I had the best part of a thousand pounds squirrelled away. I'd never left England with more than three hundred quid before that. I was on cloud nine.

But those two weeks turned into hell. Maria completely stopped talking to me, even though we were still living together. She'd lie in bed and cry for hours. I was still in nightshift mode, and I'd be awake most of the night, walking laps of the lake, which sat just behind her flat, trying to work out what the hell was going on. The longer she wouldn't talk to me, or even look at me, the more I wanted her to. I was driving myself crazy. I did understand the strangeness of the situation I'd sprung on her, which was basically: "Let's live together for four months, then I'll leave for India and never see you again." But in my young traveller's head, I thought that being open and upfront about it might possibly make it all right.

Well, it didn't. I was living with a very upset woman, and I had no idea how to handle her. Even though I'd never seen her read a book or spark up a real conversation, and had knocked out whatever sense she'd had previously with an intake of serious drugs, I'd had a lot of fun with her. She made me laugh and we had some wild nights. And she was very, very sexy.

Sean phoned me during this horrible period.

"Mark! I did it! Got kicked out of acting school. You still going to India? I'm thinking of coming along for a few months. I've got enough for a return flight and about two hundred and seventy quid. That should be enough, shouldn't it?"

The way I was feeling at that point, arriving in India on my own had suddenly become a very depressing thought.

"That's great Sean! Honestly. Bloody fantastic. I'll phone ahead and warn them."

"Yeah, sod it. Let's go, have a laugh."

"Trust me Sean, there'll be plenty of that. I'm leaving next week. Sort your ticket out. Turkish Airlines, next Thursday afternoon."

Maria's intermittent periods of silence and then crying continued right up until the day I left - either in bed, in the bath, or in the chair under the Swatch watch. All she managed to say was: "Mark, you chose to leave me."

But I hadn't. I'd chosen to leave England well before I'd met her.

I was still excited about getting to India, but I'd messed something up. I wasn't feeling free and I'd hurt Maria.

I felt unusually despondent as I hugged Mum and Dad goodbye. They were happy I was leaving Maria I think. But I felt sad saying goodbye to my mum, not knowing when I'd see her again. Damn, I was feeling vulnerable all over.

Just get me to that airport, and I'll be free again.

A year to reach Australia, a year or so there replenishing the coffers, a year or two to get home again. That was my rough plan.

At last, it was time to go back to India and Nepal. Just make sure to avoid any bloody glaciers this time. Stick to the paths. Not much can go wrong really, if you stick to the paths.

6

The Bends

The plane ducked out of the clouds and there she was: to my mind, the finest triangle of land on the planet: India.

I'd thought about this place almost constantly for over a year since leaving it as a skint, skinny, slightly deranged twenty two year old with a mate on the brink of a mental breakdown. I was now fit and strong from the hundreds of hours of bending and lifting at Tesco, my pockets were bulging with travellers' cheques, and I was there once again.

Holy cow, I'm back!

Sean and I had done a pretty good job of kicking England into oblivion at the Heathrow bar, with a six hour top up in a street bar near Istanbul airport. We awoke, spectacularly cramped and dehydrated with stuffy aeroplane hangovers.

In an unusual act of restraint, the two bottles of Blue Label vodka we'd grabbed as we'd shot through duty free were sitting unopened at our feet in their yellow bag. I nudged Sean awake.

"Sean, look - India."

Cloud shadows floated across the plains where rivers split and snaked off to the huge towns and cities that grew out of the brown land. Lines became recognisable as roads, and dots recognisable as cars, buses and trucks. We dropped lower in the sky, and flew over a line of people sitting at the airport perimeter fence.

Definitely not plane spotters.

We sat on the runway for an interminable amount of time after the engines and air con were shut off. The temperature soared as the plane roasted under the glare of the morning Delhi sun, stewing our hangovers to horrendous proportions.

Just when I thought I might die from extreme hangoverness, the doors sucked open, and out danced the cigarette smoke that we'd carried across Arabia, only to be poleaxed by the thirty degree heat of a July Delhi morning.

We were the next to be poleaxed as we made our way across the shimmer of the tarmac to the terminal through a heat that smothered us like a blanket, with no gaps for air.

We grabbed our bags and my guitar, muddled and sweated our way through customs, and finally stepped out into India. Our welcoming party was a ramshackle collection of buses, taxis and rickshaws cluttered around the exit, all beeping and revving, the drivers shouting above the din at each other, until they saw us.

"Mister - hey Mister, taxi? Yes please, Mister. Come. I take you to a very nice hotel. You will be very happy there. Very cheap. Very clean. In the middle of New Delhi." A turbaned Sikh beamed through some impressive whiskers. I was quick to block him.

"Nah, no taxi. We'll take a rickshaw, thank you."

"Hang on Mark, we've only just got here." Sean wasn't looking convinced. "We've got all our bags and stuff. And it's seriously hot. Why don't we just take the taxi. Come on, New Delhi sounds fine. Let's do that. Get settled in first before we-"

"No! A rickshaw WILL settle you in, Sean. Come on, we're in India!"

"I just think that it's our first day, I feel a bit like I'm gonna be ill, you look like you've just been ill, we've got all this -"

"Sean, quick." I jumped into the nearest rickshaw, squeezing up into the corner, making room for Sean on the very slightly upholstered metal seat.

"In you get!" I patted the space beside me. "We can pretend we're on our honeymoon."

"Fuckin' hell, Mark."

But he climbed in, just about managing to squeeze his six foot plus frame onto what was left of the back seat.

"Paharganj, Old Delhi please," I yelled into the driver's ear over the two stroke ring-a-ding-ding.

"Old Delhi?" Sean sounded confused. "I thought New Delhi sounded OK, shouldn't we -waaarggghhhh!"

The rickshaw took off up the road in a screaming fury, cutting Sean off mid-sentence, leaving behind filthy clouds of two stroke smoke, hammering along behind another black and yellow rickshaw which spewed out an equally foul cloud of muck and burnt carbon straight into our sweaty white faces. We hurtled out of the airport at a precariously zippy thirty miles an hour, headlong into our Indian trip.

"You'll love Old Delhi Sean," I coughed. "It's completely mental."

His head gave an almost imperceptible nod, so I knew he was receiving communications. But he wasn't looking happy.

The rickshaw roof did little to hinder the sun's blaze. Within minutes we were bumper to bumper in a jam of traffic that could easily have become a permanent fixture. Every day, more and more cars and rickshaws are sucked into its gravity, a black hole of snarl from which neither light nor rickshaws can ever escape. We'd just have to wait for time to wash us all away.

When rickshaw drivers - usually the kings of the rev hand and the constant searching manoeuvre - flick their engines off, sit back, spark up a cheroot and pull their filthy headscarves down over their bloodshot eyes, as our driver now did, you knew you were in for the kind of wait that would make the headlines back home.

Sean turned to me, his eyes streaming from the settling fumes. It was like being parked in a hot, gassy marshmallow.

"Bloody hell Mark! This is ridiculous. I said we should get a taxi."

"Oh come on, it's not that bad!" I coughed, trying to grin in an attempt to pretend I was enjoying myself. We sat in silence, taking in the ambience. And coughing.

We were still alive when, for no discernible reason - like everyone suddenly decided 'that's enough boys, time to go'- the blockage cleared. The silent horde of rickshaws fired up in unison, replacing the stagnant cloud of poison with a nice stinking fresh one. We accelerated away, and morphed into a swarm of angry bees fighting for space and combustible air, as we raced along beside knackered, windowless buses and trucks driven by blind demons intent on dicing with death and mayhem.

"Whooooaaaaaa! That could've sliced us into bacon!" I shouted in Sean's ear as we pulled out of a head-on crash with a thirty tonne truck loaded to the sky with thirty more tonnes of life threatening corrugated iron.

Sean's white knuckles gripped the metal frame, his jaw locked tight on whatever it was that he wanted to say to me.

An hour or so later, we wormed into what I recognised to be Old Delhi. The streets squeezed tighter around us, and the noise and heat rendered us almost senseless. My jeans were so hot that flaming denim was a possibility. Sean hadn't spoken at all since he'd spat the word 'taxi' at me.

The rickshaw screeched to a halt, and the driver stuck his hand out.

"Two hundred rupees, Mister." About twelve quid.

"What?! No way! Thirty."

The driver jumped out and started hopping around in front of me, rattling off a high velocity verbal attack, his bloodshot eyes wide with fumes and anger. He was blessed with the perfect dialect for swearing, and he splattered me with what I presumed to be carefully constructed insults and accusations. Whatever he was saying, he was saying it very well. And very quickly.

"Alright - thirty five.'. That just made him madder, and seemingly even more eloquent. It was like being shot with a machine gun loaded with curses. People started to gather around.

"Look, Mark, just pay him. Who cares. Let's get away from here. For Christ's sake, don't start a bloody fight."

"As if I'd start a fight, Sean, but he's ripping us off, and we have to stand up to…"

"Excuse me, Mister." A young man stepped out from the crowd. "He says you have been in his rickshaw for more than one hour. You have to pay the money please. Or he'll call the police. You should pay him."

"This is a bloody set up. There's no way…"

"Mark, PAY HIM!" Sean shouted, looking increasingly uncomfortable with the growing situation.

"Ripped off AND nearly decapitated in the first hour. Brilliant!"

I begrudgingly handed the driver one hundred and fifty rupees, which calmed the situation. He jumped back in his rickshaw and shot off at full throttle, screaming a parting volley rat-a-tat insult at my tight-arse, pathetic self.

I smiled at the crowd, who quickly disbanded, revealing what once may have been a footpath outside a very basic looking hotel. We heaved our bags onto our shoulders and inched past the creamy coloured cow that was partly blocking the doorway.

"Shift over Daisy, we've arrived." I grinned at Sean, trying to show that things like losing arguments with rickshaw drivers, having a crowd side against me, and manoeuvring past big cows in hotel doorways didn't phase me in the least.

This is all part of it, pal. The fun has begun.

"Namaste. Do you have a room for us?" I asked the several men that occupied the front desk. They were draped over each other in a very relaxed Indian manner. Each took it in turns to nod, shake and wobble their heads in response - a multiple-headed octopus of mixed signals.

"Was that a yes or a no?" Sean asked me.

"Maybe both, probably neither, possibly one or the other. Let's wait and see."

We stood around, sweating in the heat. A particularly small Indian man with bulging eyes sat on a block of wood beside the heavily occupied desk, staring up at us. He was slowly pulling his remaining eyelashes out with a pair of sharp tweezers, which further enhanced his goggliness.

I whispered to Sean: "If that eye pops, duck."

The small man oscillated between leering at us and shouting up the stairs in his high, keening voice, which was met with banging doors and people dragging things around corridors.

"That'll be them clearing a room out for us now," I mumbled to Sean, trying to lighten the mood. "They use empty hotel rooms to store dead bodies sometimes. Saves leaving them on the street."

No response. Not even a "Fuck off, you prat."

Small boys suddenly appeared, scuttling down the stairs with buckets of murky water that sloshed onto the floor, for which they received a thick ear from one of the many desk men.

Our room wasn't forthcoming, the heat was hideous. It was the middle of July - pre-monsoon season. The fan creaked above our heads.

"Right. C'mon Sean, let's get the hell out of here."

Sean looked eagerly up at me for reassurance. All I could do was shout at the odd-shaped man beside the desk.

"One of the prerequisites of running a hotel is that you communicate certain pieces of necessary information to potential guests."

This gave no one any reassurance, but it made me feel a tad perkier. Perkiness is a great asset in India. The desk men obviously didn't give a toss.

We headed down the tiny packed out street, past the horses dragging carts filled with rusty concrete-strengthening bars, past sleeping cows crashed out in gutters stupefied by the sun, past screaming motorbikes, wheezing cars, rickshaws, cycles, beggars, throngs of people, dying dogs still attached to litters of puppies – well, they looked like they were dying – past a thousand beeping horns, stepping over piles of roasting dung and jets of hot cow piss.

The sun was so hot that the piss wasn't even steaming. One second it was there, shot fresh from the cow's bladder in a torrent of foamy yellow, inches from our feet, next minute - gone, evaporated away, adding an extra tang to the heavy, pungent air.

Eventually we found a hotel that had a promisingly bright neon sign hanging above the door, all letters fluorescently present and correct. We managed to get a room this time, and threw our bags into a pile in the corner of our hot concrete box.

"Come on Sean - let's go out and explore, get something to eat."

"No way. I'm not going out there."

He threw himself on the bed under the fan, refusing to budge. I'd never seen Sean like this, as our relationship had been based solely on going to pubs, gigs, parties, and anywhere else that would let us in. Well, now they'd let us into India. We'd never before made such a huge effort to make sure we ended up somewhere so disorientating.

I felt bad about the morning. I should've listened to Sean and taken a taxi to New Delhi, checked into a decent hotel for a few days, found a nice bar - if such a thing even existed in 1987 - and slowly landed.

What the hell was I thinking? A rickshaw straight into Old Delhi - one of the most condense, intense, no sense free-for-alls I'd ever come across. Great if you're already a seasoned and settled India head who can handle the onslaught - but straight from Woking with a splitting hangover? No way.

I kicked around the streets for a couple of hours, not particularly enjoying what I saw. I felt confused - I thought I'd loved it here. I'd had the best time of my life in India, and couldn't wait to get back. But it all just looked like dirty, hot chaos to me now. I couldn't see one aspect of the place that held any chance of fun for us.

When I headed back to the room, Sean was lying exactly where I'd left him on his bed, staring at the creaky fan belting round over his head.

"Come on Sean, let's go for dinner somewhere."

"No Mark. I told you, I'm not going out there. It's horrible."

I couldn't help laughing. "True. It is. But we'll get used to it."

"That's what I'm worried about."

"Well, what do you want to do then?"

"Drink the vodka."

So we lay on our hard little beds in the concrete room and opened a bottle of the evil stuff, the noise from the street never letting up, the sweat never drying.

Sean had the bends: the culture shock bends. He'd changed environments too quickly. Big bubbles of conflicting cultures were lodging in his veins, popping in his head and leaving him none the wiser, and a lot more concerned. Although he was hardly speaking, his eyes clearly conveyed his thoughts, which went something along the lines of:

What have I done?!

I need to get the hell out of here.

I can't. We're stuck here now, at least for a while.

Mark is a bastard.

We drank in near silence, swatting away at the endless flies that buzzed in the air. When they finished their shift at dusk, the mosquitoes took over for the attack. Huge cockroaches flew in through the non-closing window and smashed into the walls, folded their buzzing wings up and stared at us as if to say "What the fuck are you two doing here?" I squashed the most horrible black monster that flew uncontrollably up and down the room. One of its back legs shot off and attached to my vest, still kicking and twitching.

"Look at this, Sean!" I held my vest out to him, pointing at the magic leg until its cockroach chemistry burnt out with a final flicker.

"You know, Sean," I said, flicking at the leg and the yellow goo plastered across my chest, "there's only one thing more disgusting than cockroaches, and that's the filthy stuff they're made out of."

He wasn't interested. He looked about as miserable as a healthy, free, twenty-four year old could possibly be.

We awoke before dawn, jet-lagged, hungover and dehydrated – a trifecta of feeling crap. The walls were splattered from the cockroach slaughter of the previous night, and zigzag lines of bloodied, squashed mosquito. It was like a join-the-dots picture tracking my killing rampage around the room all night.

I heard Sean sucking up the last of the bottled water.

"Oi, camel boy, save me some," I gasped, as the hot morning air rattled around my parched tonsils.

"Too late. Can you go and get some more? I feel like I swallowed a desert."

"No, Sean, you go. There's a shop up the road - just past the lepers."

"I told you, I'm not going out there. Can't you just go?"

"Bloody hell Sean, we can't carry on like this!"

He spent the rest of the day in our room, tipping buckets of cold water over his miserable head. I wasn't exactly enthralled with my re-entry back into India, but I had to try and keep cheery. If we both hit the skids, we'd have no chance of finding fun. We might as well just give up.

Wandering, it seemed, was the answer. Wandering and watching. A walk up the street in India can take hours if you let it, or a few seconds if it freaks you out. The endless commerce taking place within any ten paces is mind boggling. Money changes hands constantly, but never quietly. Rickshaw drivers, taxis, beggars' bowls, food stalls, shop owners, cafes, restaurants, money changers, water sellers, bus boys, street hawkers. A never ending flow of folded, noisy Rupees, and the goal being to hang on to as much of the wafer-thin stuff by the end of the day as possible: survival.

I ducked into a backstreet cafe for a huge dosa - a pancake on steroids, fried to a crispy light brown on a hot plate that the place must have been built around. I sat wondering what we were going to do, drinking hot, sweet coffee and crunching on my dosa and coconut relish.

Yes. I used to like doing this. Hopefully I was landing.

One thing was for certain - there were very few travellers about. I'd never factored this into my India equation. I'd just presumed there would be the usual rag tag bunch of freaks, lost souls and warped characters wandering around that helped make travel in India so entertaining. Paharganj, Old Delhi, would be where those characters would be, if they were anywhere in Delhi. You'd have to be mad to be here in July, unless you had no say in the matter.

Sean's stand-off with India lasted a few days, as he wrestled with the fact that we'd come here out of choice. I figured he couldn't keep it up for too long, and I'd just have to let him work it through. Only he knew what was going through his brain, lying under the fan all day, listening to the noise from the street and flicking the flies away.

Late one afternoon I was sitting in the cafe I'd made my second home, chatting to the owner, when the door swung open and Sean's cautious head peered in.

"Sean! You're up - come in."

I'd been telling the owner about Sean, and he welcomed him in with a big smile and a friendly head wobble.

"Namaste. Please, sit down. Welcome to India."

Sean beamed at this glimpse of the warm Indian spirit. He ordered a juice, his first transaction in the country, and I could see the possibility of a change glimmering in his eye.

So whilst he was up and moving, I needed to get us the hell away from Delhi. Our options were limited. Journeying south would just mean heading into even more intense heat. The beaches of Goa were well out of season and empty of travellers. The desert towns of Rajasthan would be unbearably hot; even the camels would be exploding. Our blood would cook and our eyeballs melt, our skin would peel off and we'd die. So no point going there.

This only left us with one destination: Kashmir.

7

Enter The Piper

We armed ourselves for the thirty-hour bus trip north to Srinagar, Kashmir. The vodka had been consumed and sweated out of our systems - time to go local: Indian Bagpiper Whiskey. On the label a lone, tartan-clad Sikh piper marched into battle; possibly straight into slaughter.

Had to be the one for us. Especially at a pound a bottle.

Next we tapped up the hotel staff for some hash - readily available - all you had to do was ask. This was followed by a trip to the chemist for some make-the-day-go-away Valium. Joints were rolled, bags were packed and we made our way to the bus station to leave Old Delhi behind and find some fun.

Outside the hotel, we watched a horse keel over and die, still attached to the cart that it had most likely been pulling around Delhi for years. The front legs flattened out into horse splits; its big worn out eyes rolled back into its knackered old head. Its working life under the Delhi sun fizzled out, right in front of us. One of its colleagues would be along soon to drag it away.

"What are the chances of that happening, Sean? Just there, just then."

The traffic built up; horns blaring. A group of drivers surrounded the skinny, virtually naked old man who, until only a few moments ago, had a horse and a livelihood. All he had now was a bag of dead bones strapped to a loaded cart that was creating further chaos in an already chaotic street. He seemed far too old and frail to deal with the fallout.

"That's just so sad. I don't know who to feel sorry for, the horse or the man."

"I know Sean. The horse will be glue by tomorrow. What's the man going to do?"

We were still mulling this over when we hit the bus station, not quite ready for the gangs of kids that were instantly onto us - crying, pushing their horribly twisted limbs our way, thrusting empty begging bowls in our faces imploringly, and following up with big, dark, pleading eyes. Their mothers crouched on the floor, holding up skinny crying babies at arm's length.

"Paise baba? Paisa baba?" Money Mister?

Sean, still unsteady on his fresh India legs, was under attack. Best keep him moving. We pushed through the crowds to find our Srinigar bus surrounded by hordes of street hawkers and beggars. Food and drinks were paraded around and pushed under our noses. Bags of chopped pineapple and watermelon, newspaper cones of warm peanuts, deep red tandooried chicken legs, big yellow hands of bananas, endless colourful sweets and curds, naans, chapatis, rotis, paper plates of dhal and curry.

We fought our way on board after throwing our bags up to the luggage boy jumping around on the roof. The din was incredible. Engines revving, dogs barking, everyone shouting, horns blaring, babies screaming.

"Bloody hell, there's more people inside this bus than there are in Woking. Come on, Sean."

I made myself big and noisy, pushing my way up the packed centre aisle to find our seat numbers, which were already taken up by two young Indian men clutching a huge hessian sack, looking like they were taking a whole year's washing home to Mum.

"Namaste! Sorry sirs, these are our seats. Look, here's our tickets. See? The numbers? Our seats." I smiled and pointed to Sean and I. "Yes? Our seats. For us…Thank you!"

I held my arm out in the universal 'please vacate' gesture.

The two men stared blankly at me, seemingly befuddled as to what the hell this hot-faced white man could possibly be on about, on this bus, waving tickets in their faces, and pointing at those two numbers which by chance matched the numbers written on their seats.

So I stared back.

"What happens now?" Sean asked, after a few noisy moments had passed.

"Er, I'm not too sure. But I think it might involve me dragging them out of our seats."

"Oh, what? Mark, are we going to fight our way round India?"

"Well it's either that or we stand our way round India. And it's a bloody big country. Ready?"

I leaned forward to politely lift the young men from our seats, when, screaming over my shoulder, came the bag boy. He grabbed the hessian sack and the closest of the two men by the arm and pulled him from the seat in a perfectly executed jettison move. The other man was up and out of there in a flash, holding his arms up to his head, fully expecting a beating from the trigger-happy young whippersnapper.

The boy then turned to me and said something which gave the old woman next to us an instantaneous hysterical laughing fit, which, judging by her tears, was the one-liner of a lifetime.

"Well that's brightened her day, Mark."

"What do you reckon he said?"

Sean gave me a thoughtful look. "Dunno. But it didn't half tickle her."

We squeezed ourselves into seats perfectly designed for anyone under five foot four with a hip circumference untainted by high-level beer consumption and nightshift custard, and jammed our knees into the backs of the seats in front.

The old lady was still cackling away behind me. It can't possibly have been that funny.

The driver climbed through his open window, gunned the engine, revved the holy hell out of the thing, screamed a very interesting combination of sharp syllables at the bag boy, powered down the engine, climbed out the window and disappeared back into the crowd, leaving the hawkers, beggars and food engulfed in a thick cloud of fresh exhaust.

"Where's he gone? What was the point of all that?" Sean was rightly bemused. "Why was he practicing his revving?"

"Shit, I thought we were about to leave then. Uh oh, what's this fella up to?"

A tall, bald man in a loose robe was standing at the front of the bus, arms tucked behind his back. He began to make his way down the aisle, eyeing the passengers with a bizarre look of intensity, which in retrospect made absolute sense because he knew what he was about to do.

"Oi Mark, is he checking tickets?"

"Well if he is, he's got a very strange way of doing it."

Sean had the window seat, and couldn't see what I could. The man had taken his arms from behind his back and held out a heavy headed hammer and two nasty-looking six inch nails. I had a fair idea where this was going.

He stuck his head forward, at Sean and I, and pushed one of the nails an inch or so up his left nostril, from where it hung for a moment - all six inches of shiny, sharp nail aimed straight into his head.

"He's not checking tickets, is he?" Sean was sounding wary. And he hadn't seen the hammer yet.

With a flurry the man swung the hammer up from chest height and connected square with the nail head, giving off a sickening *dink-thunk*, surprising the hell out of Sean, and belting the metal right up his nostril into some deep, pre-furrowed cavity.

"Oooooorrrrggghhhhhhh! I can't watch this!"

Sean quickly turned away as the hammer rose again, burying the nail up to the hilt, but this time it must've burrowed into his forehead, just where I always thought the brain started. A sickening spectacle to watch, especially as his eyeballs did a lap of their sockets on each hit. There was no fakery going on here.

He twisted the next nail into place in his adjoining nostril, swung the hammer up again with even more force and buried the nail into slot number two. Thwunk - strike. His eyes bulged and spun upwards.

Sean's face was pressed hard up against the window.

"Make him go away, Mark." He sounded tense. "Quick, give him some money."

I fumbled for a five rupee note, about thirty pence, and thrust the money into his hand.

"Please. No more. You're very good. Thank you, thank you." He pocketed his fiver, grinned, wiggled the nails out of his nose, creating a metal-on-bone scraping sound, and continued on up the bus, sending back dink-thunks and sickening groans from the other passengers.

"God, that was almost worse than watching that horse die. Imagine doing that for a job. I think I'd lose the will to live."

"I lost the will to live working in Tesco."

"Yeah, but you had a choice, Mark."

"True. And I chose to not be there anymore."

"I don't think you can compare. You earned enough money in six months to travel the world; that bloke fires metal nails into his forehead everyday just to survive."

The success of the nail-nose man was the cue for a stream of disturbing begging acts to target the trapped passengers on board. This wasn't going to be pretty. Not even the lone Bagpiper could fend this lot off.

A man waving three tiny thumbs about on one hand was heading our way. He saw us and smiled, before sticking a skewer through his cheek, then right through his tongue, and then out the other cheek. Sean had his face pressed against the window again.

"Bloody hell, Sean, it's a human face kebab. Sure you don't wanna see this?" I handed over another fiver, and off he went.

An hour later, with the temperature inside the bus near fusion point, and myself about thirty five rupees out of pocket, the driver returned, wiping fresh curry from his moustache. After throwing his chai cup to the ground, he climbed through the window, fired up the engine again, crunched the ageing bus into gear - a sound like a tumble drier gargling rocks - and nudged the old crate through the crowds, elbow firmly pushed against the horn, as we inched out into the Delhi traffic. The ninja boy hung from the open door, screaming.

"Srinagaaaar-ayyyyy. Srinagaaaar-ayyyyy."

The only other westerners on board were a bunch of young Italian couples, neatly attired in what Sean described as 'Rome casual.' They did an incredible job of not saying hello to us. Which was fine. We'd soon be in floaty Valium joint world anyway. We gradually relaxed as we slowly left the Delhi madness behind, occasionally accepting toots from the Bagpiper.

We stopped north of Delhi at a chai stall on a hillside. The sun had gone down, forgetting to take the heat with it.

"Sean, grab a joint and we'll sneak up to those trees."

"You've got them. You rolled them and put them on your book. With the Valium."

"No, I gave them to you, and you put them in your money belt."

"No. You put them…"

We dived through our hand luggage. My book wasn't there, which was bad enough. If Sean was right, it was on the bed back at the hotel with the joints and the Valium.

Bollocks. This was going to be one long, uncomfortable, wide-awake journey. We sat, silently blaming each other for this major stuff-up.

As night fell and communications were resumed, I told Sean some tales of Kashmir that I'd heard, and what we could possibly expect once it enveloped us in its high altitude bosom.

Top of my hit list were the houseboat hash treks. Beautiful little boats weave amongst the many waterways around Kashmir, so I'd been told. Possibly pulled along the towpaths by horses. Or camels. I wasn't sure about that, so I'd just invent detail to make it sound like I knew what I was on about.

For a couple of quid a day we'd float along, sipping beer and whiskey, eating curries, stopping when we came across huge fields of sticky marijuana plants towering high above us. We'd don special leather aprons and run through the headily aromatic marijuana fields collecting pollen on our special aprons – like huge, happy, upright bees. We'd then take this pollen back to our houseboats (hives), and spend the rest of the day rolling the sticky residue in our hands to make hash (honey), which we'd crumble (drizzle) onto our breakfast, should we fancy. Which we would.

"And do you know what else, Sean?"

"There'll be two Japanese hippy girls on the boat with hash dependent nymphomania?"

"Yep."

"I can't speak Japanese."

"Doesn't matter. They communicate by touch."

This mindless nonsense went some way to cheering us. We sipped from the Bagpiper, amused by the ridiculous possibilities which lay ahead, as night-time India crawled by outside.

8

Boat to Nowhere

The twenty-four hour journey took more like forty, thanks to endless rockslides on the steep, crumbling roads, which wound up from the North Indian plains to the dizzying heights of Kashmir.

In my mind, Srinagar was going to be a kind of high altitude Amsterdam, with waterways and cool cafes to lounge in for long afternoons of stoned chess, cake eating, reggae marathons, people watching and mountain staring. Not to mention the endless shagging we were bound to become embroiled in.

This hopeful notion was shattered within seconds, once we'd prised our aching arses and sore knees from the killer bus seats. We probably would have been more comfortable folded up inside suitcases and chucked on the roof. Half completed concrete buildings, dirty backstreets, and a smell of stagnant lake water pervading everything. Worst of all, there was a distinct feeling of 'nothing going on' that was more Woking than Amsterdam.

The first thing we didn't see were Japanese hippy girls with glints in their hash-dependant eyes. The second thing we didn't see were adverts for houseboat hash treks. Wrong time of year, apparently, for girls and boat treks. Wrong time of year, full stop. The best we could do was book a week on a houseboat to nowhere.

We ducked into a concrete bunker, which doubled as a travel agency, and were told, quite emphatically: "Nagin Lake is the place to be, for sure."

So we jumped in a taxi and drove out to the lake, after replenishing our supplies of Bagpiper.

We found a boat at a reasonable price run by a man named Abdul and his ten-year-old daughter. He was a big, virtually silent man whose fleshy lips let his heavy lidded eyes do most of the talking. We completed what was possibly the quietest transaction in India as we booked in for a week. Abdul, in his grey gown, was the same size as two Japanese girls put together. That was the end of that fantasy.

Our room was almost exactly the size of the two single beds that had somehow been squeezed between the four dark walls. A small curtained window, which didn't quite close properly, peeped out just above the brown waterline. I could almost see the mosquitoes dancing a meniscus dance, lining up for their evening feast. I had something in my blood that mosquitoes couldn't get enough of, some lovely sweet protein that, when sucked up their proboscis, lit up their tiny vampire minds with glorious images of distant heather, Friesian cows and the M1. Scottish blood in an English body apparently equals deep mosquito joy.

I tore some pages from a book, wet them from the bucket in the standing-room-only bathroom, and papier mâchéd the gap in the window shut. Sean looked on.

"Good to see you enjoying yourself, Mark. I'll meet you on deck."

With my preventative repairs completed, we sat on deck in our Kashmiri deck chairs and watched Nagin Lake in the early afternoon light, the sun occasionally creeping out from behind the low level clouds. The ornate wooden houseboats, like floating Romany caravans, tucked up amongst the reeds and the blossoming lotus plants around the lakeshore. Tree lined hills rose to meet the surrounding clouds. Little merchant boats paddled around looking for customers, like floating vending machines. But there weren't any. Just Sean and myself.

Our neighbouring houseboat seemed as void of life as every other boat that my desperate eyes could search out. It would appear that we'd managed to drop ourselves into one of the quietest, most romantic places on the planet.

"Oh, Christ." Sean saw the week stretching out ahead of us. "What have we done?"

A gong sounded. Abdul popped up from below deck and wordlessly invited us to follow him.

We stepped back a hundred years into the dining room, which was built around a fine old table stacked high with a mountain of scones, buckets of jam and butter, and plates of biscuits. Centre stage was a huge silver teapot snuggled in a fluffy cosy.

Sean let out a whimper. A grandmother clock ka-thunked our lives away in the corner.

We sat down, feeling awkward. Abdul hovered close by; there was only 'on top of us' and 'close by' to choose from. He pointed at the various goodies, nodding his massive silent head knowingly, which seemed to say: "This is what you've come for, boys - Abdul's jam and scone party!"

Sean reached for the teapot, and set me off with an unexpectedly cheery, "Shall I be Mum?"

I couldn't look up, and sat trying to swallow my painful snorts as Sean handed me the scone plate.

"Here you are Mark, these scones look just smashing, don't they?"

I concentrated on my clenched hands below the table as Sean slathered my scones in butter, trying to hide the shaking of my shoulders as the wheezing sniggers snuck out; my face burning with the effort.

He slapped a big dollop of jam onto his plate, turned to Abdul with a mouthful of scone and sprayed, in a very enthusiastic tone: "Mmmmmmmm, these are delicious, Abdul! Did you make them yourself?"

If I'd had a mouthful of tea, it would have shot everywhere.

Luckily Abdul left the room, and I could recalibrate myself to act like a normal human being again. But he soon returned, and fussed some more over the tea and scones and biscuits.

Now the humour had gone, it all just felt very uncomfortable. We overcompensated by saying 'thank you' a thousand times too often.

Then, unannounced, Abdul opened a cupboard and hauled out a huge water pipe, which he set about filling with sticky hash so black it was verging on green. *This'll give you smart-arsed gits something to smirk about,* his large head seemed to say.

He lit the hash, which he mixed with a plug of hard, charcoal-like tobacco, and sucked up big bubbling lungfuls which he spectacularly blew into the air with a long "Phoooooooooooohh."

We passed the pipe around until all oxygen and conversation had left the room. There hadn't been much of either to start with, so it didn't take long.

Within minutes we were bone stoned. Heavy, weighed down underwater stoned. Hang on - we were underwater! Below the plimsoll line anyway. We bolted for the door and wrestled our way up the now tricky ladder, and collapsed, four cream scones heavier, back into our Kashmiri deck chairs.

Abdul's daughter was on the lower step, cleaning plates in the dirty lake water, worryingly close to the where the bathroom waste pipe was. She grinned up at us.

Her eyes said it all. "Daddy's got you with his pipe, hasn't he?"

The lake seemed busier than before, the light much sharper. Even more of the long boats - wooden shikaras - were out. One was cutting a path through the endless green lilies, heading our way. A young man, his boat filled with flowers, was doing a good job of rowing and simultaneously frantically waving at us.

"Hello Misters! You like flowers?"

"Er, yes, they're very nice. Very yellow. And red."

We all looked at each other for a bit too long.

"You buy flowers? For your wives? Very beautiful thing to do. You will make them very happy."

"We have no wives."

He grinned at Sean.

"For your friend then?"

He rowed away after a few more minutes of silent grinning and eye widening.

"He was friendly," I offered, in a pathetic attempt at speaking again.

Kingfishers flashed by; dashes of electric blue against the grey, muggy sky. Herons waded around the reeds, occasionally striking out at the fish with their long, sharp beaks.

And that was about it. Not much else happened on Nagin Lake.

Every four hours Abdul would reload the pipe and destroy us just as we were coming back up for air. I sat around playing guitar and reading for the rest of the week, trying to fend off images of Maria sobbing on her bed, trying not to go over the same old ground. Sean sat around reading and thinking. You could almost see the cogs lumping against his brow, book folded in his lap, a look of intense, stoned, cornered boredom firmly stuck to his face.

Evenings were the worst. We'd crash out early, wrecked from Abdul's pipe, and awake in the small hours in our tiny cabin, trying to read ourselves back to sleep by the dull glow of the lamp.

But not one mosquito breached the defences of my intricate window work. They didn't need to, as the door wouldn't shut. All they had to do was fly through the obvious gap where the wall didn't meet the door, and I was all theirs. The room hummed with the high pitched buzz as they flew past my eardrum and onto an orgasmic probe under my skin to get to the good stuff.

It was a fucking miserable week on beautiful, romantic Nagin Lake.

9

The Drinking Club

After a week, Abdul released us from our silent contract and four hourly pipe of annihilation. We took ourselves back into the centre of Srinagar in search of whatever it was we might be able to find.

In a different concrete box that doubled as a travel agent, we explained our predicament to a couple of young Kashmiri men working there. The predicament being, of course, that we were bored to death.

They laughed when we told them about our week on Nagin Lake.

"No, no, no! Nagin Lake is for couples and newlyweds. You should be on Dal Lake. That's where the fun is. Plenty of parties, many people. You could even go to the Drinking Club."

Our world suddenly turned all rosy again. A drinking club. A club for drinking. And we'd just been told by these fantastic two lads who understood us completely, that we could go there. Based on this small but solid piece of intelligence, we booked another week on a houseboat, this time on pumping Dal Lake, the Majorca of the Mountains, the Ibiza of the East.

Our first impression was that Dal Lake was much busier than Nagin Lake; it felt like something could actually happen here. The houseboats were closer together, a bit more rough and ready, hopefully less likely to be decked out in doilies and overflowing with cream scones. We took a rowboat taxi to our new watery address and presented our prepaid chit. The boat was run by a couple of young men who looked surprisingly similar to the ones who'd sent us there. They welcomed us with big cold glasses of Kingfisher beer. Nice touch.

But where were the other travellers? We'd sort of been expecting heads to be popping up from boats as we rowed past, like party-hungry gophers checking out the lake's new additions. No heads popped. But it was a big lake, with many waterways leading this way and that. Maybe we were just in a quiet 'street'.

So, not to get too down, we capitalised on our earlier bout of positive action, and made an attempt to kick our new week into life with a trip to the Drinking Club that evening, it being Friday and all. Whoever was around was bound to be there.

We limbered up on deck with several Kingfisher lagers and some splendid curries and dhal, whipped up down below by the resourceful and friendly young men. They sipped chai and watched their profits soar as our afternoon flowed on. Come early evening we took a water taxi back across the lake; the orange glow from the sinking sun lighting up the underside of the fat clouds and turning the muddy lake water a slightly more appealing shade of brown. Our water taxi man was a dark, handsome old fellow in a pure white, superbly uncreased dhoti and white, fez-like hat. His two gold teeth flashed as he grinned at us from his end of the low lying boat that looked like it could have floated straight out of Biblical times. His oar was a heavy-handled bat in the perfect shape of the ace of clubs.

"I like your teeth," said Sean. "Are they new?"

The old man nodded and grinned even wider, arcing his ace of clubs deep into the reeds that choked the busy waterway.

"This," I said to Sean, as a warm feeling of content rose in me, "… is bloody lovely."

And so it was. Lanterns dangled from the eaves of the houseboats, kids splashed in the shallow waters along the shore next to half-submerged water buffalo, and the herons waded around one last time before settling down for the night in their nests buried amongst the tall reeds.

"I wonder what an Indian drinking club is like," Sean asked, as the endless line of shikaras rowed by, trying to sell us huge bunches of flowering lilies, Kashmiri carpets, colourful little hats and booklets of matches.

"Well," I chirped up, full of knowledge and happy memories, "I've been to one in Bombay. It was great. Little private wooden booths, everyone drinking whiskey. Course, it was more of a local den for Indian men, no tourists to speak of. Gareth and Paul got involved in a chilli omelette eating competition with the cooks. They payed the price later though. I only had a hangover to deal with. They had hangovers and third degree under-burns."

"Well you're a very sensible man, Mark. Not given to foolish behaviour."

"That's right, Sean. But the drinking club here should be more of a mix. Locals and tourists I'd say. I reckon it'll have a chandelier."

"A chandelier? That good, eh?" He was impressed.

"That good, Sean."

We came ashore, after folding a generous stack of notes into the strong hands of our smiling old oarsman, and stomped off in search of our first good night out in India. Our moods were satisfyingly elevated from the fine afternoon, having been free of Abdul's pipe for a whole day. As we'd just proven, we were almost capable of having a conversation again. Things were definitely looking up.

After many false leads down backstreets that led nowhere, we finally reached our destination. There she was, glistening like an oriental jewel in the dark, Indian night: The Drinking Club.

Well, it had a light on. Not a bright light, but bright enough to draw these beer moths blindly onwards. Pulled on by the light, we broke into a thirsty trot, which wasn't getting us there anywhere near fast enough. I kicked my heels and raced ahead, momentarily closer to the chandelier-lit beer fountain than Sean was. He came flying past me, elbows flailing, laughing. Alive again!

We burst through the door in a laughing heap, and came to a sickening halt. A large, under-lit room housed rows of empty tables. A lone Indian fellow stood behind the bar. The only noise was the squeaking of his cloth as he cleaned a glass.

We ordered two beers and sat by the window, supping in silence.

"Bloody hell Mark, what are we going to do?"

"… Drink up and go?" That's all I had.

"No - about this. India. We're having a shit time. There's no one around, and it's not going to change for months. I don't want this. Do you?"

No. I didn't. I wanted my old India back. I loved my old India, where every town was an adventure of some kind, with people to meet and an abundance of strange times. This new India was too hot, too depressing, and too quiet by far.

"Shit, we can't even go anywhere. Well I can't. What's the closest fun place to here? Thailand? If we flew there I couldn't afford to fly home again."

Sean had no interest in 'finding himself' in India. He wanted a laugh. And so did I. We needed fun, drinking, and, most importantly, other people. I could come back later when it was busy again and find myself when no one I knew was looking.

I couldn't give up after two weeks though. I'd invested so much time and energy over the past year to get myself back there. If Sean went home, I doubted that I'd want to have stayed there on my own.

"Look, I know things aren't looking great, but let's just see the week out here, and then decide what to do. Something will change. Something will happen. It always does. You'll see."

Sean shook his head, looking around at the empty room.

"Like what, Mark? What's going to change?"

We left the Drinking Club, never to return, and walked back towards town.

Just then, a taxi pulled up and a youngish driver jumped out.

"Did you want to buy any hash?"

"No thanks, got some."

"You want me to take you to the Drinking Club?"

"Definitely not - just been there, and it's shit."

"You boys looking for fun?" he asked, with a grin.

"Well... we want fun, yes, but probably not the kind you're offering." Maybe Srinagar was more like Amsterdam than I thought.

"You think I mean prostitute? Ha! No. No prostitute. But I do know where there are some. You want prostitute? Very young girls. Or old lady if you like."

"No no, we don't want prostitutes. We want fun."

"Yes, yes. I know. I can tell. I'll show you fun. Very, very good fun. You are lucky men. The best fun in Srinagar." Well, it was either that, or head straight back to the houseboat.

"Also, very cheap. You give me one hundred rupees, and I'll show you fun."

About six pounds. We glanced at each other.

"Ok, show us your fun then Mister," and we jumped into his cab.

We shot off into the dark, laughing at our eager desperation. He could've been taking us anywhere, but the streets didn't feel dangerous in Srinagar, and he didn't seem like trouble. Even if he did, the thought of trouble was more appealing than a big, fat nothing.

We raced through ever darkening streets to the edge of town.

"Where do you think he's taking us, Sean?"

"I reckon it's an underground gambling den. We might win someone's gold teeth!"

"Or lose our own real ones. I don't play cards."

"Nor do I. Not for teeth, anyhow."

"I hope it's not a dog fight. Do you reckon they have dog fights here?"

"Dunno Mark, I've never really thought about it. Oh shit. I hope not."

"I think dog fights are more Mexico way. That was Gate 22 at Heathrow. Tequila, cocaine, women and dog fights. We were Gate 24: houseboats, hash and silence."

The driver was slowing to a halt on the edge of a dark field. He turned around, grinning.

"Ok. Tonight is full moon. Keep watching the clouds, you will see. Today there was a wedding. When a man marries a woman in Kashmir, there's a special place they go alone when the full moon is out."

Sean dropped his head into his hands. I couldn't tell if he was sobbing or laughing.

We parked up beside the field.

"You see that tree? Way over there? That's where you'll hide. Very soon, a boat will come down the river and stop near that tree. The married couple will then do the fucking."

Sean let fly a huge snort.

"What? And we watch them?! That's the hundred rupee fun?"

"Yes. It is very good. She is very beautiful. He is very tall. When the moon comes out, you will see everything." He made an obscene gesture with his arm and hand, like an elephant's trunk shooting up through a drain, accompanied by a noise that sounded like a squid being trodden on.

"And do they get the money?" I asked, laughing.

"No, no. The money is for me. I wait here for you and then take you back to the lake. You see the fucking, I get the money. Everybody is happy. Especially the tall man." He did the disgusting gesture again, grinning and winking at us enthusiastically.

"See Sean - I told you things would look up," I laughed. "Sean?"

Sean still had his head in his hands. He spoke from behind his outstretched fingers.

"Mark. That is not my idea of fun. Is it yours?"

"Nooooo," I lied, "but it is something to do…"

The driver was tapping his watch.

"Quickly, they will be there soon. Run now. Run to the tree, but don't be seen. Hide properly. If they think someone is watching, maybe they won't do the fucking."

No, I'd gathered that.

"Look, thanks for the offer," Sean said to the driver. "But can you take us back to the lake please."

The driver seemed quite stunned at this suggestion.

"What? You don't want to see the fu-"

"No, can you please just drive us. Thanks." Sean wasn't having any of it. I would've happily ran across the dark field and hidden in the bushes, if only for the fact that it was way more exciting than the alternative. But I didn't think it was worth arguing over.

An hour later, we were dumped back at Dal Lake again, and took a silent water taxi in the dark back to the houseboat. Things didn't seem quite as endearing as before. Bed by ten. Awake at two.

Uh oh. Here comes Maria, sneaking into my thoughts again. I couldn't shake her. The treat-Mark-mean routine had really worked its magic on me. Was that her spell? Simple, but very effective. I lay on my thin mattress in the dark, listening to Sean laying on his thin mattress in the dark. He was awake too. I could hear his brain wrestling with itself. It was like listening to a crocodile taking a fisherman under.

Next morning, up early, we tried to remain positive about our situation. After all, we had been close to almost having a laugh last night. That in itself was something. A hopeful glimmer, albeit a very desperate one.

Over breakfast of curd and chilli omelettes we hatched a great plan, which involved going back into the ever disappointing Srinagar.

We borrowed the houseboat's rowboat and I rowed us ashore; the dark, smelly water bubbling up around our feet through a small hole, which Sean scooped out with a little plastic beaker.

We bought a pad of paper and coloured pens in town and wrote out our great idea in big, let's-have-a-laugh lettering:

TRAVELLERS WANTED FOR DRINKING PARTY ON HOUSEBOAT NEPTUNE.
WHEN? SATURDAY NIGHT (TONIGHT) 6PM.
BRING DRINKS AND HAVE A LAUGH WITH MARK AND SEAN.

We pinned these desperate little gems all around town where we thought any young travellers might wander. Post office, outside the bank, on lamp posts, near the water-taxi jetty.

Mission accomplished, Sean rowed us back across the lake towards our houseboat, the lake water still bubbling up through the planks of old wood under our wet feet.

"I think you should do something about that water, Mark." Sean was sweating in the muggy heat, pulling hard against the oars to speed us along.

"Like what? Drink it?"

"No, scoop it out, you git, like I did. What do you think that plastic tub is for?"

"Oh. What, this plastic tub?"

My scooping wasn't as good as Sean's though, and the water was definitely on the rise. Either that or his rowing wasn't as good as mine.

"You're not rowing fast enough, Sean."

"Well you do it then!"

"I can't. I'm scooping."

"Don't fuck around, Mark. Get that water out."

We made it to the houseboat, just in time, as my ankles were almost submerged. Without thinking I jumped up and leapt from the front of the rowboat onto the steps of the houseboat, causing the nose of the rowboat to shoot skywards, and Sean and the boat were tail flipped backwards towards the stinking brown water that made up Dal Lake in 1987.

Within seconds he was up and running towards the houseboat like a Jesus Christ lizard, using the sinking row boat as an underwater platform, screaming "DOOOOON'T!" as he ran himself under, until I could just see his head and shoulders propelling forward. Luckily the two houseboat lads were on hand to help pull him out, and refloat their boat.

I laughed myself sick as Sean was hauled onto the deck, covered in brown gunk and lily leaves. I hadn't seen anything move so fast for days. It was the only time in my life I thought he might actually hit me. But you couldn't hit a man who was laughing as hard as I was.

"I'm sorry Sean. That was stupid, I know. I'm not very good on the water. You'll be OK - your head didn't go under, did it? I wouldn't be laughing if your head went under, promise."

"Fuck off, Mark. You're a bloody idiot. I could catch typhoid in there. There's a shit pipe just by that bog window."

The image of Sean running across the water screaming "DOOOON'T" - with his his arms straight out like Shaggy escaping the ghostly janitor in Scooby Doo - kept me buckling over long after I should've stopped laughing.

"You just looked so surprised and… submerged. Sorry, Sean."

He disappeared below deck to scrub himself pink under a thousand buckets of cold water, which was pumped straight from the lake anyway. I thought it best not to mention that.

He threw his sodden, smelly clothes in the bin, reappearing on deck sometime later.

"Cheer up, mate. We've got the houseboat party in a couple of hours. Our guests will be arriving. I hope they embark more gracefully than you did."

"Well they won't if they arrive with someone who's as big a prat as you are, Mark."

I laughed.

"Oh well, at least things are happening now, eh? Look how far we've come since leaving the Drinking Club! Told you things would look up."

"Yes, it's great, Mark. I don't know why everyone doesn't come here on holiday."

Six o'clock came and went, and of course, no one arrived for the drinking party. Not one desperate soul. We sat on the deck peering across the lake, looking for signs of life that could bring us any amusement.

The lake traders were all we could see. And we were all they could see, because we were the only ones around. Early night again.

Twice more during the week we put up posters, desperately imploring anyone to come and drink with us.

No one did.

On our last full day on the boat, a water taxi rowed along with a western couple and their bags, checking out the houseboats. They pulled up next to ours. I felt like a puppy in a pet shop window.

"Is this a good boat?" They called up to us.

"Yes! It is. Really, really good! We've had a fantastic week here."

Please, please stay with us!

They did, and we were pathetically ecstatic.

Once on board, we gave them three or four minutes to settle before we pounced.

Clink clink. "Beer?"

Chai suited them just fine. He was Australian, she was English. Sure, they were finding the heat a bit much, but the out-of-season thing didn't bother them. They were a couple enjoying a quiet time in Kashmir.

Without being asked, we filled them in on our trip so far, from arriving hungover, to Sean's shock at Delhi, stupidly forgetting the Valium and joints for the bus journey, the bone-crushingly boring week on Nagin Lake, the painful disappointment of the Drinking Club, and the desperate cry for help from our poster runs around Srinagar. We didn't mention the potential honeymoon voyeurism.

She summed us up perfectly.

"You two are definitely in the wrong place - you should be in

Torremolinos."

I felt like an absolute prat. Not only should we have gone to Torremolinos, we were acting like we had gone to Torremolinos, and no one had bothered to tell us we'd caught the wrong plane.

10

The Gulmarg Shuffle

We learned from the insightful boat couple about Gulmarg, a mountain village west of Srinagar. I was sure we'd get some views of the Himalayas from there, and convinced Sean to give it a try. We set sail for land, and made our hopeful way into the sweltering bus station. If in doubt, keep moving. I knew that seeing the Himalayas would cheer us up, and help Sean make sense of why I'd brought him there.

The bus slowly wound its way west towards Pakistan, through Kashmir forests and over mountain rivers. Again and again we had to stop to help clear landslides that had only recently crashed down the hills, depositing piles of rocks across the road that were big enough to wipe you from the face of the world, if the timing wasn't on your side.

The first thing I noticed in Gulmarg completely surprised me.

"A golf course? What the fuck is *that* doing here?" I spluttered, as we lifted our bags from the bus.

"No idea. Let's ask. Someone's bound to know."

The village itself was very mountain pretty. It'd be great in winter, with a girlfriend. Probably shit in summer, with an already bored mate. Wooden lodges were scattered amongst the trees, and even what could hopefully be classed as a bar. Well, it had a shop with a faded picture of a bottle of lager in the window. That'd have to do.

We walked past a uniformed guard standing outside a lodge near the store.

"Namaste," I smiled to the guard as we entered. He nodded in neither a friendly nor an aggressive way. Just a nod. We nodded back. Nod nod.

"I suppose they need guards because we're close to the Pakistani border," Sean mused, as we approached the desk. "Can't imagine much trouble round here - an irate golfer, maybe?"

"Oh! Hello sirs. Will you be paying for the whole week?" The attractive Indian woman running the place was all smiles. She seemed as surprised at seeing us there as we were at seeing the golf course.

"We'll just pay for a night, please."

That took the smile off her face. Her eyes narrowed as she tilted her head back, baring her teeth, as if she was about to spray me with some viper venom that she'd squirrelled away in her jowls for such an occasion.

"Certainly," she spat, "the menu is on the wall. The best food in Gulmarg. Thank you."

'Thank you' was accompanied with a dismissive flick of her chin. Thank you. Now fuck off out of my sight.

"Shit, she didn't like you Mark, did she?"

"No she did not. She wanted us to pay for a week."

"I'm not staying here a week."

"No. I can guarantee that. Fuckin' golf."

We parked our belongings in our small wooden room and headed out to explore. Well, we headed straight to the shop with the faded beer picture in the window - after another nod nod with the guard - and waited half an hour for someone to pop their head up from behind the counter and actually take our money. We stared at the golf course. We stared at the trees. And we stared at the clouds shielding the mighty Himalayas from view.

"Maybe China has learnt to make clouds, and they're pumping them over the mountains to block the view," I offered.

Sean let out a sound like a small animal being snared. He gripped his temples, trying to rub away the scream of frustration that was building inside his head.

We sat for a while in silence.

"OK Mark, and why would they be doing that?"

We sat in silence again, sipping our beer. No point rushing.

"I dunno. Maybe they're up to something. Pulling Everest over the border?"

Sean gave me the look.

"What?" I laughed. "They might be. They could give it a fresh coat of paint. Or put some wheels on it and spin it round so the easy side is facing China. Then they'll get all the money from the climbing permits. Good money in permits nowadays, so I hear, Sean." I smiled, pleased at my ludicrous ponderings.

We returned to silence as we finished our beers.

"Want another?" I asked.

"What? Another conversation? No. I don't think you'll beat the last one, Mark."

"No. Another beer." I clinked our empty bottles in a cheery kind of way.

"Nah. I'm going back to read. Coming?"

We loped back to the lodge, went through the guard nodding routine, then past the venom-spitting owner into the dining room, and stopped dead in our tracks - not that we were moving particularly fast anyway. A blonde girl looked up from the long table that spread the length of the room. It was obvious she'd recently spent some money on new Kashmiri hippy gear. Her red embroidered tunic and colourful headscarf still needed some wearing in before it would cut the mustard on the beaches of Goa or the hippy cafes of Kathmandu.

"Hi guys! I'm Aimee. Join me for a chai?" Canadian. She jumped up, all smiles and openness. Reflected light glanced off the little cosmic mirrors stitched into her new tunic.

"Oh 'allo. I'm Sean." He'd suddenly brightened up.

"Hi Sean!" She sent out a beam of love and gentle understanding. I wanted one too.

"Mark. Hallo! How you doin'?"

"Hiiiiii!!"

Oh, that felt good. At last, someone to talk to. Apart from the couple on the houseboat, she was the first traveller we'd actually spoken to since landing.

"We've just been wandering around the town. It's very quiet, isn't it?"

She gave me a quizzical look. "Of course it's quiet - Gulmarg in August! What did you expect? Party town?! You should see it when the snow comes in October though. The place is packed."

Damn! Only out by about two months. I tried to not catch Sean's eye.

Aimee wasted no time in filling us in on her thang. It was impressive how many questions she could get into a sentence without actually asking anything.

"Yeah, I'm on vacation, I guess you'd say? Do you say that? In the UK? Vacation? I work in advertising. I just kinda came to India to, I don't know, explore myself a bit more? You know what I'm saying?"

No. We didn't know. But we presumed, correctly, that she was about to tell us.

Sean was in straight away. "What, you work in advertising, and you're here to... Do what? *'Get deeper?'* They'll sack you when you get home. You'll break the industry. Put a big hole straight through the middle of it."

His cynical words didn't make a dent. The cosmic mirrors were doing their job, reflecting away all that negative energy.

"Ha! You're funny. What do you guys do?"

"I work in Tesco," I piped in.

"Neat!"

"Not the shop part though."

"OK."

"Or the office part."

"No?"

"No. The other part."

"Ohhh! So you work in the *other* part of Tesco? That's great!"

"No. It's shit."

"Oh." She looked over to Sean for help. "So, do you both work in the other part of Tesco?"

"No," Sean smiled. "I'm a concreter."

"I thought you were a hod carrier?" I butted in.

Aimee did one of those faces that you can only do when you are truly taken aback.

"What - he carries pigs?"

"Hod! Not hog. You know, H O D - the *hod* carrier, for bricks."

"I've never carried a hod, Mark," Sean said. "Or pigs, for that matter."

"Ohhhhh! OK." Aimee looked confused, understandably, but quickly recovered. "That's great. So are you guys going on a retreat?"

"A what?"

"A retreat. You don't know what a retreat is?"

"Er, when it's time to turn around and run away? Usually in battle?"

"It's a retreat from the *world.*"

"Ohh. We've just been on two of those," I nodded. "They call them houseboats now."

"Ha! No, not quite. There's retreats you can do all over India in Ashrams. Yoga retreats. Meditation retreats. I'm meeting some friends here, and we're going on a meditation retreat. This is my fourth one. I'm doing ten days of silent meditation. It's should be a-mazing."

Sean was looking at her like she'd been describing his own death. It was his turn to use a 'What - you carry pigs?' face.

"Hang on. So you sit in a room for ten days - TEN! And you don't talk?

That would send me mad. I bet everyone says that, but it really would. I'd go mental. They'd drag me out in straps and have to put a bag over my head. Come to think of it, they'd have to drag me *in there* in straps with a bag on my head."

"That might be a bit off-putting for the other students, Sean," I laughed.

Aimee smiled knowingly, letting us have our fun.

"Well, different things come up for different people. It's kinda challenging, sure."

"And there are other people in the room with you?"

"Yes, of course."

"Wouldn't you just be peeping at them the whole time? Or does everyone get a big pair of blinkers? Like they put on race horses."

She sighed, shaking her head. "You close your eyes, Sean. But yes, you can look around if you want. There's no rules. Well, apart from not talking."

"That's a pretty big rule though. What happens if you do start talking? I bet I'd just start shouting out words if I wasn't allowed to talk for ten days. Cabbage! Monocycle! Feet and inches!" Sean boomed.

"It's not that you're not *allowed* to talk... You *choose* to not talk. That's why you're there. You watch your thoughts, you acknowledge them, and you let them go." Her hands flowered open, releasing an imaginary pigeon to flap around the very real room.

"But if my thoughts thought someone was watching them, they'd just put on more of a show. They'd think they were on telly and come out all dressed up, blowing trumpets."

"Sean," I piped in, "you'd have to sit there with a big pair of ear muffs on, eye blinkers in place, and a leather muzzle on to shut you up."

"I'd need more than that - I'd need a brain muzzle." We laughed.

"A brain muzzle! Yes! You would! Maybe one of those old diving helmets would do it. The round brass ones that you bolt onto your suit. You'd have to black out the glass though. You'd look the part, sitting there at the front of the class. The poster boy for the meditation retreat. *'Come meditate with us! All equipment supplied.'*"

Sean and I were cracking up. Aimee waited for us to finish before adopting the tone of a Kindergarten teacher.

"There are techniques there to help, like counting to ten slowly in your mind. That helps. You repeat the numbers, slowly, and you learn to observe the space between the numbers, until the numbers... Simply... Disappear!" She released another pigeon. "Then, you just calmly observe the quiet space left behind. The valleys between the mountains. It's very powerful."

It was my turn for a story.

"I knew an Irish fella that tried meditation, using that counting trick. He said the only way he could concentrate on the numbers, and not all the other stuff racing through his brain, was by having the number light up, like a huge glowing sign in big, bright colours. Then he'd make the number jump around in his head, like a neon jackhammer, squashing everything else, 'till it was time for the next number to light up - which wasn't very long. He put big explosion noises in to make the changeover more exciting, and shouted the numbers out in his head as they bounced around. ONE ONE ONE BANG! TWO TWO TWO BOOM! THREE THREE THREE BANG!"

"I hope I forget that story Mark. I really do," Aimee winced.

"Sounds like punk meditation." Sean turned to Aimee. "So, how does all this inner peace help you sell more margarine? I just think it's a bit of a stretch to be working in advertising AND chasing the inner light in India. Shouldn't you be doing either one or the other?"

Aimee closed her eyes and gave a supremely knowledge-heavy shake of her head. She leant forward again, to give us her earnest truth.

"Balance is very important, as is self-knowledge. That in itself can bring a lot of peace."

"And a lot of money when you fly home to sell a shed load of chocolate fingers to people that thought they wanted jammy dodgers. What would your ideal campaign be? Imagine if you got the contract to advertise chai! You could have someone sitting cross legged, possibly hovering, with a diving helmet on. And they flick open the little glass window, and you just see their lips reaching out to sip on their chai. *'Namaste! Go deeper - with Chai!'*"

She smiled and half lifted her cup to her lips.

"Think on this: the Beatles went home to sell more records after their India meditations. Why is that any different to what I do?"

"Er, because they also went home to write songs that changed the world, rather than just sucking on the devil's co-"

"Sean!"

I thought I'd best jump in - not that she needed my help. Aimee seemed blissfully unfazed by our Woking cynicism. I just knew that if the vein in Sean's forehead started to worm around, like it was just beginning to, it was probably time to stop him. Aimee gulped down her chai and stood up, stretching her arms as high as her cosmic tunic would allow.

"But hey, thanks for the chat guys! I really hope you find what you're looking for in India. Goodnight."

We watched her stride out and head off down the dark corridors to her room, her aura lighting the way.

But she'd got me thinking.

"Didn't the Beatles write 'Yellow Submarine' after India? There you go! It's all about getting deeper."

"I don't think Ringo ever got deeper, Mark. The others did. They used Ringo as a periscope."

We lay on our beds, reading. Or, in my case, staring at the words stuck to the paper. Aimee's parting comment about hoping we find what we were looking for in India had kind of flattened me. Again, we sounded like we should've headed for Torremolinos. Our day in Gulmarg, like the rest since we'd arrived in India, ground to a steady, silent halt.

That was until a noise - no louder than an ant in bed socks tiptoeing across a wet sponge - ripped the Gulmarg silence apart. A small, but very distinct noise. A cross between a clip and a swish. We sat up in our beds like startled meerkats, more alert than a pair of wartime submarine radio operators.

"Did you hear that?" I whispered, my eyes scanning the room. "Sean. Look!"

Between our beds, at chest height, a hole had been cut in the wood. Not a big hole. But big enough for ONE eyeball. Another noise, definitely coming from what lay beyond that hole, confirmed what our brains were already one hundred percent sure of.

A zipper was being lowered.

We shot from our beds and raced for the hole, arriving at the same time - two arrows vying for the same bullseye - sniggering like a pair of kids. I pushed Sean out the way.

"Shhhhhh. Go and roll a joint, Sean."

"Fuck off, you go and roll one! Move over."

Before I was knocked sideways by Sean heaving his shoulder into mine, I got to see - at very close hand - Canadian Aimee's red hippy tunic being opened, though details were hard to make out in the dim glow of the twenty watt light bulb.

We snorted and shhhhh'd and pushed each other away, fighting for the hole. I wrestled my way back in with a schoolyard dead leg - not full force, obviously, as the resulting scream would blow our cover - just in time to see her walking out the door, wrapped in a towel.

We collapsed back onto the beds, laughing.

"Oh God, we can't be doing this! It's pathetic."

"I know Sean, well at least it's stopped now, she's…"

Then a noise from the opposite wall. Water flowing. We were across that tiny room as quietly as two big lads moving at speed in an enclosed space could possibly be. Another hole had been cut in the far wall. There she was again - totally naked in the annoyingly dimly lit bathroom, pouring buckets of water over her head. My eye strained at its muscles, my pupil opening as wide as the heavens to take in as much light as possible before - *whumpf* - I was whacked out of the way by Sean's head, which took over where mine had left off.

We played head-conkers until the light was clicked out in the bathroom, then turned round and raced back to man the other wall hole. At least we were getting some exercise.

In the morning, I strolled up to the desk lady.

"Can we pay for a week, please?"

That put the smile back on her face.

We had breakfast early, though not in the lodge restaurant.

"We can't go in there, Mark. Aimee will be there. I can't look her in the eye."

"She probably can't look *us* in the eye! I reckon she was watching me in the bathroom this morning. There's holes in every bloody wall! Have you noticed?"

"Maybe everyone is watching somebody watching somebody else. A perv circle."

"Well there's only three of us here. And I definitely wasn't watching you."

"I know. I was watching you. You were busy watching her again. Actually, there's four of us here. The desk lady. Do you reckon she makes the holes?"

"Dunno Sean. But someone must have. We should measure her eye to see if it fits. You distract her, and when she's not looking, I'll measure it. Christ, how are we supposed to resist the temptation? I'm not strong enough, I know I'm not. Here, you don't suppose the desk lady is perving on *us*, do you?"

"No Mark. I really don't think she is."

After our egg and chapati breakfast at another eating place, we walked around the empty golf course. The only way you could tell the fairways from the greens was from where the holes were situated. The flags had seen far better days, and hung low and lifeless in the hot, mid-morning air. We walked from one sweltering hole to the next, slowly turning in on ourselves over the previous night's perving.

The surrounding valleys rolled away towards Pakistan, the clouds stubbornly concealing the space where the the Karakoram mountains were supposed to be. I could very easily still be lying over there, mummified beneath a glacier, my death mask a final scream of *"IDIOT!!!!"* The thought gave me the creeps, but at least I wouldn't have turned into a high altitude Peeping Tom.

We returned to the lodge - nod nod with the guard - and hurried back to our rooms for the obligatory mammoth reading and lying down session. As we walked past the restaurant we saw Aimee chatting away to three other western girls.

"Oh no! Look, Mark. Her friends have turned up."

Aimee saw us and waved. "Hi guys! Been playing golf? Ha ha!"

We muttered and stumbled away to our room, too ashamed to speak, and threw ourselves down on our beds.

"There's four lovely women out there Sean, and we can't even face them. Possibly the ONLY four single women in Kashmir."

"I know. Bloody idiots. OK - listen. No more perving. Seriously. I don't wanna be doing this. It's pathetic. And what if we get caught? There's that guard outside. Bloody hell, Mark, they cut the hands of thieves, can you imagine what they'd cut off if they..."

A noise. From the bathroom. *Swooosh.*

We were up and running for the hole before we knew what we were doing, sniggering and elbowing.

Dinner time came, and we snuck out past the dining room and the laughing, chatty Canadians. Our paranoid nod to the guard wasn't returned.

"Did he scowl at us, Sean? He did. He scowled."

We roamed around for a while, looking for a bite to eat in the quietest town in the world. The rest of the week became increasingly worse as our paranoia grew with every joint we smoked on the fairways - or greens. We became more miserable by the hour. We actually stopped what we called the 'Gulmarg Shuffle' on the second day - not just because it was so pathetically pervy, but also because we were convinced that we'd given the game away, and the guard *definitely* wasn't returning our nods.

"I think we should stop nodding at him, Sean."

"But then he'll think we're feeling guilty about something. I think we should keep nodding."

"OK. You nod. And I won't. That might put him off our scent."

The girls didn't even acknowledge us as we scuttled past them that evening, which we obviously took as a bad sign. Even though we'd paid for the week, stopped the 'Gulmarg Shuffle' and had reduced our nodding by fifty percent - we were still considering sparing everyone, and leaving town early. And maybe we would've done - except that we were *told* to leave.

One morning, as we were trying to commando roll past the potted plants in reception, the attractive Indian lady called out to us:

"Hey - excuse me!" She sounded very terse.

The Canadian chatter around the communal table dropped to a hush. I whispered to Sean to keep moving.

"Hello! Misters. Please. Come here." All eyes were on us. It was so quiet you could've heard a crumpet being buttered.

"Go and see what she wants, Mark!" Sean hissed.

"Fuck off! You know what she wants. She's probably going to hand us over to the police."

We looked towards the ever present guard, who was staring at us from the doorway, daring us to nod, casting glances at the Indian lady owner.

"We have to go and talk to her. Both of us. We'll just deny it."

We slunk over, stupid grins plastered to our stupid heads.

"You two are no good for this place."

I let out a small bleat.

"You have to leave - today!"

"Um... OK." I could see the guard paying greater attention now. He'd probably been pre-warned of the up and coming showdown. I didn't dare look towards the table, but I swear I could feel the claws of an imaginary pigeon scraping on my scalp.

The desk lady leaned forward, her eyes narrow. "We've been watching you two!"

Christ, maybe Sean was right. Everyone was watching everyone else.

She raised her voice. "You have only eaten one meal here and you've been here almost five days. You eat everywhere else, drink beer everywhere else, but spend no money here. Please. Now go!"

I could've kissed her. But that would've been inappropriate behaviour.

11

The Magic Man from Pahalgam

We were on the first bus out of town, greatly relieved that we'd escaped any public shaming or retribution. For the sole reason of just being somewhere else, we headed east, past Srinagar, and from there the bus climbed steadily up two thousand feet to Pahalgam, a village set amongst mountain forests of pine trees, streams and lakes.

The bus deposited the pair of us at the side of a very quiet village street.

"At least it's much cooler here. There'll be fewer flies. And mozzies."

Sean looked around. "I can't see anyone - I think it's deserted."

The only other visible sign of life was a horse that was slowly chomping on the healthy grass on the banks of the shallow, rocky river.

"Maybe it's closed on Wednesdays. We should've checked. Still," he said brightly, "we could always go looting!"

We wandered through the empty streets until we found a lodge, whose owner was incredibly eager to take our money. I doubt a paying guest had stumbled through for weeks.

We reluctantly settled down to a few days of majorly quiet inactivity. Boredom levels were becoming obscene. Several times I caught myself sitting under a tree, my head slumped over the guitar, not moving, not even staring at my boots - like I'd turned my eyes off to save energy. Sean said I looked like I'd died mid-song. He'd read the same paragraph of his book so many times he was muttering it in his sleep. I was itching to know what was going to happen next.

We were so bored we were in danger of getting ill. Conversations were reduced to the basic essentials.

"Hungry?"

"Suppose."

"Shall we eat?"

"Yep."

"Shall I roll a –"

"Arrrgghhhhhh."

I couldn't even be bothered to talk bollocks. The Chinese could do what they wanted with the Himalayas. Let them have them. Shift all the mountains across the border. Eat them. Fit them with matching wigs. I didn't care.

One day, trudging from tree to tree on one of our walks to nowhere, we met a man who asked us what we were doing in Pahalgam. We glanced blankly at each other.

"No idea. We might be mad."

He laughed, and told us about the most exciting thing to do in Pahalgam. Or, at this time of year, the only thing to do.

Please, no more perving.

"You have not seen the donkey trek? Everybody does the donkey trek. It is my brother's business, he owns *all* the donkeys in Pahalgam."

The chances of bumping into the brother of the man that owned all the donkeys in Pahalgam, with a population of about eight, were incalculable.

We managed a smile. Sure. We'd love to go on a donkey trek. Why not? It certainly sounded a lot more exciting than not going on a donkey trek, and we'd done plenty of that.

The donkey-monopoly man was easy to find if you knew where to look, which we did because his brother took us straight to his house. He awoke his donkeys from their enforced, but probably very welcome off-season hibernation, saddled them up, and attached all the bells and colourful dangling bits you'd expect to feature on a donkey ride.

"This should be fun, eh Mark?"

"Yes, Sean, this should be fun."

Our guide joined in.

"Oh yes, it is four hours of very happy times. Where are your wives?"

"We haven't got wives."

"Oh! OK. Never mind. You will have to be happy with the donkeys then."

"God, I hope it doesn't come to that, Sean."

I re-engaged my eyes as he pushed us on board the well-worn animals. The poor donkeys received a resounding WHACK from his belting stick which instantly turned their legs on, and the whole show jolted into action.

I've never felt at ease on a four-legger. As a kid back in Derbyshire I'd seen my brother flipped from the back of a cow and land upside down on a barbed wire fence, where he'd hung, screaming, until Mum managed to unpick him.

"Have you ever seen a cow with a saddle on, son?"

"*Nooooooo!*" Eric had sobbed, upside down.

"Well, now you know why, you silly wee devil."

So I hung on tightly as we clip-clopped out of Pahalgam and down a track. The donkeys knew exactly where to go. They also knew just what to do when they received a crack across the arse bone with the belting stick.

"Ooh, easy pal. We're in no rush," I winced. "You don't need to hit them, really."

"Yes! Yes I do. They are donkeys," he beamed.

"I know. But please, don't hit them today. My friend here works for the UN." I pointed at Sean.

"Do you put petrol in your car?" he asked, laughing, waving his stick in the air. "This is donkey petrol!" *Whack whack whack.*

Streams trickled along at twice the speed of our hobbling. Ferns and thick moss covered the ground, and creepers and vines hung from the trees. We lolled back and forth with every lumping step as we slowly navigated the uneven track, all the while dreading the next whack on each donkey's arse from the guide.

On and on we went, almost entirely in silence. It was as if he was escorting two near dead men to a double execution in the woods. After two long, thigh-sore hours, we popped out from the forest into a wide clearing, with a stream running by and pine covered hills either side. We might have been surrounded by white-peaked mountains, but we'd never know, of course. The cloud curtains were still firmly drawn.

Our donkeys stopped and we sat there quietly as the flies buzzed around our four low hanging heads. I lifted my eyes and looked over at Sean. He looked absolutely ridiculous - six foot and a bit of slumped misery, like a human version of the creature beneath him. I must have looked the same, only an inch less miserable. There wasn't a shred of joy left between us.

From a canal side pub in Woking, to here.

Is this the end of the line?

Suddenly the guide twisted around to face us, his moustache widening into a grin.

"There! That was fun, wasn't it?"

It was like he'd lobbed a laughter grenade that detonated between us, blowing our sanity and lack of joy to smithereens. All our indulgent needs and our bored misery were obliterated in a hilarious flash, and into the vacuum roared an unstoppable explosion, the force of which sent us rolling from our donkeys, heaving coughs of uncontrollable laughter and filling the crater of silence with sidesplitting madness. We flipped onto our backs, our legs kicking and flailing as we tried to force some air down our windpipes, which were choked by snorts, guffaws, unidentifiable barks and chesty trumpet honks - the sound of which only made things much worse.

"I... can't... stop... *Arggghhhh!*" Sean squeezed out over a two minute period, as I lay face down, trying to eat the rich Kashmiri soil, as I'd now gone mad.

"Stop... Mark... *Stop!!*"

But I was nowhere near finished, and nor was Sean. My sides and back ached so badly from laughing that I had to crawl up the trunk of a nearby tree and hang from a low-lying branch to straighten my spine in a desperate attempt at getting some air back into my lungs. I swapped from one hand to the next, pumping my knees up and down, throwing my head back, grunting and parping from the middle of my chest as Sean crawled around and clawed himself back from the brink. But one glance at the hairless, deranged baboon dangling from above set him off again, and I dropped back to the ground on all fours to carry on snuffling around in the dirt, where I now belonged.

There. That was fun, wasn't it? No! It was NOT fun, we were screaming inside. It wasn't!

But for some fantastic reason, this is!

After maybe fifteen of the maddest minutes we'd ever experienced - like a long weekend in Amsterdam condensed into a morning tea break - the world started to right itself and we looked up from where we were lying, next to our donkeys' hooves. Our guide gripped hold of his saddle as he looked down at us quizzically. He'd been in the donkey trek game long enough to know that something wasn't quite right here. One more squeak from us and he'd be off.

He opened his mouth to speak, but thought better of it.

"I'm... I'm sorry," I heaved, wiping away the dirt and tears, "it's not you. Or your donkeys."

His eyes scanned between us, making sure we weren't trying to trick him into saying something hilarious that might explode us again.

"... S-sorry," Sean managed, still sniggering, "We're OK now. It must be the altitude. Very clean air you have up here!"

We hauled ourselves up onto our saddles and steadied ourselves for the long climb up to Pahalgam. There was no denying that something weirdly pivotal had just happened. Those six little words from our guide had achieved what we had failed to do ourselves. We were no longer two lost souls stuck in a holding pattern somewhere above Torremolinos. We'd somehow managed to pass through the eye of a needle and finally pop out into a peaceful glade tucked away up in Northern India. We really had arrived, at long last.

The guide delivered us safely back to the village as two completely different men to the pair he'd met earlier that morning. Turns out the donkey trek actually was the best thing to do in Pahalgam. I can't recommend it highly enough.

We tipped him generously, and, feeling a ton lighter, sailed back to our room. Later, over dhal and rice, in the shade of a huge tree amongst the cool hills of the lower Himalayas, we made some real plans.

"Sean, you're right. We shouldn't be in India. But I think I know where to go."

"Really? Where?"

"Kathmandu, Nepal. You'll love it. It's not like India. It's... It's more magical."

"Magical?!" Sean snorted.

"Yep. Magical. The Himalayan Kingdom of Nepal. Sounds magical, doesn't it?"

"The Isle of Skye sounds magical, but I'm not going there."

"And here's the best part: I'm pretty sure Nepal is actually in season. We'll go trekking. There'll be no clouds - we'll see the Himalayas at last. That'll be a highlight. I promise."

Next day, we rode the Valium bus back to Delhi, leaving Kashmir behind as the sun set over distant Pakistan.

I sat in the dark as we whisked through endless villages, watching the chai stalls rolling by, gas fires illuminating dark faces, and started thinking about Maria again. Maybe the continuous banging of the bus, or the Valium, had unseated her from the place I'd been trying to tuck her away.

"You're very quiet." Sean's voice floated out of the dark.

"Hmm. I was just thinking about Maria."

"Ah. Don't blame you. Mind if I join in?"

"Be my guest. Did I ever tell you about her witchy aunt? Taught her a spell to keep men away?"

"So were those tiny skirts and stockings part of that spell?"

"Ha. Yes, I never thought of that."

"You're thinking of them now though. Maybe she put a spell on you."

"What? So I'd leave her?"

"No. So you'd become a terrible, voyeuristic pervert if you did."

"Shit. What's your excuse?!"

"Boredom. Any whiskey left?"

I reached under the seat. The Bagpiper played well in the Valium fog. Not a bad way to get round India.

"What you gonna do when you go home, Sean?"

"Well… I've been thinking about comedy."

Now that surprised me.

"Didn't look like that from where I've been sitting."

"No, I don't suppose it has. But I'm going to try some stand-up. There's loads of places round London to do it."

The cogs in Sean's brain had forced out an idea. All those stoned, endless days, all the hours of doing absolutely nothing, all the head-crunching boredom. Maybe it had actually amounted to something.

Slowed by the Valium to almost contemplative levels, I didn't feel like being a smart arse. It made sense - Sean, a comedian. I'd seen him keep whole groups of people in hysterics many a time when he'd struck a vein. Who knows, he might even do well.

"I reckon that's a great idea, Sean."

"Well, it's gotta be better than being a bingo caller. Or a concreter."

"Or a hod carrier," I laughed.

"What, carry pigs around? I could try the donkey line out. Do two hours of absolute shit, then when everyone's about to kill themselves, just say: 'There, that was fun. Wasn't it?!' I'd be the funniest show on earth."

"Hey, maybe that's what that boy said on the bus in Delhi to crack that old lady up?"

"Nah. It was definitely something to do with your yellow T-shirt. And your yellow shorts."

"I wasn't wearing yellow shorts!" I perked up.

"Yes you were. And yellow socks. You looked like a canary going on holiday."

"Fuck off. I haven't got yellow shorts."

"Well, they're definitely yellow-ish, Mark."

"Khaki."

"Yellow."

"Khaki."

The sun came up, sending hot, orange rays over the northern Indian plains as the roads grew busier and the towns larger. And as the sun rose, I too had an idea, which completely surprised me.

The bus crawled into oppressively hot, stinking Delhi. Dogs lay half dead in the shade of cows that were sprawled across footpaths. Newspapers ran stories attributing numerous bizarre murders to the pre-monsoon tension. The rains surely had to come soon, before the cities cracked under the pressure.

I scurried off to a post office to phone Maria.

After many wrong queues, I finally had the number of her Woking council flat ringing away.

"'Allo. Maria speaking." *Ahh, that lovely accent.*

"Maria, it's Mark."

There was a moment's silence as my words clattered across the globe, gaining delay before tumbling into her pretty little ear.

"… But you are in India!"

"Yes. They've got a phone here now, Maria. They're letting me borrow it."

I waited a moment, whilst she thought this through.

"Oh! Haha. How is India then, my darling smart arse?"

Darling! That's a good sign. This might just work.

"Well, it's been pretty miserable actually, but it's almost monsoon time now."

"Oh… What's that?"

"When it rains a lot."

This brightened her up.

"That's good. It'll wash all the shit away from the streets. Are you phoning to say that you're missing me? Are you? Mark?"

"Well, yes, I am. Maria, I've had an idea."

Here goes. The unveiling of my crazy Bagpiper-Valium induced plan.

"Fancy meeting me in Australia?"

"Australia? That's a clean place isn't it? A good country."

"I think so, yes. We could get a flat in Sydney, see what happens?"

"Ohh. Um, well - there's something I have to tell you. My family are moving back to Gran Canaria in November. I'm going with them."

Bollocks.

"But why don't you come and live with me there instead?"

I don't want to live in Gran Canaria, that's why.

"Well I'm supposed to be heading for Australia. I'm meeting my mates out there. Have you written me any letters?" I asked.

"Of course not! You stupid idiot, Mark. You left me and you went to shitty India! What address would I put? To Mark, in Shitty India?!"

Maria had a Pakistani friend in Woking who had told her horror stories of Indian poverty and squalor. She could never understand why anyone would want to go there.

"Well no, that probably wouldn't work. But remember, I explained to you about 'Poste Restante'? You just put my name on the envelope, then 'Poste Restante', followed by whatever city you're sending it to. And the country's name. Like: Mark Giblin, Post Restante, New Delhi, India."

"What? And then someone comes and finds you, like magic? Don't be a stupid boy."

"Never mind, Maria. I'll send you an address."

"OK my darling. Are you eating?"

"Yes, of course I'm eating."

"Well, be careful. Don't get sick."

"I won't. We're off to Nepal tomorrow."

I may as well have said that we were leaving Moon Base Alpha 1 and heading for Moon Base Alpha 2, for all that 'Nepal' meant to Maria.

"Do they shit in the streets there too?"

"Oh, Maria." But the phone had died. There was no way I was going to join another queue, so I cleared off into the steaming heat to sort out our bus tickets to Kathmandu.

The phone conversation hadn't quite gone the way I'd imagined it on the bus that morning. It was a selfish plan - to keep travelling until I was ready to go to Australia, where I'd meet Maria. I'd not really considered the fact that flying to Australia was a bloody long way to go, just to 'see how it goes.'

A few tiny splats of rain dashed around me as I passed through the roasting streets of New Delhi. I ducked into a jeweller's shop, and asked the Sikh behind the counter if he thought this might be the monsoon breaking.

"I do not know, Mister. You will have to ask the meteorological society," he informed me through his whiskers.

The sky was dark and heavy; surely something had to give. The thick, weighty clouds looked as if they'd sucked up half the water from the rivers that were overflowing from the melting Himalayan snow. There was no way they could hold onto that load for much longer. I wandered off down the street through the almost electric air. Dogs crouched low in the gutters, bristling with tension, sniffing up at the thick, heavy sky. Cars and rickshaws were pulling over, people stood around expectantly, peering upwards, waiting for what was about to come. Everyone seemed to know - apart from that bloke in the jeweller's.

I found Sean in a coffee shop near our hostel, sipping a chai, rolling a fag, watching Delhi melt. He looked happy. The magic from the donkey trek was still there.

"Did you get through to her?" Sean asked, wiping the sweat away from his brow.

"Yeah… I asked her to meet me in Australia."

"Really? Bloody hell! What did she say?"

"She's moving to Gran Canaria with her family."

"The Canary Islands?" Sean was smiling. "You should go and live there with her. Bring your yellow things. You could become Lord Canary." That tickled him.

"Sean! I do not have any yellow shorts. They're khaki."

Just then an almighty bang split the sky apart. The air was filled with the gush of water hammering down from above - sheets of it, soaking everyone and everything in an instant; bouncing back waist-high from the pavement. The noise was deafening.

The sky echoed with a rolling, rumbling thunder, and sharp, head-ducking whip-cracks as lightning ripped through the black clouds.

Shop owners ran out into the streets as awnings buckled under the weight of the water. Cars were beeping, kids shrieking with joy, dogs biting at the falling, jumping rain.

It was fantastic. Rivers of water flooded the roads, washing away the dust and the heat and the filth. A look of sheer, joyful relief was on everyone's face. Even the cows seemed to smile.

We danced in the streets with the kids, laughing, soaked to the skin with the warm monsoon rain. Nature had let us all off the hook.

Delhi was reborn, and we were off to Nepal.

12

Hava, Nagila Hava

Unsurprisingly, there'd been no let up in the level of mayhem we'd first encountered at Delhi bus station almost a month before, but the monsoon now added a carpet of mud to the mix. This time round however, we'd acclimatised somewhat, and toughened up. The man with no nose pushing his wheezing, rattling, skin-covered hole into our faces wasn't that shocking anymore.

Sean wished him a friendly 'Namaste' and folded a few rupees into his outstretched hand. We squeezed our way through the wall of passengers and beggars, looking for our bus to Kathmandu. Or, as Sean was calling it, our 'escape pod.'

"Holy Moses! Sean, check this fella out."

A Sadhu, coated in white ashes and wearing only a small neck pouch from which poked out a well blackened hash pipe - his sacred chillum - was holding the crowd at bay with his backstreet version of The Nutcracker Suite. His eyes were wide and bloodshot, possibly from the hash, but probably not. Between his shins dangled a hefty looking metal weight tied to what looked like an ostrich's neck in crisis, but was actually his massively overstretched penis. He bent his knees, dropping the weight into a large puddle between his feet, before straining and stretching and hauling the muddy lump of lead up to his knees, almost strangling and decapitating his ostrich in the process. Then - splash! Back down again.

Up. *Oooaarghhh!*
Down, splash.
Up. Oooaarghhh!

Down, *splash*.

Then, with the weight in its splash position, he gripped his balls, pulled a 'ready for this, everyone?' kind of face, and applied a liver-shrivelling twist to the left, before yanking them viciously the other way, giving the poor abused devils no time to settle into their new unnatural position.

"Ooohhh!" We buckled.

"See, he didn't need to do that. I was quite enjoying watching 'till he started twisting his nuts around." Sean shouted over the hammering rain.

"Pardon?" I'd heard him, but it's the kind of thing you'd rather hear someone shout twice.

"I SAID, I WAS QUITE ENJOYING WATCHING THAT 'TILL HE STARTED TWISTING HIS NUTS AROUND."

"I agree. He should leave the poor things alone. Shall we tell him?"

"I think he should change the colour of the string. Doesn't go with his knob."

We were pretty chirpy as we boarded the super packed, Super De-Lux tourist bus, but our ticket numbers guided us to a pair of seats torn apart by sharp metal springs; the ripped vinyl coverings soaked from the rain which was dripping down from the hole in the ceiling above.

Sean was horrified. "We can't sit there! Not even that Sadhu would sit on those springs. Well, he probably would…"

I raced off back to the office to find the ticket man, sticking my head through his open window.

"Namaste. We need to change our seats. Or change buses. What else do you have?"

"You don't want those seats? Fine, Mister. Come back in two days' time. No more seats till then. Everything booked. Very busy." He continued to pore over his sales ledger, cooing with pleasure at the countless columns of neat entries spread out before him.

"But the seats are torn and the springs are sticking up like bloody razor blades! They'll ruin our bottoms."

He looked up, wobbled his head and stuffed a big wad of betel nut into his mouth.

"Do you read? Sit on a book. Goodbye." And he slammed the shutter down.

"And the roof leaks!" I shouted at the closed hatch.

Sean was standing outside the bus, watching the driver practice his revving.

"Bloody hell! What's he doing?" I spluttered.

"He's been doing it since you left. He's worse than that other one. Maybe he's deaf."

"He will be soon. Maybe he's trying to reduce it from a Super De-Lux tourist bus to a clapped-out pile of shit."

"Well he hasn't got far to go. I'd be happier to see him practice his braking before we left. Or steering. Any luck with the tickets?"

"Nope. Lovely bloke though, really neat handwriting."

We found some cardboard and attempted some repairs on our sliced apart seats. The revving died down, and we were finally off to Kathmandu, rain dripping onto our heads, down our necks, and into our laps. The rest of the bus was perfectly dry, and no other passengers were wriggling around like Sean and I.

"Thirty six hours of this?"

"Get the Piper out," Sean suggested.

We were excited to see a few fellow travellers on board - even a couple of girls sitting a few rows ahead of us. I passed the whiskey over to a middle-aged Indian man who was smiling our way.

"Please, have a drink."

"Oh, thank you very much. That would be very nice." He had a drink. His friend had a drink. The man behind them had a drink, though I noticed he never offered it to his female companion. The bottle did a quick tour of the bus. A smiling group of Tibetan monks decked out in purple robes occupied several seats to the rear. They laughingly declined the whiskey, but smiled and clapped at the range of squirming faces being pulled in the bottle's wake. At a pound a bottle, it really was a vicious drop.

"Lucky we bought two, Sean," I said, holding the near empty bottle up to the light.

Sean ignited the whiskey trail with a chorus of the Israeli song 'Hava Nagila' that caught on after a few false starts - especially with the monks, who stomped their feet and clapped along loudly.

"Hava, Nagila Hava, Nagila Hava, Nagila-" STOMP STOMP STOMP!

We never got beyond that line, just repeating and stomping, repeating and stomping. Sean sat back down on his cardboard, pleased with his handy work.

"There you go Mark, Tibetan monks singing Israeli folk songs. This is more like it."

Two seats down from us sat a happy-faced hippy with long, sun-bleached hair tucked behind his ears, turquoise pendants and bracelets jiggling against his deep brown skin. His stripy, baggy harem pants flowed out into the aisle, where a pair of dusty feet sat in some well worn, Jesus-type sandals. He had to be a good ten years older than us.

"Fancy some whiskey?" Sean asked, stretching forward with the bottle. The hippy man looked around tentatively, as if he was trying to make sure no one would see him.

"Go on, have some. Quality gear, this," Sean prodded.

"Well, erm, OK. Everyone else seems to be." A mad kind of giggle bubbled up and out of him, which seemed to take him by surprise, and make him giggle again.

We all laughed.

"Been here a while, have you?" Sean asked. "You look like you have."

He giggled again and his eyes darted around the bus - up to the ceiling, out the windows; his eyes all merry and playful.

"Y-e-s," he said slowly, possibly only just realising how long he'd actually been there.

"We all have to be *somewhere*. Otherwise - " his eyes widened, "we'd be… *Nowhere*."

He nodded the last part out, and carried on nodding, just to make sure he was correct. Then he took a huge slug on the whiskey, before handing it back.

"Namaste. My name is Dave." He pressed his hands together and gave us a little head bow.

"Hallo! I'm Sean. This is Mark. Where you from Dave? Your accent… I can't place it. Kiwi?"

Dave smiled, tilting his head in a thoughtful way.

"Ommm-teresting…" He kind of hummed the 'Ommm' sound, to make sure we picked up on his unique wordplay. *"Ommmmmm-teresting."*

"You're Australian, aren't you," I twigged. "I bet you you don't say 'Ommmm-teresting' down there!"

"No bloody way, mate. I'd get my hippy arse kicked! Any chance of, erm, you know, another?" He nodded at the bottle, took another huge swig, then leaned out into the aisle, twisting in his seat to give us his full attention; his Australian character slipping back below the surface after having taken a quick look around.

"In Hindi," he began, his eyes widening with wonder, "we believe the Om was the first sound in the universe."

"Do you?"

"Om."

"That's the first time I've ever heard 'Om' used as an answer, Dave."

Sean laughed. "Anyway, I thought the first sound was a massive BANG!"

"In Hindi, we believe the 'Om' is the start of everything." He closed his eyes and let fly another longer *Ommmmm.*

"You're like an 'Om' generator, Dave. An 'Om' owl."

"An 'Om' Owl! Ha, yes! I am, Sean. The 'Om' Owl of Peace." He laughed his funny giggle; his eyes twinkling at the notion, before a more important thought invaded his brain.

"The West..."

Dave paused dramatically.

"... Is a state of mind."

We nodded for a while, digesting this bombshell.

"I never said it wasn't," Sean pointed out. "But I'll tell you what Dave - the West ain't ready for the Om Owl."

"The West..." Another long pause as he nodded the truth into his words.

"... The West is an *illusion.*"

"Wahey! That means Woking might not be real. Cheers Dave, nice to meet you."

"Well, paths cross for a reason." Dave smiled, nodding at the whiskey. Sean laughed and passed the bottle over.

"Cheers, maaaaaate!"

"Hava, Nagila Hava, Nagila Hava..." The monks were off again.

Sean knelt on his wet seat, waving his arms round, conducting the sing song as the bus ploughed on through the afternoon rain, the whiskey making its way round the bus in ever widening circles. The local women were laughing and pointing behind their hands, apart from one older lady who stared daggers at us, like we were a two-headed demon. The chickens stuffed into a basket by her feet looked suitably concerned.

Endless chai stops, however, meant our journey slowed to a crawl. The driver and his surly assistant had a seemingly unquenchable need for chai, and would stop the bus and huddle roadside under plastic sheeting, nattering to the local chai stall men for half an hour at a time, forcing all the passengers to sit by and wait.

A boy selling newspaper cones of warm peanuts did a roaring trade at one particularly long stop. When the bus finally took off again, the little kid in front of us peeped up between the seat and flicked a peanut right between my eyes.

"Why you little..." I shot one back, bouncing it off his little brown nose. Flick flick flick, and it was all going on. Sean joined in, flicking one at the kid's brother, and pretty soon warm peanuts were dinging from the windows and the roof, as the kids squealed, and the mums laughed.

I'd noticed Dave looking on in horror. He jumped up, waving his hippy arms around.

"No, no, no! This is very bad, stop! In Hindi, we believe food is sacred. You are being very disrespectful. Food is a gift fro- *wooaaaarrghhh!*"

He wasn't up for long. Peanuts rained down on him, from all corners of the globe. Muslims, Hindus, Buddhists, and even a few lapsed Catholics joined in. The monks looked like they might burst with joy.

"Hava, Nagila Hava, Nagila Hava…"

This motorised tin can packed with merry Kathmandu pilgrims - and one sulking 'Om' Owl of Peace - wound its noisy way onwards as the afternoon drew to a close. But the driver's need for chai increased in direct proportion to the amount consumed. The constant stops were getting ridiculous.

"If we don't hurry up, Sean, we'll miss the border crossing for the night. That'll add another fifteen hours at least to the journey."

Just before sunset we did manage to leave India via some remote border crossing, and inched our way across the strip of no-man's land to the Nepali border, just in time for the 'CLOSED' sign to be slammed down on Nepal's customs window.

"Told you. The driver did that on purpose. He'll be getting a kick back from whoever runs that eating house over there."

"Oh well," said Sean, "at least we're not in India any more." A thought suddenly occurred to him.

"Oi, Dave, look! We're literally nowhere! We might not even exist. C'mon, that's gotta be worth an 'Om.'"

13

Highs and Lows in No-Man's Land

Dave was still smarting from the multi-faith peanut shower, and wasn't having a bar of us - though he never refused the whiskey, whenever it passed his way.

A wooden shack jutted out from the trees, and was lorded over by a seedy looking man dressed in a dirty white vest and a sarong. A goat was tethered to a nearby post, bleating and yanking anxiously at its moorings.

The bus slowly emptied and the shack filled up with the hungry, thirsty travellers. The party atmosphere was still bubbling away, so we set about rolling some joints, which caught Dave's attention. He sidled in to sit down opposite us.

"Sorry if we ruffled your feathers earlier," Sean smiled. "I didn't think the 'Om' Owl could get grumpy."

"Well," said Dave, eyeing up the joint, "you can't be grumpy if you're nowhere. We're between paradigms, we've slipped through the cracks."

Yes you have Dave. That's exactly what you've done. You've gone for a metaphysical walk on a metaphysical glacier, decked out in Indian sandal skates and draw-string pants, and you've taken a tumble. Only time will tell if you'll ever be rescued.

"Well, it's a funny old world, eh Dave. Here, you want some of this?" I handed him the joint, which he puffed on as eagerly as he'd attacked the whiskey bottle.

You could almost see his brain conjuring up its next whirlwind of revelatory epiphanies. He leaned forward over the flickering candle, his eyes twinkling. *Uh oh, here we go.*

"In Hindi, we say: the World…" He paused to gather all the energy in; a cosmic boxer about to deliver the knockout punch to our defenceless, unenlightened minds.

"The World… is ROUND." He rolled his hands in front of his face in a circular motion, outlining the shape of a ball to help us understand.

Even the goat shut up.

Dave's eyes jumped from mine to Sean's, gauging the impact of his ancient, spherical wisdom.

"Ever think it's time to go home, Dave?" I asked.

He laughed his hearty giggle before sitting bolt upright, the cosmic glare vanishing with almost no trace. Aussie Dave was back.

"Yeah, I do sometimes. But I haven't got a ticket, and I can't really ask my mum. She's a nurse. Lives in Melbourne. You should go to Melbourne. It's a cool town, mate."

"So, what will you do?" asked Sean. "You can't just hang around in India forever, can you?" You could see the horror in Sean's eyes. Hanging round India - indefinitely.

"Well, I suppose I'll have to. At least it's… *Somewhere!*" His eyes widened again, super chuffed at the way this had all come round, full circle. He nodded happily, having made complete sense of his world. Cosmic Dave was back.

We joined a table of Indian men sharing a bottle of whiskey over their meal. It wasn't long before Sean had them in absolute hysterics, asking about the Himalayas - the magical mountains he'd still never seen.

"I hear they're really big."

"Oh yes, Sean, they are really, really big."

"But they're invisible, so how can you tell?"

"Noooooo! They are not invisible!" They laughed, playing along.

"What, they're hiding? Are they hiding in the kitchen?" He made as if to get up and go towards the kitchen.

"No, they cannot hide! It is not possible."

"OK. So which direction are these Himalaya things?"

"They are over that way." One of the laughing men was pointing north, towards the Nepali border.

"What, those?" Sean pointed to the speed bumps on the road joining Nepal to India. "That's the Himalayas? Really? They're not as big as I was expecting."

"No, no, Mr Sean! The Himalayas are…" But he'd turned into a giggling jelly.

"Wow." Sean carried on. "Which one is Everest? The third one?" He ran over to the speed bumps, measuring each with his fingers, his face pressed against the tarmac.

From his crouch, he shouted back into the shack in his booming voice: "Yep, this one is Everest." He held up his thumb and finger. "It's half an inch bigger than the others."

Tears were rolling down the Indian man's face as he banged his hands on the the table, trying to get a breath, as the owner of the shack untethered the poor goat from its peg and dragged it, bleating and crying, round the back of the shack.

"Dinner is served," said Dave.

"Dave!" I cried, "that's horrible. I'm not eating that goat. I feel like I know it now."

"Well," he continued, eyes wide, "in some religions, we are actually helping the animal attain a higher spiritual standing. By eating it we can help it come back as a higher form in its next life. Eventually it can become human, and begin its path towards becoming pure and enlightened."

"Ommmmm-mazing! A helping-hand-up pie! Brilliant!"

"I bet you won't be giving that cockroach over there a helping hand up, Dave. So what animal is one up from a goat? A cow?" Sean was immediately in on this one.

"No," I pondered, "I reckon goat and cow are on the same level. I think horse is next up the line."

"No way. What about donkeys?"

"They're stuck," I said. "Who's going to eat a helping-hand-up donkey pie?"

"True. Chickens are in a good position though. Lucky buggers. They're on the fast track to enlightenment."

"You've almost gotta stop them jumping in the pot."

"What's above a chicken?"

"Fox."

"Shit, this is complex. Is that why foxes eat chickens?"

"It's a system fraught with trouble. You'd wanna get in the right lane. Trouble is, all lanes have to lead to monkey, don't you think? They're one down from us."

"Maybe that's what monkeys are trying to tell us. 'Oooh Ooh Oooh' actually means 'EAT ME! EAT ME!' They're begging for it."

"Ooo-beee-do-ooo-ooo, I wanna be like you-hoo-hoo, doo-bee-doo."

That set all the westerners in the shack off.

"I wanna walk like you, talk like you, doo-doo."

A perfect moment in no-man's land.

Oddly though, if its perpetual bleating was to be believed, the goat was still alive. Something very peculiar seemed to be happening.

"Sean, have you noticed all these men turning up? You watch those bushes over there."

Local men had been scurrying out from the bushes for the past half hour, and they'd lurk around just outside the shack until the owner approached them. Money changed hands, and then, in maybe ten minute intervals, one man would be led around to the back off the shack.

"What's going on?"

"No idea Sean. But that's where the goat is being kept."

"No... You don't think they're..."

"I wouldn't like to say. But listen to the poor thing."

We observed the bizarre process for some time, becoming convinced that we'd stumbled across a goat prostitution ring.

"Is that why the driver was going so slow, do you think?"

"Dunno Sean. This is truly 'orrible. Hey, you don't think they've just got it wrong a bit, and they think they're giving the goat a helping hand up the ladder, do you?"

"Oh Christ - surely they're not going to eat it later?"

"Nah, no way would he cook his main breadwinner. Look at him." I pointed over to the owner, who was drinking whiskey and counting his cash with his cronies.

We were very stoned, of course, but it all made sense. We stared in equal measures of hilarity, disbelief and horror at the line of men who were continuously emerging from the bushes.

Over the next couple of hours we kept an eye on things, until the comings and goings from the bushes died down. The goat didn't stop its pained hollering, but we soon stopped our musings and sobered up sharply, horrified, when a woman appeared from the back room, looking completely exhausted and utterly miserable.

"Shit Mark - they were queuing for her, weren't they?" Sean said.

The owner rose from his table and started shouting at her, pointing to the tiny kitchen and the piles of dishes. She never raised her head or spoke a single word, but squatted down and set to work scrubbing the pots and pans.

"Oh god, this is terrible," Sean said. "I can't sit in here. Not near that bastard. He ain't getting any more business from me."

What else could we do, apart from feel ashamed at being witness to such awful misery? It was one of those tragic situations that we knew we wouldn't be forgetting.

Everyone that was still in the shack from the bus left straight away, looking disgustedly at the owner, who didn't bat an eyelid or even look our way. There was no more joking around from our gang. It was time to crash. The clouds had cleared throughout the evening, leaving the Milky Way stretched above us, shooting stars pinging from all corners of the heavens. It was the first really clear Himalayan sky we'd seen all trip. There was a good possibility we'd see the mountains in the morning.

"I'm gonna sleep outside, Mark. On the roof. Gotta be better than those seats we've got. See you in the morning." Sean climbed the bus ladder, and wiggled into his sleeping bag under the starry sky.

After a very uncomfortable night of continuously wrestling with the seat springs to keep them from tearing up my backside, like ferrets on a mission, I awoke to find Sean sniffing and coughing in his sleeping bag outside the whisky shack. A low mist clung to the ground and the surrounding hills, hiding Sean's speed bump Himalayas. The clear night sky had been replaced by dark clouds that were hiding the real Himalayas. Nothing magical was going on here this morning.

"You look shit, Sean."

"I feel shit. It rained and I couldn't get back on the bus, so I slept under the back wheels. I'm freezing."

Reluctant as I was to give the pimp man any more money, I ordered some chai. The woman was already up, cleaning more dishes and tending the fire, though it was barely past dawn. We'd be gone from here soon. There was no escaping for her.

We had to sit around for hours waiting for the Nepali customs officials to arrive, then watch as they dragged all the bags from the bus and directed endless questions at the poorer passengers. Money was passed around and bags were eventually placed back on the roof.

We cleared the border with Nepal, and from there slowly, slowly wound our way towards Kathmandu. Sean's cough worsened, as did everyone's mood, as the bus took forever in the drizzling, hot rain. On and on we crawled, stopping at almost every chai stall we passed, which were many.

"This is mental, Sean," I moaned, "this bloke is like a bloody chai hoover. And why does he need to chat for so long at every sodding stall?"

"Yeah, well, you going on about it isn't helping anybody." Sean fidgeted around on his piece of wet cardboard, coughing and sneezing. The whole bus seemed to have a hangover, apart from the monks, who sat quietly observing a very good reason for not drinking. They knew the *Hava, Nagila Hava* party was over. Dave was very quiet too. Whiskey beats 'Om' hands down. Especially the cheap stuff.

By mid afternoon my patience was all but over. Half an hour drive, half an hour stop. The driver's apparent disdain for his passengers was really getting to me. By my reckoning, we should have closed in on Kathmandu hours ago, with time for an evening stroll round the temples of Durbar Square to stretch our legs and ease our sore bottoms, and then relax with an evening beer and a good sleep in a cheap bed.

We crawled along a windy road, past terraced rice paddies and low lying green hills. The driver pulled over again and jumped out for more chai.

"*Arrrrgghhhhhh!* Fucking hell Sean, that's it! I've had it." And I was up and off, powering down the centre of the bus aisle like an angry buffalo with a chilli up its rear.

"Mark, don't…" Sean shouted after me. "Mark!"

I jumped down the steps and ran round the front of the bus, where the driver was settling himself down for yet another lovely cuppa. I presume he got a surprise when he was hoiked up from his roadside stool by his vest, and dragged back towards the driver's side door by a curly haired, steaming ball of red-faced fury, screaming "GET BACK ON THAT FUCKING BUS AND DRIIIIIIIVE!!!!!"

This, funnily enough, didn't go down very well. He did not do as I'd suggested. Instead, he went absolutely crazy, which started off with him screaming back at me, then progressed onto pushing me hard in the chest with a lot of jumping about and swinging of arms. His assistant joined in, and suddenly all the Indian men in the bus emptied out and took sides. Half of them, it seemed, wanted to kill me, and the other half were undecided. I was jostled and pushed, grabbed and yelled at.

I could see Sean on the peripheries, shaking his head at the chaos my temper had caused. Luckily no one took a real swing at me, because I would've swung one back and the whole thing would escalate into a roadside slaughter, with me being the slaughtered one. Instead, the assistant driver climbed onto the roof, undid the load and chucked my bag and guitar down onto the verge.

"I'm NOT getting off here!" I bellowed into his face, as I grabbed my belongings and tried to climb through the crowd onto the bus, which started off a bi-lingual comedy exchange of 'Oh Yes You Are!' 'Oh No I'm

Not!'

The driver was still hopping from foot to foot, totally incensed at me. Then, out from the pack came the man than Sean had reduced to hysterics over the speed bump Himalayas. It took him a further five minutes, but he did manage to convince the driver and his assistant that they couldn't possibly leave me here, miles from anywhere. My guitar and bag were tied down again and I climbed back on the bus, to much muttering and eye aversion from my fellow passengers, whom I knew all thought I was a right cock.

I brushed past Dave as I swept towards my sodden, cardboard mess of a seat.

"In Hindi, it is very-"

"Oh fuck off, Dave." That was unfair of me, because he was right. I'd brought a little piece of Woking to Nepal.

Sean shook his head as I sat down.

"You're a fucking idiot sometimes, Mark."

"What? Come on, someone had to do something, Sean!"

Tensions remained high for the rest of the long, quiet trip. The journey had turned sour, and Sean's coughing had turned gurgly. We rolled into Kathmandu almost seventy hours after leaving Delhi. It was supposed to take about thirty-five.

14

Followed by a Lung Shadow

Sean's disappointment at our first view of the city of Kathmandu was palpable. Scavenging through the mounds of rubbish piled knee high on the street corners were packs of wild dogs that glared at us with menacing eyes as they tore through the muck. It was as if the city had set up a breeding programme to populate the streets with an army of mangy, aggressive canines of every shape, size and colour - a dog orgy to create a new species: the street-brute. I was sure they hadn't been there the year before. Either that or I'd been so excited to be in Nepal at the time that I somehow never noticed them.

Traffic jammed the narrow streets, filling the place with noise and fumes. Even the temples with their big, benevolent Buddha eyes and strings of colourful prayer flags didn't seem to cheer the city up. I couldn't imagine Buddha being very happy with the state of things. Or, being Buddha, I suppose he wouldn't really mind.

We made our way to Thamel, a district of Kathmandu with plenty of cheap beds, eating holes and, hopefully, other travellers looking for fun. I picked out a scruffy little hostel from the swathe of fairly shoddy looking establishments, all proudly trading off the magnificent surroundings. The Everest Lodge. Yeti Lodge. Roof of the World Hotel.

I could have been more sensitive to Sean's growing cough-bark, and taken us upmarket. But I'd never been upmarket before, had no idea where it was, and, if I did manage to find it, would've said something wrong and we wouldn't have made it past the door.

We chucked our bags into the absolutely bare-minimum room, stared down the cockroaches in the grotty shower block - squashing a few to help lighten the mood - and headed into the Kathmandu evening.

We found a cafe that served beer and ordered some buffalo noodle soup. I noticed Sean itching around on the hard wooden bench, pulling a range of faces I hadn't seen him use before. Something was clearly afoot.

"I feel shit Mark. And there's something wrong with my bum. My buttocks are killing me."

I nosed my way through the soup, still grumbling over the bus journey. "Fancy another beer, Sean? Or should I go and buy some weed?"

"No. I'm going to bed," he coughed. And sneezed. And coughed. And wiggled.

There ended our first night out in Kathmandu.

Next morning, after a fitful sleep due to Sean's hacking cough and frequent complaints about his sore bum, I went out for breakfast in Freak Street - so named after the hippies that set up camp there in the '60s and tripped and smoked their western reality into oblivion. Maybe I'd see the ghost of young Dave ambling around and let him know that 'The World was round,' but that would spoil the surprise for him.

I'd had some good times on Freak Street with my mates the previous year. Great times. We'd arrived at night, not having any real expectations about the place. We'd sort of aimed ourselves towards Kathmandu after leaving Istanbul several weeks previously, and finally waking to see the Himalayas powering down on us the next morning had blown my mind. It was the most beautiful sight I'd ever cast my happy eyes over. The whole month was spent staring up at the mountains in varying degrees of pleasure. Everywhere we went, there they'd be - huge, silent and totally breathtaking.

Skateboard man was still there - an extraordinarily cheerful fellow with a tiny body on a pair of skinny, useless legs, living on a makeshift skateboard that he strapped himself to with a piece of old rope.

When we'd first met him, he'd pleaded up to us for money: "Paisa Baba?"

Being the prat that I was, I'd looked back at him and asked: "Why?"

We all looked at each other in confusion, not quite knowing what to do or say next.

I was about to apologise for being such an awful git, when he burst out laughing.

"...Why?" He laughed, slapping his withered legs. "Why?! No one say this to me before!"

We'd sit chatting with him, and bring him chai and food. Of course, now he didn't remember me. After eighteen months of trundling around the city on his skateboard, surviving day by day on hand outs, battling through a freezing Nepali winter with only a pack of dogs to keep him warm, why would he? And, I wasn't wearing my rainbow yak this year.

Freak Street was a different place now. No giggling, stoned young travellers gorging on huge pieces of banana cake; no eager trekkers taking off for the Himalayas; no strong armed climbers with gaunt, sun burnt faces telling stories of ice falls and sheer rock faces.

There was no-one around. No colour, no Himalayas, no magic.

I wandered back to our room through the dirty streets, kicking out against the street brutes where necessary. I found Sean coiled over, sweating and feverish on his bed.

"Mark," he coughed, "can you have a look at my arse? It feels all lumpy."

Could my day get any better? I braced myself as best I could for the ringside view of his derrière, the sight of which damn near burnt holes in my retina and knocked me through the closed door and out over the balcony to a premature death. An army of big, red, angry boils were marching from the top of his thighs up over the slopes to his lower back, scores of them going to war on his cheeky pale buttocks.

"Bloody hell Sean! It's like a relief map of the Himalayas back here."

He slumped forward onto his sweaty bed, revealing valleys of angry pain that no one in peacetime should ever be exposed to.

"It's bloody agony. There's definitely something wrong with me."

"There is. It looks like you've been farting out live hornets into your pants."

"Shut up, Mark. Please."

He coughed some more, and groaned. I brought him aspirin and water and sat with him until he crashed out again, which wasn't very long. I couldn't see any point in observing him in his sweaty sleep, so I wandered outdoors again, trying to forget just what was occurring on Sean's backside.

I sat in an empty cafe, maudlin over a solitary bottle of beer, watching the rain drizzle down through the yeti painted windows as I pondered over our latest travelling let down. I had to admit - I'd royally messed up the trip so far. India and Nepal, in August? In my mind, Kathmandu was meant to be the answer. But that was looking very unlikely. Where could I go to escape the heat and rain, and find the fun? What had happened to my notions of riding from village to village on an old thumping Royal Enfield bike - crossing into Tibet and back down the coast of India with a gorgeous hippy girl and my guitar, reenacting the advanced techniques from the

Karma Sutra in our cabin bed? Instead, I was holed up with a bloke with a miner's cough and a raging battle between good and evil going on in his underpants. And in his head, for that matter.

I was facing months of lonely boredom, as I assumed that Sean would surely give up on the trip and head home, once he was back on his feet. I couldn't really blame him.

I was beginning to feel really glum about the whole dismal situation, when a voice boomed over my head, snapping me out of it.

"Hey - mind if I join you?"

A thickset, balding American sat himself down at my table and launched into an excited rant before I'd even had a chance to reply.

"Man, you should see the butcher's shop I found! There's four buffalo legs - chopped off at the knees, standing outside in the street, like they're waiting for the body to be reattached. It looks like a giant eagle dropped out of the sky and - *whoooopff!* Ripped the top half off and fucked off on a Himalayan thermal. You could put a plank of wood across the four legs, and you'd have yourself a buffalo-leg coffee table. And the lungs are hung up in the window, covered in flies, like a pair of spotted yellow curtains. It's carcass decor, man! The new Kathmandu scene. I'm Rob by the way - pleased to meet you. Isn't this place brilliant?!"

And he stuck out a hairy hand.

"Mark - how you doing?" That cheered me up a bit. It was just the kind of thing that I would have ranted about the year before.

"You here on your own?" Rob asked, pouring himself a beer.

"Nah. I've got a mate back at the room. He's got a bad cold from the bus, he smokes too much and his arse is a city of festering boils. But he'll be OK."

"Arse boils?! Cool!" Rob laughed and banged the table.

We spent the early afternoon hanging around the temples, watching monks and monkeys going about their business, and the locals darting around in the Kathmandu rain. Rob was living in South Korea, after turning his back on America some years before. We talked guitar, which he'd been struggling to learn.

"Fancy coming back for a smoke, Rob? I'll teach you some blues. You can meet Sean, he'll be glad of the company. Poor sod must be sick of looking at me. Maybe he'll let you have a look at his backside battle ground."

"Count me in, man. He sounds like a true gent. *Whoa!* Look at that freakin' dog, it just ate a carpet! What kind of a town is this?"

We headed back through the late afternoon traffic, stopping to buy some weed from one of the many street dealers running around looking for tourists.

I called to Sean as we ran up the stairs to our room.

"Yoo-hoo, Sean! You've got a visitor. Are you decent?"

I opened the door to see Sean curled up on his bed, just finishing off a wet coughing fit. Rob took one look at Sean with his grey, sweaty features and his sputum bucket, writhing and groaning in his pit, and turned to me.

"Mark, your friend is really sick! He obviously needs a doctor. Hadn't you noticed?!"

Oh.

Shit.

No, I hadn't. But now that Rob mentioned it, Sean was clearly in a bad way. The boil army was rampaging. His lungs were wheezing and gurgling inside his chest. His hair was soaked with sweat. I'd been so preoccupied and confused by the effect that Kathmandu was having on me that I'd somehow failed to notice my old mate going down the gurgler.

We dressed him and rushed him down the stairs. The rickshaw ride for Sean was hell, as sitting on the new version of his arse was clearly not an option. He grimaced and hollered, like he was lowering himself into a bucket of fire ants.

Rob took us to the American hospital in Kathmandu - a shiny, clean clinic in the expat end of town. A doctor did a quick once over examination on Sean before sending us away for chest X-rays - which, unfortunately for Sean, meant travelling to the other end of town.

"Ahhhhhhh-ow-arghhhh! Ow-ow-ow-ow-ahhhhhhhhh," Sean moaned, as we hurtled through the backstreets again.

I looked at Rob guiltily.

"He wasn't this bad when I went out this morning. Honest!"

Many hours were spent waiting in a dingy, poorly lit, run down clinic before we took the X-rays back to the American doctor, all the way across town again, who then pointed out the dark shadows on Sean's lungs.

Pneumonia.

Sean was put on a huge dose of antibiotics - both for the pneumonia and his arse boils, and I was put on my best behaviour to look after him. A few hours on a drip helped to rehydrate him. But as neither Sean nor I had any medical insurance, he wouldn't be staying there overnight.

The doctor didn't recommend checking into a regular hospital. In Sean's weakened state he would be open to all manner of dangerous diseases. Well - other than the one he already had. I don't think the arse boils were a disease though - more of an occurrence.

So we ferried Sean back to our shabby little room, attempted to fluff up the hard foam brick pillow on his bed and did our best to make him feel comfortable.

"I can't believe you've got pneumonia, Sean." I said, unhelpfully.

"I can't believe you didn't notice." He coughed back at me, holding his chest.

Rob popped in and out over the next few days as I sat with Sean. Maybe he was checking that I hadn't just cleared off and left him to die. I made sure he drank enough water, took his prescribed drugs, and even helped dab soothing cream onto his bum boils. His fever bubbled away under the skin, which led to many ranting sessions that made absolutely no sense, but helped to keep me amused. The sweat poured out of him, and by Christ, the weight had just dropped off him - like someone had snuck in and stolen it when I was out mooching around. His face seemed to be sucking itself away and wrapping around his skull. It was a particularly unpleasant little room to be sick in, but the thought never crossed my mind to move him elsewhere.

Sean responded very well to the drugs. His temperature soon dropped back from above-boiling and his eyes started to clear once the fever subsided. I was hoping it hadn't jumped into me, but I felt good and strong - not even a sniffle.

As Sean recovered, Rob and I had a few parties in our room, drinking beers and smoking the hooch. He'd found a local whiskey-like spirit that made The Piper seem like holy water. We called it The Scorpion, because one little nip was all you'd ever need. Or want. If seeing Sean's naked, boil-sprouting arse fall forwards onto the bed hadn't sent me blind, drinking this stuff just might.

Sean lay under his filthy, sweat-stained top sheet, sucking on his water bottle, grinning a kind of semi-insane grin, as Rob and I passed the guitar back and forth, rolled joints and dared each other to take nips from The Scorpion. We sang songs to celebrate his illness and recovery:

His arse-boils were rampaging, pneumonia fever raging
He couldn't walk, or talk, or cry or sing
But his illness went unnoticed
By his friend, in the remotest
City that young Sean had ever been...

It was a great road to recovery for Sean. Along with his humour came his appetite; the colour returned to his sunken cheeks, and his eyes started to make their way back out from the deep holes that they'd receded into, like a couple of badgers coming back up the burrows after the dogs have been called off.

"Hallo Sean! You're back!"

His chest sounded much better, and the arse boils were disappearing back beneath the surface. Another visit to the X-ray clinic confirmed that the pneumonia had cleared up, and he was pronounced healthy again - or at least, on the way to recovery.

It's good to watch a friend recuperate, especially when it's your fault they'd ended up so ill in the first place. He was actually starting to look pretty pleased with himself. Not deranged pleased, like after the donkey trek, but something new - like he'd just been somewhere you wouldn't normally go, and had come back with a secret piece of the puzzle in his head.

15

The Red Man

Sean was so chuffed at feeling better that, much to my surprise, he was keen to make plans to go trekking.

"Really? I thought you'd be on the first plane out of here."

"Nope! Where shall we go? Everest?"

"Nah. It's probably not a good idea. We'd have to walk for a week before it'd get interesting. I reckon we should go to Pokhara and head to Jomsom, or do the Annapurna circuit."

I knew about the well-trodden treks in western Nepal that wound up through some incredible valleys into the Himalayas. At last - a chance to show off my travelling knowledge.

"OK. Let's clear off tomorrow. Quick, before I change my mind. How long is the trek?"

"Depends."

"What on?"

"How quick we walk, obviously. What else could it depend on?"

This decision called for a celebration. Sean wasn't strong enough for The Scorpion just yet. He had a better idea.

Every street corner near our hovel had a street dealer, and ten or twenty times a day they'd whisper: "Hello. You want marijuana? Opium? Brown sugar?"

Sean surprised the hell out of me: "Brown sugar, please. How much for brown sugar?"

I'd never tried the stuff, but the past month of unrelenting boredom and the shock of Sean's sickness now made anything seem worth a go. But the dealer freaked.

"No! No have Brown Sugar."

"But you just offered us some!"

We asked another, and another, but they all backed away from us pretty quickly. Sean did look quite scary, in a kind of gaunt, not fully recovered way. I doubt I would've sold us any strong drugs either.

"OK - opium then. We'll have some opium please."

"No! No opium. Police big problem."

Shit. Kathmandu had changed. The year before I'd bought some opium from a street dealer, and ran back to our room to share the booty with my mates. We heated it up over a candle and smeared the sticky sweet goo up and down a Rizla, forming a hard black line of liquorice down the length of the paper. We really didn't know what we were doing. Chucked a pile of tobacco over it and sparked it up.

Waited.

Nothing, except the usual coughing and dizziness from the super raw Nepali tobacco.

We tried again. Nothing.

I legged it down to the street and found the dodgy bastard I'd bought it from.

"You sold me a lump of shit," I yelled, waving the thick black lump in his face.

"No, no Mister. This is Nepali opium, from the mountains. The best. Number One!"

"Rubbish, I've smoked stronger rubber. You know what rubber is?"

"Like on car tyre?"

"Yes. You've sold me rubber. This stuff is crap. Doesn't work. Take me to your boss."

"Oh no, Mister - you don't want to meet my boss. No no no."

"Yes I do. He's selling shit and I'm going to tell him."

The poor man was not only confused, but scared. "OK, but I'm not coming in."

He took me down a side alley off Freak Street, then down an even smaller, darker alley. He banged out a rhythm on a door tucked behind some bins.

The door edged open and a few words were passed, the street dealer scarpered and I was led down some concrete stairs into a cellar.

Several nasty looking fellas stood around a table piled high with wads of rupees and dollar bills, and behind these sat the boss; his clothes stretched tight over a large, barrel body. He looked like he'd seen too many gangster films. He lifted his bald head and looked me in the eye.

"What do you want?" He barked from behind his line of men.

"Your opium... is shit."

His jaw flopped open. I'm not sure if his men could speak English, but they shuffled around uneasily, possibly reacting to their big boss' surprise.

"What did you say?" He leaned forward. I repeated myself, this time speaking louder and slower.

"I said, your... opium... is... *shit!*"

His jaw was hanging down where his neck would've been, if he'd bothered to grow one.

"You come to me and say my opium is shit?"

"Yep, it's shit. Doesn't work. I've had two joints of it. It's rubbish. It's like smoking a car tyre."

The boss looked at me and then at his men, which was when I realised that coming down here probably wasn't the smartest move of my life. He mouthed something to his men, which could've been "the bloke is mental" or "kill him." I don't think a phrase book would've helped me to clarify.

"Well -" I decided to follow up, after a lot of tense silence and shuffling, "that's just my opinion, of course."

He stared at me, leaning even closer. Then he burst out laughing.

"This is number one Nepali opium, from my village. This is not shit! Show me how you smoke."

Grinning with relief, I pulled a chair up to the table and showed him how I smeared the opium on the paper and covered it in tobacco.

"No, no, no. Stop! Give to me."

He crumbled a small piece of aspirin onto a bubbling drop of opium, which he dropped into a tiny headed pipe with a long, curved neck.

"Smoke that."

I did, and it tasted sweet, like molasses crossed with a woodbine. *"Ahhhhhh!"*

He made up another pipe for me as I felt my whole body start to smile, and all the dormant little receptors in my brain reached up to grab hold of the passing cloud of delight; their tiny mouths opening up to sip from the glorious Himalayan nectar. I saw a thousand rhyming words flow up from the middle of my brain, like smoke signals popping out of a hole in a teepee, which my lips didn't quite know what to do with, so they just went *"Oooooooooooooohhhh"* instead.

The big boss very kindly let me recalibrate before bothering me.

"You still think my opium is shit?" He smiled.

"Nooooooooo! No sir, I do not. I think... *Aaaaaaahhh.*"

A few pipes later, I did my best to convert my inner smoke signals into a big 'thank you' to them all for not killing me and leaving me all murdered and minced in a backstreet gutter, like a butchered two-legged water buffalo, before I floated back up the stairs into the cold Kathmandu air, which filled my lungs with the purest collection of molecules ever inhaled by any creature anywhere in the universe.

Oh well. No opium this time. Probably a good thing, in Sean's condition. We had to make do with the usual Himalayan offerings - Iceberg beer - guaranteed to leave you with a blinding hangover - and the local marijuana, guaranteed to make you laugh and eat like a stoned hyena. No more Scorpion though - the next day effects were only a shade above total organ failure.

We ended up dancing around our room in the late afternoon to an old Muddy Waters tape. There was more fun to be had there than in any of the empty cafes around town. Rob came by to celebrate, and our belly laughs and guffawing attracted another American fellow who we'd seen hanging around the place. We called him the Red Man because he wore red baggy pants and a red hippy top below a thick clump of ginger hair. He was staying on the next floor up from us.

"Come in, come in!" Sean welcomed him with wide arms and drunken legs.

"Hi! I'm Jim. Sounds like you guys are celebrating," The Red Man observed, very astutely.

"Yes. We are. We're going trekking! *Wahey!!*"

Sean whacked on James Brown and went into wild dancing mode, throwing himself around between the two smelly beds, flicking his legs around like he'd just discovered that they were hinged in the middle.

"Yeeeeaaaaahh Seany baby, back from the dead!" Rob was nowhere near as nimble - more John Belushi than James Brown, and he dragged himself across the floor on his backside like a dog with worms, in time to the music.

Get up ahh, get on ... Drag drag.

Get up ahh, get on... Drag drag. All the while he smiled up at us like a big, happy baby that'd just discovered the world is a great place to be alive in.

The Red Man sat back with a few beers, and did what I'd discovered a lot of American college kids liked to do: roll endless joints and laugh at mental English men.

"See," I yelled in Sean's ear, "it's all been worthwhile. Don't you think?"

"Yes, I never knew I loved going trekking so much," he laughed.

We slowly came to rest as the afternoon took its toll. Rob stood in the doorway, saluting his farewells.

"It's been an honour knowing you two fine gentleman. May your travels be as interesting as your dancing has been. Quick, march!" And he was off, disappearing back into the Kathmandu streets that he found so fascinating, maybe stopping to pick up a buffalo lung to feast on before his head hit the pillow.

The Red Man - Jim, stood up to leave.

"Wow, if this is you guys celebrating going trekking, I'd love to bump into you on New Year's Eve," he laughed. "Man, I've gotta crash too. Good luck. Might see you again somewhere."

He weaved his way between the door posts and staggered off up the stairs.

We lay on our beds, feeling the Iceberg beer enter its secondary stage, unlocking the doors to the part of the brain where the headaches are kept.

"Quick Sean, I'd best roll us a joint before we can't function - chuck the papers over."

"They're in my money belt, hang on." He scuffled around behind the door, then dived under the bed.

"Shit, where's my money belt? It was hanging on the door."

"Errrr, no idea, Sean." I didn't even bother looking around, as there was only behind the door, under the beds, or on the tiny table to choose from.

"It's gone! Shit, Mark, everything's in there. Travellers cheques, passport..."

"Fag papers..."

"Quick, pull the mattresses up." Sean decimated the room even further, to no avail. This was not the time to remind him that I'd told him earlier to put his money belt in the safe downstairs.

"Sean, I told you earlier to put it in the safe downstairs with mine. Remember?"

A lost passport and no travellers cheques would be a whole new world of pain, and would mean weeks of hanging around Kathmandu waiting for missing faxes to never show up, police reports to be filed, and an infinite amount of frustrated boredom that would send us over the edge.

Sean's face suddenly changed.

"The Red Man must have taken it."

I cracked up. "Sean, the Red Man did not take your money belt! You've left it somewhere, you idiot."

"He did. He took it. Don't you think he looked dodgy, sitting there for ages? Bastard."

"He was just sitting there drinking. And smoking. You can't call him dodgy for that!"

Sean's eyes widened as it all began to click into place for him.

"He kept rolling joints - so we'd get smashed and wouldn't notice."

"We were smashed when he got here, Sean!" I pointed out, correctly.

From the pile of mess on the floor Sean grabbed one his walking boots and shoved his fist deep into the place where you'd normally be putting your foot. He waved his booted fist around in front of his drunken head in what I presumed was meant to be a menacing gesture, reducing me to a laughing heap on the bed.

"What you go gonna do with that, Sean? Challenge him to a wall climb?"

"Come on! I'm going up to his room. Fuckin' thief!"

Boot-wielding Sean looked ridiculous, but nevertheless, quite scary. His face was still gaunt from the pneumonia, his dark eyes still a little on the sunken side. The badgers weren't fully out yet. And after several hours of drinking, dancing and smoking, he was unsteady on his feet.

I tried to distract him.

"You should put a sock on your hand at least, don't want him to think you're crazy. Shame we haven't got any gloves. You could put them on your feet. He'll think you're upside down."

Sean looked down at himself and laughed, before catching me unawares and lunging for the door and running up the stairs towards the Red Man's room. I scurried after him in pursuit, whispering loudly at Sean to hold his wayward horses. I reached the top landing, and peeped out along the corridor to see him crouching like a drunken, badly trained commando outside the Red Man's door. Shit, he was going to do it for sure, and it wasn't going to end well.

"Sean, you prat, come here!" I hissed, trying to be as quiet as possible, which was difficult after the intake of the afternoon.

But Sean was busy readying himself for the charge: knees bent, holding his booted fist in front of him like it was a real weapon - which it obviously wasn't. He backed away from the door, hoiked up his jeans that were hanging off his skinny backside, lowered his shoulder for the impact, and tucked his head down low. But then, he turned and looked at me with a pained face, and hobbled back along the corridor, clutching his tummy and whispering loudly.

"Hang on, I've got to have a shit. You watch his door."

I was in hysterics in the shadows as he scuttled down the stairs on bowed legs, holding his boot to his tummy. But I had to think quickly - I couldn't let Sean burst in on the Red Man. He'd be lying on his bed now, head spinning, almost passed out, probably still giggling. The poor bloke was about to get the fright of his life when his door smashed open and Sean came sprawling and crashing into the wall by his bed, shouting "Fuckin' thief," tripping over his legs and ending up in a heap on the floor, waving his boxing boot around.

"Mark!" Sean whispered up the stairs. "Mark. Come down. Quick!"

I dived down the stairs.

Shit, what's he gone and picked up now? A bed post?

Sean stood on the bottom step, grinning stupidly, his money belt dangling from his thumb.

"… I'd left it in the bog. Sorry."

16

Bagpipe Burp

The highlight of the twelve hour hungover bus journey to Pokhara the next day, a couple of hundred rainy, very bumpy kilometres west of Kathmandu, was the joy in finding two hard-boiled eggs for sale in a roadside stop that I called The Town With No Food.

"Will you look at that, Sean." I peered into a fly-mesh covered cabinet beside an empty chai stall. "I've been here twice before and never found a thing to eat. God knows why the bus stops here."

Sean didn't find this as interesting as I did. He looked up and down the strip of empty shacks.

"I bet this place comes alive at night. Sure you don't want to book us in for a week here?"

Feeling lucky, we nibbled our eggs away to nothing as the bus ploughed west, eventually dumping us in a drizzly Pokhara bus station in the late afternoon. We headed off to a lodge I knew, run by a friendly ex-Gurkha called Charlie, who was on his veranda drinking chai.

"Hello Charlie - got a room for us?"

"Hello! Yes. I have room - very nice lodge!"

"Yes, I stayed here eighteen months ago."

Charlie was still looking strong from years of training in the British army, a permanent grin spread across his broad, handsome face.

"Aha, yes! You stayed in the front room downstairs! Charlie never forgets a face."

"Um, no - we were upstairs at the back."

"Yes, yes, I remember! With your girlfriend."

"Nope. With some friends."

Charlie slapped his thigh. "Yes, you had happy times."

Well at least he'd got that right. From the roof of the lodge I remembered seeing Mount Machapuchare staring down at us in the distance - a sharp-ridged mountain rising like a pyramid from the line of its white coated neighbours. Its colours and shades changed throughout the day, with an orange glow in the mornings and early evenings; the snow of the high peak shining in the bright sun. At night the moon reflected its silver light onto the snow; a direct hit.

Sean and I clambered onto the roof of the lodge.

"What, behind those clouds there?" Sean pointed, "or those ones over there?"

The only changing colours we could now see were varying degrees of grey and dark grey, to the almost thunderous black of the never shifting cloud line.

"Come on, Sean. Let's go up to the lake. That's where all the bars and cafes are. Maybe we'll get lucky again."

We'd learnt to lower our expectations to a minimum, but still, the sight of all the empty bars lining the water front was a disappointment.

"We had such a laugh here last time," I grumbled, as we walked up the empty, muddy street. "We sat in that bar for hours, smoking with a naked, one-legged Sadhu. When we left, Gareth was convinced he saw the Devil hiding behind those bushes, squatting down and waving to him."

Half the bars were boarded up, awaiting busier times. It was so quiet now, even the Devil had left town.

"Well, Mark, we know no one is around. Let's stop going on about it and get the hell out of here. We're here to go trekking, not mope around in bars waiting for the Devil to show up. He'll be back in Woking by now, anyway."

There was no quick escape though, as we had to sort out our trekking permits, which could mean a couple of days of irritating waiting until a man in a uniform would stamp a piece of white paper that allowed us to head for the hills.

Next morning, I woke up feeling slightly sick, which was my fault for drinking on a one-egg tummy, as my appetite had completely vanished the night before. I lay in bed, feeling a bit weak, as Sean pored over endless maps of the surrounding region.

"I fancy a long trek, Mark. Go right in, right up into the mountains." He ran his fingers over a dotted line that wiggled across the map. "Let's aim for Muktinath. Look, it's not far off the Tibetan border. That's at least a two week walk."

Since the pneumonia, Sean had cut back on the ciggies, and I could see he wanted to test this new, leaner version of himself out on the mountain tracks.

"That's a month of walking, Sean! There's no bus home when you get there, you know. That dotted line you're following might look easy from here, but you're gonna want some new knees by the end of it, believe me."

Sean leaned over the map, his eyes widening at the prospect of an adventure. Or maybe it was simpler than that - he was just excited because we finally had something to do. I had to hand it to him; he'd stuck it out on this miserable trip, and had never given me a hard time for bringing him here. The laughs had been few and far between, and he would've been well justified in using the pneumonia as an excuse to get the hell out.

"Yeah, OK, let's do the big one," I said, dragging myself out of bed, "but only if you promise to always say 'Muktinath' in a Yorkshire accent."

We visited the Trekking Permit Office, asked for "two returns to Muktin-ath, please," in broad Yorkshire accents, and headed off to practice our walking round the lake. But I didn't get very far.

"I'm going back, Sean. I still feel a bit sick. Maybe my egg was off. God, it could've been there for months."

"OK mate, I'll practice for both of us. See you later!"

I went back to bed and crashed out. Sean woke me at dusk, bright eyed after his big walk.

"Come on, let's go for a bite. I must've walked fifteen kilometres today."

But I still wasn't hungry.

"No, you go. I might just stay in tonight and read. Still feel a bit icky."

Next morning, I found it difficult to get out of bed, which was a worry. Trekking, I knew, was hard work at the best of times, and the best of times can be few and far between once you start to gain altitude. The thought of facing some of the bigger climbs was not filling me with the jollies. But slightly more worrying was that I also had a strange feeling of discomfort around my stomach.

Sean went off to pick up our trekking permits as I pondered over my sore abdomen. I sat with Charlie, moaning about my tummy and my lack of energy.

"My friend, she is doctor in the hospital here," Charlie offered, possibly in an endeavour to get rid of this miserable Englishman. "She is Scottish. If you are worried, you should go see her."

I figured Sean would want to head off the next day - we had no reason not to - so I decided to have a quick check up. Better safe than sorry.

I took a taxi to the hospital on the outskirts of town, and spoke to a nurse, who sat me down in a packed corridor adjoining the waiting room, which was full of young and old from all over Nepal. Most would've had to walk there, sick or injured, days or even weeks from their homes up in the mountains. There were no roads north from Pokhara in 1987 - just endless miles of severe tracks winding up and down the hills throughout the lower Himalayas. Consumptive coughs filled the air of the hospital and deathly sick characters curled up on the floor. If you weren't ill when you came in, there was every chance you would be by the time you left. No wonder the American doctor had advised Sean to avoid hospitals.

I felt ridiculous being there. In comparison to most, I looked like the healthiest creature on the planet, still pretty fit from the year working in the different part of Tesco. But I sat in turn and waited for a few hours, dangling my head out of an open window whenever possible.

Eventually the red-haired Scottish doctor called me in to a cramped, messy room.

"Right son, what's the problem?"

"Well," I said, "I don't feel that well."

I sounded pathetic. All the misery and calm suffering I'd been observing all morning put me to shame.

"In what way? Tummy? Let's have a quick look at you."

She poked around my tummy and had a good listen with her stethoscope, before telling me that everything was fine. I pressed on.

"I'm starting a trek tomorrow, and I'm not sure whether I should go or not. I feel a bit weak. I'm worried about going."

"Och, you'll be fine. Go away and get some fresh air. Enjoy yourself. Stop worrying. Go on, off you go."

I slunk off, nodding to the scores of ill Nepali patients that had been staring at me all day.

But I was still worried. I took a taxi back to the lodge and sat on the roof, watching the clouds gather, the distant lightning crackling through the low light. I wasn't accustomed to this feeling of worry. I just felt as if something bad was going to happen, though I couldn't picture what. And it wasn't tangible enough to chat to Sean about. Maybe the ominous feeling in my stomach was a hangover from the glacier attack. Being so close to the mountains again had triggered off my jelly wobbles.

So I did something that I hardly ever did in all my years of travelling: I walked into town and phoned my mum.

It was so good to hear her warm voice coming down the wire - the second Scottish woman I'd spoken to that day.

"Och hello son, how are you?!"

I filled her in on our trip so far, and told her we were about to go trekking. I would usually be babbling with excitement at the prospect.

"Well you loved that last time son, so that's nice. You just be careful now. I saw Gareth's mum, he's made it to Australia and they're all looking forward to you getting there."

"How are things at home?" I asked.

"Och, you know." She wasn't saying much.

"He's not drinking again is he mum?'

"Mmmm hmmm."

"Is he drunk now?"

"Mmmm hmmm."

"Oh Mum, I thought he'd stopped."

The thought of her sitting in the lounge, with Dad incoherent in the chair, slumped, staring blankly at the TV, or, more likely, completely unconscious, was a profoundly saddening, familiar image.

And there was me, moaning about my slightly boring jaunt around Kashmir. The best thing that could happen for her was that Dad would fall asleep, and then at least she could put some music on, rather than the Friday night telly. She told us that when she'd met Dad she'd thought he was the deep, silent type. Once they were married, she realised he was just silent.

"When did the drinking start again?"

"Listen son, don't you worry. I should nee have said anything. It's just the way it is, Mark. He's not a bad man, and there's nothing we can do to change things. Anyhow, son, tell me about Kashmir again. Och, I'd love to go there."

I didn't want to tell her that I wasn't feeling well. I knew she'd only worry.

I was low when I came off the phone. Maria had popped into my thoughts again, and I had Mum going round my head. And I was anxious about this trek.

Then I burped. And I burped again. I sat watching the clouds covering the western Himalayas, burping, burping, burping. That's odd, I thought. I'm breathing in, and burping out. Breath in. Burp out.

I wandered and burped my way into town to find Sean in a cafe by the lake having an early evening beer.

"Oh hello, Mark. Feeling better?" I told him about the Scottish doctor at the hospital.

"But she said you're fine, though? That's good. You don't look ill, if that helps. You'd know if it was pneumonia by now. Shit, I wouldn't fancy getting that in the middle of a trek. Anyway. Ta Daaaaa!" He held up our trekking permits. "You up for leaving in the morning?"

"Yeah. Course, Sean. I'll be fi-"

BUUUUUUUURP!

"Christ," Sean laughed, hanging onto the table, "where did THAT come from? It sounded like an old walrus farting."

"I know, I think I'm evolving. Or de-evolving. It started about an hour ago. Then it stopped for a bit. I did one earlier on that sounded like a bagpipe dying." I let out another long resonator.

"Lucky you didn't do that in front of the Scottish doctor. She'd think you were taking the piss."

I was considering ordering some food when two blonde girls turned up, sat at the bar behind us and ordered some beers. English. I groaned and whispered to Sean, "Oh Christ, bloody typical! Two beautiful girls turn up and I've turned into a wind generator." Sean saw the opportunity, grinned, and invited them over.

"Oh, thanks! Hi, I'm Sarah; this is Lucy. We've just got here. Quiet, isn't it?"

"I'm Sean, this is Ma-" Before he could finish, I let fly a four pint burp.

"Sorry. I've got a funny tummy. Mark. Hello."

"Mark's learning to talk in burp. This is his first day, so he's not making much sense."

"Very funny, Sean. I ate a dodgy egg, that's all. Why don't you tell them about your sea of boils. That's a good story."

"Sounds like you two are having a good trip then!" Sarah laughed. God, she was gorgeous. Blue eyes with a cheeky twinkle; a touch of the hippy, but no try-hard hippy clothes.

"How's your trip going?" I managed to ask, without expelling unnatural amounts of tummy gas.

"Ours has been pretty shit, actually. We've met no one. Apart from that funny old Aussie hippy in Kathmandu, what was his name, Lucy?"

"DAVE!" We all shouted together.

"You met Dave! Right," said Sean, "that calls for a real drink. I'll get some Raksi." Sean was always quick to bring out the big guns. He ordered a bottle of the local spirit - much smoother than the Piper - more like vodka with an edge. I took a sip.

"Mmmmm, you know, I think this stuff might just settle my-"

BUUUUUUUUURRRRPPP.

"Now, I think what Mark is trying to say…"

"Shut up, Sean-"

BUUUUUUUURRRRRRPPP.

Luckily, the girls found this not only extraordinary, but very funny.

How bloody brilliant to bump into these two. My mood brightened nicely, the burping peaked at its funniest and died off before it ruined everything, and I managed to eat some rice and dhal between drinks.

"So, you boys are off trekking tomorrow, are you? Where to?"

We filled them in on our big, manly plans to do a four week trek to Muktinath and back. I saw an opportunity here to turn this trip around, to give us something special, something memorable.

"Why don't you come and meet us? Get your permits, set off in a few days, and meet us at Jomsom. We could walk back together!"

"What do you reckon, Lucy," Sarah laughed, "fancy meeting these boys in a remote mountain village?!"

"Only if Sean promises to show us where his boils were."

Excellent! Lucy wants to see Sean's boil scars, and I can try and tempt Sarah into an extended trip across India on the back of a Royal Enfield motorbike. Playing guitar… searching out erotic temple carvings… cabin beds by the sea…

We drank more Raksi, made vague plans, joked and laughed.

This is it. This is finally getting good.

It wasn't just the vague possibility of high altitude sex in the middle of the Himalayas with two funny, good looking girls - at last we were meeting the kind of characters we felt we should be meeting: Cosmic Dave, American Rob, the Red Man, Lucy and Sarah. The sex we could just about do without - the laughs, we couldn't.

The girls and the Raksi did help to dispel my sense of foreboding. Later, Sean and I lay on our beds at Charlie the Gurkha's, smoking a joint.

"Do you reckon they'll come trekking, Sean?"

"Nah. Well, yeah, maybe."

"Make your bloody mind up!"

"I don't really care, Mark. I just wanna get up into those mountains. Can't wait."

"Yeah. Same." I lied, thinking of Sarah. I fell asleep telling myself I'd be feeling fine in a day or two. Half pissed, I could believe anything I wanted to.

We woke early in the morning to the usual grey skies and hangovers. I lay in bed feeling a bit sick, thinking of excuses to wiggle out of the trek. My optimism from the previous evening had totally disappeared.

But now the time had come to head back into the mountains.

17

Blood On The Rocks

After I finished struggling through some chapattis and eggs for breakfast, we set off for Sarangkot - a steep hill rising six hundred painful metres up from Pokhara. This should be a good way to push the legs and lungs into gear for what lay ahead. The air was thick and muggy and the sweat poured from me as we trawled up the endless steps. Sean went ahead on almost the first corner.

Good. Let him go. I'll just take it at my own pace.

My bag felt heavy, my legs heavier still. I'd climbed this hill barely eighteen months previously, but I was like an old man now, grumbling, groaning, puffing and panting. A few hours later, I met Sean at the top. He'd ordered some food and drink from the hut, and waited whilst I recovered.

"You alright Mark? You look knackered." Nice of him to notice.

"I dunno Sean… Not great. But I'll be okay."

The views to the south, overlooking the town and lake, then onto low-lying terraced hills beyond, were almost worth the struggle. Treetops spread out below us and Pokhara Lake glinted up through the leaves.

To the north, east and west – clouds, clouds and more clouds. They didn't look as if they'd be shifting anytime soon.

After a rest and a couple of boiled eggs, I felt slightly better. I couldn't handle the thought of any spicy food, and my diet was heading for the blander end of bland. Eggs, curd, rice, toast. Sweet fizzy drinks. I'd fantasise about drinking Cola and Fanta as I dragged myself up the hills.

We trekked on. Sean was busting to get his thighs working again, like a bloody jack-rabbit.

After Sarangkot, the next few hours walking weren't that bad. Plenty of ups and downs, but nothing too severe. I let Sean pull ahead – well, I couldn't keep up, but that was fine. The mostly shady track just rolled on and on through the afternoon, snaking further and further into the quiet of the hills.

So long as I kept my egg-powered knees working, and sucked on my sweet drinks, I could handle it. Every couple of hours I'd come across Sean sitting on a boulder, waiting for me, taking in the view - or really, the lack of a view. But then he'd be off again, and I'd just roll along, roll along, till the next meeting. It was maddening to know that behind that unshifting line of cloud was one of the most spectacular visions on this old planet. To see the Himalayas from Kathmandu was one thing, but to pop your head over a ridge after a back-breaking four-hour climb, and have the jagged white range open up right in front of you, was something to remember for all your remaining days. Ah well - things could only get better the further in we went. Some puff of wind would surely blow the clouds from our line of vision for the big reveal.

We'd agreed to stop for the night at a tiny village marked on our map. I arrived about four; Sean had been there a while.

"Alright tiger?" He called, as I puffed and panted the last few yards out of the woods; wiping my hot, sweaty face with my wet, sweaty t-shirt. I couldn't even manage a growl.

I noticed the steps that disappeared down the ravine behind Sean. Far below, a river cut its way through the rocks, straddled by a rope bridge.

"Oh gawd, look at that, Sean. Straight down, first thing in the morning. That's gonna be fun."

Tomorrow, I knew, was going to be hard.

After forcing some more eggs down my egg hatch, and some dhal and rice for Sean, we bought a bottle of Raksi and a bag of weed for about thirty pence. Both were obviously the last things I needed, but both were completely necessary. Sitting on the top of the ravine that evening with Sean, I began the ongoing process of convincing myself that I actually felt fine. So long as I could laugh, all would be well.

Make me laugh, Sean, for god's sake, make me laugh.

The moon shone down, illuminating the valley and the treetops below. *All will be well tomorrow, Mark. Just relax. Breathe, be strong.*

We fell asleep in our sleeping bags in a tiny hut, worn out from the day's hike, surrounded by the absolute peace and quiet of the hills; the nearest road now a full day's walk behind us.

After a good sleep we awoke at dawn, stretching and yawning in the cold, fresh mountain air. We had breakfast and chai by the fire with the smiling family that lived there. Fresh chapattis smoked on a plate over the fire, and the ancient, grinning granny niggled away at her last remaining tooth as she poured out the fresh pancake mix onto a sizzling griddle. I loved banana pancakes. *But not today I'm afraid, gran.* The little kids, rugged up against the morning cold, couldn't decide what was more fascinating – Sean and I, or that tooth. We'd be off soon, but that tooth still had days of fun in it, so they settled on just staring at us.

We ate up, paid up, packed up and left. I chucked a couple of bottles of Cola into my pack and readied myself for a never ending thigh trembler.

"You go ahead, Sean. I'll take my time." My energy levels were low, but I blamed it on the Raksi and the grass from the night before.

The tiny cobbled steps twisted back and forth; nothing remained constant for more than a few paces. Nepali men, women and children overtook me effortlessly – each carrying what looked like a tonne of goods on their backs. I swear a bloke went past me carrying a fridge.

When I saw a man carrying what was probably his mum in a sling strapped to his head, I felt like giving up. Jesus, how could I feel so weak? All I had in my backpack was a couple of books, some extra clothes, a sleeping bag and a towel, which doesn't weigh anywhere near as much as a mum - even a tiny Nepali mum.

Hours later, I met Sean by the rope bridge beside the river that I'd glimpsed the night before. I dropped down beside a grinning Sean. The clean, fresh air in his recently diseased lungs must've felt great. He was strong and well again. Match fit. Lucky bastard.

"Sean, do you think you could carry me in a head sack?" Depressingly, I was only half-joking.

After stringing the break out for as long as possible, we had to make a move onwards. There's only so many places to sleep on these treks. Being caught out and stuck between lodges after dark would be unwise, unless you knew what you were doing and were well prepared, which clearly neither of us were. We didn't even have a torch. I didn't want to get myself into any more strife in the mountains. My experience on the glacier was more than enough for one lifetime.

On the last trek I did with Gareth, we didn't even have a drinking bottle - just a plastic bag we'd found to scoop water out of the mountain streams when we came across them. I'd reached states of extreme happiness on that trek: bounding along, the Himalayas to my left; endless green, terraced valleys to my right; arms in the air, singing old punk songs at the top of my voice in rhythm with my step.

Pure bloody freedom.

I could see Sean was heading for that feeling. His boots grew wings as he took off up the track, away from the rope bridge.

"See ya at the next pit stop, Tonto!" He hollered.

The track climbed way up high, with freaky drops to the rapids below, before diving back down to the river, which was high and wild in places. Several times the track nudged along the bank, the white water gushing only a couple of feet from my boots.

A few hours later I rounded a bend and saw Sean sitting by a lodge, boots off, trousers rolled up to his knees, green t-shirt on, holding a chai.

He waved at me, encouraging me on, until I collapsed beside him on the chair.

"I feel fantastic. This is brilliant, Mark."

Luckily the mountains weren't visible - he might've exploded.

I felt like weeping.

I don't know why I didn't turn back. Probably because every other part of the trip had been such a failure, and I was still searching for that highlight. I knew I wouldn't feel bad for too long, so I'd have to just hang in there.

When all comes good I'll be well on my way to Muktinath, and on the way back, probably bump into gorgeous Lucy and Sarah.

That'd be a highlight. Surely.

"We'd best get a move on, Mark. It's still a few hours walk to the next stop. Are you sure you're OK?"

"Yeah, I'm fine. I think the burping bug tired me out. Go ahead, I'll meet you there."

I dragged myself away from the chai-stand and carried on doing what the track demanded of my concrete weighted boots, the roar from the river never too far away. I made it to the next set of lodges, perched on a hillside above the river, just as the sun was setting.

Sean was sitting there drinking beer with a couple of German girls - the first westerners we'd seen since leaving Pokhara. I can't have impressed them much when I stumbled in. Sweaty, pale, exhausted and surrounded by my own ever growing fart cloud. During the afternoon, my burp bug had returned and brought along its stinking cousin, the fart bug.

Breathe in. Burp out. Breathe in. Fart out.

I slumped down beside Sean and the girls.

"Hi," I groaned, desperately trying to contain whichever end needed containing. "I'm Mark."

I could feel twinges in and around my abdomen. Sudden little flaring stabs, like someone was striking matches on the inside of my lower ribs.

"Hallo Mark. Are you OK? You are looking at your stomach a lot."

"Am I?" I said, glancing down at my stomach.

"Yes. You just did it again."

"Did I?" I said, pretending to pick some fluff off my sweaty t-shirt.

"Mark has been having wind problems," Sean thought it best to mention, "I wouldn't sit there if I were you."

"It is OK. We have brothers."

"Not like him, you don't," Sean laughed, "he's the Wind King. He's got little wheels on his boots and he blows himself along the track. He's like a trekking yacht."

Sean and the German girls had some dinner. I didn't. They ordered more Raksi, so I joined in for that, hoping it'd dampen down my insides. Possibly not the wisest move.

Even though I was well on the way to feeling awful, having the girls there to have a drink with was most welcome. We had a funny old session up in that tiny village somewhere beside a river, a few days walk from Pokhara, but during a laughing fit I felt a surge in my stomach and legged it to the toilet: a hole in the ground behind a tree.

Blood. Lots of blood.

I was shocked, of course - but not that shocked. I'd had this before in Pakistan, after eating a mutton curry swimming in grease in the desert.

The trouble was, that this seemed like *just* blood.

I joined the others and carried on, the little voice in my head telling me all was OK, I'd just eaten some dodgy food or something. That was actually very unlikely, because I'd hardly eaten anything except for a few eggs over the past three days. Anyhow, the Scottish doctor in Pokhara had told me I was fine, nothing to worry about. "Go and get some fresh air," she'd said. "It'll do you good." She hadn't heard my bagpipe burps though.

The girls were a good match for Sean on the drinking. Foolishly, I did my best. We all crashed in our huts well after dark, the roar of the river replacing the peace and quiet of the night before.

I awoke during the night, worrying, listening to the river. Several times I had to get up and visit the hole in the ground in the dark. The birds were beginning to call out when I managed to fall asleep again.

We'd arranged to have an early breakfast with the girls, but by the time we were up and running, they'd long gone. They were wise to leave early because a ten-hour day lay ahead to Ghorepani - almost straight up a vicious looking hill, after re-crossing the river high up on a wobbly rope bridge.

"I shit blood last night, Sean."

"Oh, really? That's not good."

"No. But I don't feel that ill. Just tired. And hungover."

"Well, you're hardly eating. And you still keep looking at your stomach. Like you're expecting something to pop out and say hello."

"Do I? Oh. No, I'm not expecting anything. Come on, let's get cracking. I'll be OK."

Through the woods we climbed, leaving the river well below us, my pack heavy with water and Cola. All I'd see of Sean occasionally was his pack high above, as he boinged away like a mountain goat in spring. I had to stop several times to crouch behind trees and leave little puddles of blood along the way.

I eventually dragged myself into Ghorepani, about three thousand metres above sea level, just after sunset. Sean and the girls were already tucking into Raksi and dinner, and I joined in with them as best I could, but they were too far ahead and I just didn't have the energy.

I crashed out early. I could hear Sean and the girls' laughter cutting through the quiet of the tiny mountain village. The Milky Way shone through the bedroom window as I curled into a ball in my thin sleeping bag, feeling cold inside.

Damn, I just wanted to be like them. Healthy, happy and enjoying the trek.

After the exertion of the last couple of days, the following day was almost a blessing. We had a slow morning in Ghorepani, waiting to see if the mountains would appear – they didn't – followed by a five hour walk down, down, down to Tatopani, the next village. Seventeen kilometres I'd been told. Again, I watched Sean galumph out of sight.

I stopped at a hut serving food and chai half way down the hill. Rhododendrons were everywhere, though spring was still a way off. All I could see above me was the high canopy of the trees, and all around was just forest, long grass and flowers. The smell of the smoke from the fire welcomed me in.

After giving up on the soup, I walked on for ten minutes and lay down under a big tree in the soft grass and fell asleep with the birds twittering in the criss-cross branches above me. It was like being a kid again, back in Derbyshire.

I awoke not feeling too bad, which was the step up I desperately needed to convince myself I'd come through the worst of it, whatever *it* was. I'd not passed any blood since the night before - a hopeful sign.

I made my way down the steep hill on the endless stone steps to Tatopani, towards some hot springs. Sean was there with the girls, and they greeted me into the riverside village. The river was strong and turbulent from the melting glaciers. Lines of flapping prayer flags were stretched out between the spring baths, which were full of hot, steaming water. Sean and the girls jumped in for a soak. I was still feeling well, with no more blood attacks, but I thought it wise to avoid sitting in the hot springs and possibly dramatically ruining everyone's experience.

The drinking began late afternoon, all in a great mood from the surroundings and the joints that Sean was rolling. I ate some more food, pushing myself to see if I could take it. The seals held, and no gurglings arose within me. I'd even stopped farting, burping, and constantly looking at my stomach.

Another trekker came into town before dark from the other direction, having just walked from the village of Jomsom, where we were heading. He told us a landslide had swept away a section of the path, high above the river. A stretch of maybe twenty metres was really precarious, and a couple of trekkers had turned back. I felt the fear return. There was no way I could put myself through that, especially as I wasn't feeling very strong.

"I can't do it Sean. I can't cross that track."

"Bollocks, course you can! You've done worse before, surely?"

"Well yeah… I have."

I reminded him about the glacier; of jumping across big cracks in the ice. Dangling by one arm from the rocks. Careering down the hill on my pack, heading for the sheer sided lake.

"Honestly Sean - I can't go across that ledge. I don't want another mountain freak-out. Sorry pal. My rule is to stick to the track where it's safe. I'm going to have to turn back."

I'd been dying for an excuse to turn round, and here it was. Glacier Day had actually served a purpose. Here was my get-out-of-trek-free card.

I could see the light spark up in Sean's eye. The same light I'd had when I had been left alone in the Karakoram mountains, before the glacier nearly stole me.

Freedom. Excitement. An adventure all on his own.

"Well, that's a shame, Mark," he lied. "Would you mind if I carry on? I love it up here. I'll meet you back in Pokhara or Kathmandu? You'll be OK, won't you?"

My thinking was that I'd turn around and slowly make my way back to Pokhara, - no rush, take ten days if necessary. I was feeling better than the previous few days, no bleeding - maybe I'd even enjoy the solitary walk at my own pace.

"I'll be fine, Sean. Honest. I'll wander back slowly and hang around till you show up."

We were still drinking well after the hut had closed its kitchen doors, even taking a bottle to bed with us, still laughing as we passed out in the lovely, cool, night-time air, miles from anywhere, springs bubbling outside our room, the prayer flags flapping in the night breeze.

Morning came, and we were a bit hungover, as we often tended to be. Sean was in good spirits as we sat beside the river, gnawing on our breakfast eggs and rehydrating on chai. And then - the most fantastic thing happened. The low-lying clouds up ahead parted, and the bulking, giant, rocky mass of Mount Dhaulagiri peeped out from behind the misty curtain. It was so unexpected and so powerful that it almost gave me a fright. The high slopes were covered in thick snow, and wispy trails of high mountain wind licked around the peak. And then it was gone again, swallowed up by the fat, grey clouds.

"Bloody hell! Did you see that, Mark?!" Sean was suitably awed, although he refrained from spilling out the word 'magical'.

Yes, I'd seen it, and it had given me a fright, because it was the first mountain I'd seen since running from that glacier. And it was surprisingly close - like it had snuck up on us when we weren't looking. Murder in the dark, Himalayan style.

If I'd been superstitious, I could've read this sudden reveal as some kind of bad omen. But I wasn't, so I didn't.

"That's where you're heading, Sean. Say hello from me when you get there."

Sean was chomping at the bit to hit the track, especially after finally seeing for himself where we actually were in the world.

"Are you sure you'll be alright, Mark? I'll walk back with you if you want."

"I'm fine Sean, just fine. I'm gonna stroll back up the hill this afternoon. No rush. I'm actually looking forward to it."

He packed some chapatis in his bag and checked the map. I knew I wouldn't be needing it. There was only one track back.

"OK mate, see you in about ten days. Take care. Hope you feel better."

We sang a quick verse of our "I like trekking" song, Sean gave me a hug and then set off. That was probably the first time we'd ever hugged. There had never been much call for it, growing up in Woking.

I walked down to the river with him and watched him go.

Out of the village.

Along the river bank.

Up the hill.

He turned to wave as he reached the rocky corner. I could sense his grin of freedom from where I sat. I was genuinely happy for him. If those clouds cleared again he would soon be having the time of his life.

I waved back as he rounded the bend, his backpack bobbing out of view.

18

Flap a Little Prayer for Me

With Sean well out of view, I felt a slight nervousness at being left alone in the mountains again - it hadn't exactly ended well last time - but also, it was good to have a bit of time to myself. No need to rush or push myself too much. I turned around to head back up to the stone brick room.

That's when it hit me.

A violent eruption, high up in my stomach, similar to the one that killed the dinosaurs off. The shock threw me to my knees.

I vomited uncontrollably as my bowels roared like an angry elephant, and I crumpled into a ball on the floor as an intense pain ricocheted around my abdomen. Less than two minutes on my own and I was now severely, completely ill. My throat burned from the acid as I retched and retched, tears rolling from my eyes.

I looked up, desperately searching the track where Sean had just gambolled off.

Was he definitely gone?

Of course he was - totally out of sight, free as a bird, punching the sky and kicking his heels. I rocked to and fro on the ground, unable to move out of the foetal position, let alone stand upright. There was no way I could catch him.

The Nepali woman from our lodge hurried over and helped me to my knees.

"You ok? You sick?"

I looked up at her weakly, and gained no encouragement from the intense look of concern on her face.

"I… I'm fine. Can you help me to my room? Please." The lady and her husband half carried me, leaving my mess of expelled fluids behind us on the stony path.

This was something way beyond the Curse of the Kathmandu Quickstep: the destroyer of dignity and faith in your exit valve. Whatever this was had come from deep inside me and was seriously, acutely painful. I could hardly lay my hands on my abdomen.

So that's why I keep looking at my stomach. THIS is in there!

But what is IT?

Two minutes earlier and Sean would have been there to help me. It must have been karma - payback time for not helping Gareth in Pakistan when his brain broke, and for missing Sean's pneumonia. And his arse boils.

Just like on the glacier, I was suddenly very, very scared.

I sweated and groaned on the stone hard bed, shaking with shock, before another explosive attack sent me stumbling and vomiting to the hole-in-the-ground toilet.

I heard a gentle tapping at my door, and the lodge lady appeared again, hovering in the doorway.

"Are you ok Mister? You need something?"

I crawled on all fours from the toilet across the cold floor, inching past her feet, and stopped when I reached the bed.

"I'm fine - just a bit sick. In the tummy."

I don't think she believed me. She closed the door on her way out.

What else could I say?

There's been some kind of mass explosion inside of me and I have a really bad feeling that I am in deep, deep trouble?

There was no point. I knew where the nearest hospital was - I'd been there only six days before. And I knew EXACTLY how to get there.

That doctor had TOLD me to go trekking. Get some fresh air, son! So I did. The only way I could have been further from help was if I'd galloped away on horseback into the Himalayas.

OK Mark, think. It's at least five days' walk back to Pokhara - five long days for a healthy body. There's no way I'll make it walking there, not like this. I'm not sure I can even stand, never mind get out of this room. There's no roads. No buffalo carts. I can't imagine a donkey climbing those steps, or crossing the rope bridges. And I couldn't sit on one anyway. It'd be agony. And they'd never fit me into a head sack.

But hanging around waiting to feel better was not an option. I could tell that wouldn't be happening any time soon. I needed medical help.

So, as hard as it was for me to admit it, my only option was to start climbing the massive hill that we'd descended the day before. At least, I lied to myself, it was only a four or five hour walk. I didn't think of it as being seventeen kilometres, straight up. That was too much to consider.

After an hour or so, I was able to unfurl myself from my foetal curl up. Slowly, I began to pack my bag, crying out each time I had to bend at the waist. After a few false starts, where I didn't even make it past the toilet, I pulled my backpack on in super slow motion and struggled out of the door. No strength; fever building; dehydrated; in shock.

Hang on - there's something else there… Something I recognise: a hangover! Yes!

Incredible that on top of everything else, I could actually feel the mighty power of a hangover.

That's it Mark, you've given yourself a stinking hangover, and because you already had dodgy guts, you've made it infinitely worse! Respect to the Raksi. You stupid, bloody idiot. Wait 'till Sean hears about this.

I slid along the stone wall towards the kitchen and eating area.

The lady was shocked to see me with my backpack on.

"You are going Mister?! But you are sick!"

"Honestly," I panted, "I'll be ok." I pointed at my stomach and shouted: "Raksi!!"

Beads of sweat were dripping down the sides of my pale head as I contorted and buckled in front of her. She blinked at me, unsure what was required. I handed over the money for the room.

"No no. You must keep money. Please."

I didn't even have the strength to argue.

"Oh, thank you. I go now. No more Raksi - very bad!"

Her husband stood by as I think she explained that the last batch of Raksi might have been off.

"Well…You take care, Mister."

I staggered out the door onto the uneven path. The village soon gave way to the unrelenting climb back up to Ghorepani, and I left the bubbling hot springs, two confused lodge owners and the flapping prayer flags behind.

Flap a little prayer for me. I think I'll be needing it.

I couldn't stand upright as the pain - no, the hangover - in my abdomen was so great. My pack acted like a lead weight, pushing me down. Within minutes of starting the climb, my stomach cramped up, sending me crashing to the ground in a shrieking heap. I looked around, wild-eyed, not knowing what to do.

Once the pain had subsided enough for me to breathe again, I pulled myself up and staggered around in circles for a while before - BANG - over I went again, clutching at my aching ribs, delivering to my lovely surroundings a brutal mixture of diarrhoea, blood and vomit.

Staggering round in circles between attacks clearly wasn't getting me anywhere, as I was still within shouting distance of the lodge. The owners were probably watching me falling over. Crawling around. Fighting off the Raksi demons like some backpacking alcoholic. So when I managed to get moving again, I tried to move forward. Forward and up. One step a time.

I had some water with me, but every little sip would tie my abdomen up in knots and lead to a huge stomach cramping and vomiting spree. Surely by now I had nothing left inside? I lay in the grass, trying to understand. I'd hardly eaten all week, so what the hell was I bringing up?

I was soon to learn that no matter what I expelled, there'd always be something more disgusting, more worrying and more painful hidden away inside that I could hurl to the surface - it was just a question of which exit it would choose.

Unsurprisingly, the longer I climbed, the harder things became. The pain grew worse, the vomiting deeper and stronger and more desperate; the diarrhoea more severe. But up I continued to go, step by tiny, knackering step. Hour after hot, sweaty hour. I actually crawled up the steeper sections, terrified that if I fell over from an attack - which was happening more and more - there'd be no stopping me and I'd tumble down the hill, all the way back to Tatopani, like I was on a real life Snakes and Ladders board. It was almost evening when I reached the village halfway up the hill where I'd stopped for a rest and some soup thirty hours before; the peaceful huts set amongst the flowers, where I'd awoken the previous afternoon, thinking I was back in Derbyshire.

The calm village tranquillity was ruined as I came blundering towards the huts, red-faced, with wild, bloodshot eyes, squeaking, grunting and groaning like some kind of plagued zombie. But presumably a zombie would smell better, unless it had shat its pants.

The worried faces of the Nepali proprietors spoke volumes. The man and his wife rushed down and helped me up the last few metres of the track. Their kids gave me a wide berth. I collapsed outside the lodge and wiggled my backpack from my shoulders.

"You are sick?"

"Yes. Tummy." I'd given up on the hangover subterfuge. It wasn't fooling anybody. All I could do was crawl into a room and curl up on the bed, my knees lifted up to my stomach in an effort to gain some relief. The lady tapped on my door and brought me some water and a bucket. She lit the oil lamp on the bedside table before she left. I lay there for hours, staring at the flickering light, absolutely exhausted from the ten hour haul up the hill. In the morning I'd have to try to make it to Ghorepani, which was the highest point I'd have to reach on the trek back. That in itself was a bit of a boost - the hardest climb would be tomorrow. I didn't even let myself think ahead to the five hundred metres of steps straight up the side of the hill that was two or three days' walk ahead of me - the same steps that I'd had a hard job handling on the way down.

I crawled under the covers and lay shivering and sweating by turns, clutching at the very necessary bucket. It must've been late when the oil lamp burnt out and I lay in the darkness, shivering with fear and fever. What with the pain, vomiting, incessant toilet trips and continuous worry, I barely slept. It was a long, cold night. Dawn couldn't come quick enough for me.

As soon as the birds kicked off and the light changed, I was up. I lay back on the bed, wiggled my pack onto my shoulders and kind of commando-rolled to my feet, squealing and crying with every movement. I knew exactly what the day had in store for me: up, up, up to Ghorepani.

The Nepali family were already awake, sitting around the fire eating breakfast.

"You go doctor?" The lady asked.

Hang on a minute - I'd never even thought to ask!

"Yes! Yes! Doctor."

They pointed up the hill towards Ghorepani. Oh thank God. Imagine if they'd pointed down the hill to Tatopani!

"Doctor in Ghorepani?"

"No no no. Pokhara. Doctor in Pokhara."

Arrrrrrgggggggghhhhhhhh.

Their attempts to have me stay and eat with them were comforting, but eating was never going to work - so off I went, stumbling out onto the track; their anxious expressions following me out the door. I left a wake of worried looks behind me from that point onwards.

I'd told myself I could do it in five hours – it had only taken me about two to reach the flowery village on the way down from Ghorepani. Leaving so early would hopefully give me most of the afternoon to rest. Up the path I headed, frequently diving behind trees and bushes, hoping someone didn't come around the corner and surprise me. Mind you, they'd get a surprise from what they saw coming out of my body. But I can't remember passing anyone in either direction. Maybe they heard me coming and hid. I dragged myself on and up, sweating and groaning, eventually crawling into Ghorepani not long before nightfall.

It had taken me two days to walk from Tatopani.

Shit. Two days in and already one day behind.

I knew I didn't have ten days' walking in me.

By this point, the pain in my guts had changed. No longer was it spread over my whole stomach, but had now localised into an area of agony that sat high on my abdomen, sort of beneath my lungs, and slightly to the right of centre. I knew the liver was around there somewhere.

I revisited the alcohol subterfuge, and convinced myself once more that what was happening must have been the result of the dodgy Raksi I'd been drinking. Maybe I was allergic? A rest from the booze might just fix me up.

But I had lost an awful lot of blood. Along with the fever and the cramping, I was growing increasingly weak. The diarrhoea was causing me to dehydrate. And I couldn't hold water down for any longer than it took for the reject switch in my stomach to activate, which was approximately one minute.

I took my ridiculous notion that I was suffering from a post Raksi attack to bed with me as soon as I arrived. The day was closing and another long night loomed. The owners of the lodge in Ghorepani kindly offered me food and chai, but all I wanted was to be left alone in my small, dark room.

I heard a bunch of trekkers turn up around dinnertime, and they chatted for a few hours into the evening. German voices, and maybe a Swede. Thank god they weren't like Sean and I, trying to turn every night into a party. Bob Marley was still on the cassette player, and his reggae tones screwed their way into my massive headache. At least it wasn't more bloody Bob Dylan. That really would have been too much. Him and that sodding tambourine man. I'd have happily hoofed the bastard over a cliff in those days. Everywhere I went in India and Nepal, Bob Dylan was strumming and honking through a pair of cheap cardboard speakers. Travelling isn't always fun.

I squeezed the pillow against my tummy all night as I lay simultaneously sweating, vomiting, and wiggling another twelve hours away, mostly in the pitch black after the generators had been turned off and the oil lamp exhausted.

I must have fallen asleep for some time after that, because I woke just before dawn with the threat of the day ahead banging its way around my muddled head. There was no avoiding the fact that what lay before me was one hell of a long walk. Down the hill from Ghorepani, to the river, across the wobbly rope bridge… and then along for several more hours to the huts where we'd met the German girls, back where I'd first noticed the blood.

That walk had taken a good twelve hours a few days before, and I wasn't exactly well then.

In the condition I was in now, it didn't bear thinking about how long it might take.

19

A Room Between Worlds

Again I stumbled out into the early light, before the birds were even considering a sing-song, doing my best to concentrate on the only positive thought I could muster - namely that today's walk was mostly downhill. At least as far as the rope bridge, anyhow. All I had to do was set off, keep my balance, and let momentum do the rest.

But no track in Nepal is an easy walk. Endless twists left and right as the path cut back on itself soon had my thighs trembling in an effort to slow my pace for the sharp corners. Some sections were so steep I had to take them on sideways, like a trekking crab, one careful wobbly step at a time.

Down and down I went. The beautiful maze of endless rice terraces held absolutely no interest for me. Workers popped their heads up from their back-breaking positions as I steamrollered past, grunting and groaning. If they were unlucky, they might witness one of my crashes to the ground, followed by the inevitable explosion.

Once moving, the trick was to somehow protect my stomach from the jarring bang bang as my legs stomped forever downwards. Each jolt was hitting me high in the stomach, up near my damaged drinking organ.

I developed a strange walk to help the pain: kind of half-bent forward at the waist, with a slight twist to the right, which somehow helped. My pack seemed to weigh a tonne, though I'd emptied my books out, and chucked away whatever else I could. I groaned and moaned and sometimes almost rolled down that track through the woods, until a kind of trance took over by mid-morning. My head hung down, eyes locked on the path immediately ahead of my stomping boots.

Hours after setting off, I stonked onto the rope bridge, not really aware of where I was, or what I was doing. I stumbled after two or three mistimed steps, and crashed down to my knees on the narrow planks. I was still close enough to the edge of the bridge to not start up a rope bridge death wobble. But I rocked and swayed, clutching at ropes till I managed to get a grip.

That snapped me out of my trance. The river was way below; white and gushing, just the way you'd expect a river to be that had a rope bridge strung over it. I sort of knelt where I'd stumbled for a good few minutes, until I got the nerve to try and stand again. The fall did the pain in my guts no good whatsoever. In fact, the whole thing did me no good whatsoever. It greatly unnerved me.

Once I made it to the far bank, I had a long rest against the bridge support, trying to make myself understand that I had to be more careful.

Up I clambered again and launched myself along the track, trying my best to remain upright, especially when the river was close by. I was back in trance land before long. I can't remember anything about the next two days, but they must have happened because it says so on the map. All I know is that I sort of came to just before the next rope bridge - at the base of the five hundred metres of steps that I'd slowly climbed down several days before.

It was about midday, and I must've left the hut from the previous night at dawn to arrive there. I sat in a chai house beside the bridge looking straight up, knowing I had to climb to the top of those stairs, lie in a hut for another long, cold, dark night, and then walk at least two more days to reach Pokhara. I ordered chai and some eggs from the young woman that lived there; I was going to need strength for the climb.

But the egg touched my stomach and my gaskets blew. I fell over, face first, screaming as I hurled the egg back up, along with some burning green bile. I rolled around the floor as the spasms pulled me this way and that.

When I'd stopped snivelling and whimpering, the shocked young woman helped me up and mopped up around me. She asked me if I needed help.

I didn't know the Nepali word for 'helicopter'.

I said I was just a bit sick in the tummy, and paid her for the tea and eggs as quickly as I could. Then I stumbled off again, over the wobbly rope bridge, to begin the slow attack of the stairs.

Ten steps up I fell against the wall, heaving and groaning as the single egg molecule that was left within me went into particle accelerator mode, clattering around inside, as my intestines worked their way through the Book of Knots.

A young Nepali lad was unfortunate enough to be sitting on the wall where I went over. When I calmed down a bit and the remaining egg sub-particle had been firmly evicted, I sat on the floor looking up at him.

"You are sick, Mister?"

"Yes, I think so."

"I help you. I carry your bag for you to the top. Very long way."

What a great idea.

The weight from my pack was pushing through to my stomach and adding to my pain. Not having to carry the bloody thing would be such a relief. Of course, he'd want paying, but I didn't need my money anyway.

But somehow, none of that came into my head.

"Thank you - but no, I'll be OK."

I rolled the bag back onto my back and headed off again, clearly quite deranged by this point. Four days of virtually no sleep, no water, no food and endless agony had made sure of that. I was becoming delirious. I'd lost so much weight that I knew I must have looked awful to anyone coming my way. And I was terrified of what would happen next. All I knew was that things were getting worse - and that was the really scary part.

But, I wasn't giving up and I was steadily, painfully inching closer to Pokhara. I knew everything would then miraculously be alright.

Of course it would.

But the little fella inspired me by running ahead and waiting on the corners as we zigzagged our way ever higher. He left me after a while and scampered back down the steps to his home.

The climb took about four hours. I crawled up into the mountain village that Sean and I had spent a night in barely a week ago.

But I had no eye for the view, and no intention of stopping for the night there - though the idea of lying down and never getting up again was very appealing. I'd worked out on the climb that if I carried on walking, I could hopefully reach a small village that I'd remembered passing with Sean, a few hours away.

And that would leave me in shooting distance of Pokhara. Well, not quite shooting distance - more like a fourteen hour, very unpleasant walk. But it seemed a possibility. A glimmer of hope.

If I could be strong, I'd make it in the foreseeable future. *Phew!*

I grabbed a local gal and waltzed her round the village square, bought bottles of Cola for all the young kids, climbed the flag pole, wrapped myself in coloured prayer flags, and led the whole village in a Birdy Song conga as the Raksi began to flow.

Course I didn't. I barely stopped for breath.

Keep moving, Mark.

My mind had tricked me into thinking that these extra few hours would be an easy walk. In fact, I remembered it as being an almost pleasant stroll before, if such a thing is even possible in Nepal. But in the hideous condition I was in, the reality was that every step brought more of the same up and down, up and down.

The sun dipped behind the not so distant hills. The climb had taken so much out of me, but I carried on, helped by the thought that after this mammoth effort I had a good chance of reaching Pokhara the following evening.

As night fell I made it to the next village, but I was in no mood for self-congratulation. I was in a terrible state - bent over, crying out in pain, burning up. I found a room for the night up some dark, creaky stairs that ran off the back of a lodge. The owner brought me some chai and soup, which I didn't dare touch.

My eyes were wild. My hair was wild. God knows I must've stunk something rotten. I curled up on the bed and waited for what I knew was coming. I was in for the worst night of my life.

Worse than the night after the glacier. Much worse. Something really terrifying was building up inside me, all around me, and it felt so real - like something was sharing the room with me. I drifted in and out of a nightmarish sleep for a few moments; the efforts of the past few days finally winning over. But I kept snapping awake, as the oil burner flickered lengthening shapes onto the darkening walls and door.

Each time I'd almost fall sleep, something seemed to grab me, pulling me into a dark, bottomless well and I'd have to drag myself awake, terrified. I was convinced that ghosts and spirits - none of them bearing me any good will whatsoever - were moving around the room as I huddled, shivering and sweating on the bed, exhausted yet too scared to sleep.

Everything built up as the night stretched into the small hours; the ghosts became more threatening and my thoughts and half dreams more entangled. Worryingly, the pain from my upper abdomen had grown so bad that breathing was becoming a real problem.

Then my guts heaved and I had to make it to a toilet, or tree, or hole - fast. The only light was from the tiny oil lamp, and reaching out to grasp it was like reaching out to where the ghosts were waiting for me. I was sobbing and whimpering in sheer violent pain as the cramps twisted my guts round and around. It was like someone had laid a never ending series of mousetraps throughout my abdomen. Probably the same person who'd been striking matches in there a few days earlier. CRACK! Sharp, sharp pains would come from nowhere and render me shocked and senseless. I felt like I was in a room filled with death: a room between worlds.

But, I still had to shit. It seemed to me that the floor was covered in snakes. I picked up the oil lamp and slowly lowered my feet over the edge of the bed. CRACK! The pain doubled me over.

Something had changed in my guts. The lump around my liver area had grown - I knew it. I could feel it sitting inside me.

I shuffled through the snakes to the door, holding the oil light ahead of me, and felt my way down the dark wooden creaking stairs. The blood was seeping out of me, I could tell, and I desperately didn't want to cover the stairs in my mess.

I couldn't find a toilet, but I made out the shape of a tree and crawled towards it. Trouble was, the tree looked as terrifying as the room had been, with its branches waving eerily in the cold night wind. After a mass explosion, I had to crawl back up the stairs again, into the hellish room and cower in my bed, awaiting the next attack.

For the first time, I really broke down and cried. But not for long, because each sob tore through my guts like a knife. This set off another set of snapping mousetraps on my traumatised organs, giving me only a few moments to drag myself out of bed again and crawl over the snakes, past the ghosts to the outside hell of the stairs and the tree.

I didn't make it.

The stairs were absolutely covered in my blood. I lay on the top step, not knowing what to do. My options were either to crawl back into the room full of horrible ghoulish things, or to stay sprawled out on the cold stairs surrounded by my stench, watching the horrible, ghostly tree waving its creepy black arms at me.

I eventually made it back into bed, and curled into a position that allowed me to breathe - just.

The ghosts were waiting. They shifted around me until the flickering from the lamp died as the oil ran out. I lay there in the dark, hearing whispers and feeling things move near the bed, trying hard to keep on breathing.

You've got to walk for fourteen hours tomorrow.

At least I knew that was real.

20

Cross Country

When the grey dawn came I was frozen to the bone, but at least the ghosts and the snakes had cleared off. The room was just a small bare wooden box with a dirty old cloth for a curtain.

But dark bloody goo was spread across the room in puddles and piles; like an alien autopsy had just taken place. I'd obviously been crawling around on the floor during the night, searching for the door.

I did my best to try and clear the bloody mess up, with the help of the curtain, but bending over was well beyond my range of movements. I was sort of locked in my weird, hunched angle, which seemed to be the only way I could breathe through the pain.

The owners had an unpleasant day ahead. I don't remember seeing them as I side-crabbed away from the hut, just after dawn. If I did, I hope I apologised and left them some money for a new curtain. And bed. And floorboards.

Fourteen hours to go.

Fourteen more hours of this shuffling along, and you'll be safe Mark.
Just keep at it.

Bent forward, my pack pushing down on me; eyes following my boots on the stony track beneath me; I managed to remain just about upright, with all the skill of a well practiced drunkard.

A long shadow of madness stumbled along beside me that day as I staggered down the mountain path - muttering; yelping; sobbing.

I'd left headaches and migraines behind long ago and reached a whole new level of squeezing, thumping, brain-belt torture. Someone was tightening a thick, leather belt around my head, twisting it tighter and tighter. Bastard.

"Brain belt bastards, bastards, bastards, brain belt bastards…" I muttered away, under my breath.

The brain-belt head squeezing probably had something to do with the fact that I could still barely consume any water without immediately expelling it in some revolting way. I'd almost given up trying.

Or maybe I'd picked up rabies? I hadn't been bitten by anything that I could remember. Plus, I wasn't frothing at the mouth, and I was nothing like the black and white footage I'd seen on World in Action years before of a girl with rabies flinging herself off a bed, Linda Blair style. I'd somehow made it to a point where the thought of actually having rabies was a welcome distraction.

On I went, hour after hour.

Brain belt bastards, brain belt bastards…

Then, later that morning - a vision.

Two beautiful blonde girls were walking along the track towards me.

Hang on - are they waving at me?

Who the hell could know me up here? Are they even real?!

Sarah and Lucy! Jesus, they're even more gorgeous than I remember.

They pulled up some yards ahead, trying to make sense of the twisted up creature lurching their way.

"Oh my God, Mark?! What's wrong? Are you OK?!"

No. I'm not OK. I'm half dead, and the half that isn't dead is half mad. Must be time to go home.

I slumped against the wall beside them, noticing that they hadn't come any closer.

"I'm… not good."

Please don't vomit. Please don't crap. Please don't explode.

"Where's Sean? Are you on your own? Mark, you look… terrible. What the hell happened to you? Oh… you had the burps, didn't you? Christ, they must've gotten a lot worse."

Much as I wanted to, I could hardly speak or look at them. They weren't supposed to be there. This wasn't helping me. I needed to walk. Or I'd die.

"I've got to get to Pokhara."

"But where's Sean? Didn't he help you? Why are you carrying your own pack, you crazy man?"

"He's walking. He didn't know. I have to go."

Please, can I borrow some health? I'll pay you back. Promise. I might need some blood as well. Just a nip to get me going.

"How far have you walked on your own?" Lucy was looking me up and down, clearly trying to work out what might've happened to me.

"I think… four days. Maybe five. I'm not sure. Last night, I…"

Nooo! Stop. You don't need to tell them about the ghosts. Or the curtain.

"We have to get you back. Come on, Mark, give us your bag. We'll walk with you."

Not for one second did I even consider their offer. I'd made it this far on my own. Whatever I'd decided back in Tatopani had got me to this point, and I was just about alive. Help was waiting for me *in* Pokhara, not before. I'd made it off the glacier alone. I could make it out of these mountains alone. If I accepted help too early, I knew I'd start to crumble. Then I'd die. Simple as that.

Not that these thoughts actually occurred in my head in any rational sense.

"No… Thanks. I'm OK. Two more days. That's all. I have to go."

And I was up, Quasimodo-ing past them, hoping they didn't get a whiff. "Mark! Stop. Stop. What are you doing? Wait!" They came running after me. "Did you say two days' walk?" my gorgeous Sarah asked. "We know a quicker way. You could make it tonight."

I stomped to a halt.

"*Whaaaaaaaaaaat?* You're kidding me. Tonight? How?"

"About two hours from here, there's a track that goes off to the left. It winds down through a forest to a river. Follow the river downstream for a couple of hours and the road starts. Didn't you know that?"

Course I knew! I just fancied the scenic route, you beautiful, blonde haired angel with lovely tanned skin that I want to stroke and green eyes that I wanna fall into and by the way, do you fancy me?

I twisted my head up from where I was keeping it on my chest, one eye squinting up at them. "Did you say 'road'?" I mumbled, as liquid air bubbled around down below.

"Yes, ya big banana! But you'd better get a move on, I think the last jeep leaves for Pokhara at five."

"Jeep? Jeep?" I tweeted, "Jeep?" *Oh god, I can be there tonight?!*

We all hugged and laughed and span in crazy circles, whooping at the insanity of the situation. Well - we might have done, if I hadn't screamed and dropped to one knee, trying with all my willpower to not foul the track, and their feet.

"I've gotta go." I was up and moving as quickly as possible. "Thank you."

"Oh Mark, please let us-"

"Bye!"

And I was off again. Clomp clomp clomp.

A jeep! A jeep to take me into Pokhara - tonight. I'll be in Pokhara tonight. I can make it. I'm going to make it.

I felt lonely after I'd left the girls though. But I was pleased to know that I still fancied them, which cheered me up, ever so slightly.

On and on I staggered, as the morning disappeared behind me. I didn't have a watch, but by now I was relying on the position of the sun for time checks. These were crucial, because time was playing tricks on me. I'd be head down, stomping along, clutching my stomach for what seemed like hours, only to look up at the sun and see it in exactly the same place as before. Other times I'd collapse behind a tree for what I believed to be a few minutes, and emerge to find the sun had traversed a whole rock line.

In this dazed state, I was about to go down a track that I'd only just heard about. A track down the side of a huge hill, through heavily wooded forests, for which I had no map, and out to a river I'd never seen, to a magical place where jeeps could be found.

Nice one.

Sure enough, after a few hours of walking, there was the track. I flung my boots in its general direction and began the downward stomp through the ferns and long grasses, past the towering marijuana plants that no longer held any excitement for me; past the little streams and brooks that on any other day I would have stopped at to dangle my hot feet in the icy water.

The longer I walked, the more hidden the sun became behind the thick foliage. I began to worry that I might have made another classic Mark mistake. Was I heading for another glacier moment, this time not just lost, but in a seriously bad way? The horrors of the previous night began to creep back into my head again. I could feel the fear rising as I made my way through the shadows. I tried to think of things to distract myself.

Just keep going.

A river, a track, a jeep. A river, a track, a jeep. Blonde girls!

The path was steep and uneven, and nowhere near as well trodden as the other tracks I'd been on. I was in no condition to be going cross-country. I fell against trees and into bushes several times, and would take minutes to recover.

After a couple of hours of very unstable galumphing, I heard faint trickling sounds coming from below, and my spirits lifted slightly. The river.

I tried to move faster; I had to be close now. I practically threw myself down the track; desperate to be out of the woods. And then - an opening in the foliage. I scrambled through and stumbled out through the giant ferns onto a flowing, rock-strewn river bed. Panting, I collapsed onto a shady rock.

Bloody hell, I'd made it down from the hills. I was on the Nepali equivalent of flat ground. It was the most incredible feeling of relief not to be sick, lost and alone in the quiet forest.

But then I remembered what the girls had told me: there were still a couple of hours further to walk along the river. Well - a couple of hours for a healthy pair of legs. I'd hidden that minor piece of information somewhere behind my brain muzzle, but now it flew out like a chicken being chased by a slavering panther.

They'd also told me that the last jeep left around five o'clock. Shit. Another vital detail conveniently tucked away. I had to get moving. But I couldn't see a track - only the wide, mostly dry, rocky river bed.

Had they even mentioned a track?

Or did they say just follow the river?

I headed downstream, keeping the flow of the river to my left. The sun was heading for the late afternoon sky - I probably had two or three hours of daylight left. I had to keep up a steady pace, which became harder and harder as I continued. The rocks were growing in size, forcing me into meandering zig-zags.

Every ten minutes or so I'd collapse with exhaustion and pain; head to the ground, bum in the air, as my guts twisted and raged inside. Several collapses later, I just had to stop. I found a big flat rock and lay down in the shade, trying to give my massive headache some relief. My eyes were spinning in my head, my body was desperate for water - but *still* I couldn't drink.

I had no energy left to carry on. I couldn't even stand. I lay there for some time, rolling around as the cramps and the firing mousetraps tore through me, trying to find a position where I could actually breathe. I slowly blinked up at the sky, my heavy eyelids drooping…

I snapped awake.

No - don't sleep you nutter. Keep moving. Mark, you have to keep moving.

I dragged my pack onto my back and began to crawl over the stones. Walking was a thing of the past. I crawled and crawled; snivelling, cramping, muttering. This really was starting to remind me of being stuck on the glacier. I began to panic.

Surely they said "follow a track" - didn't they? They never said "crawl along an almost impassable stretch of rocky river bed."

Oh God. I've messed up. I have. I know it.

I can't spend the night out here.

I'll have to go back the way I came and try and find the path up through the woods again.

But it'll be dark by then, and I'll be stuck in the woods.

Oh shit Mark, shit shit shit! You can't walk!

How am I supposed to climb a hill again?

I couldn't possibly turn back, so I carried on. I don't know how long I crawled for. It doesn't make sense that it took hours, but it felt that way. Eventually I came to a meander in the river, and dragged myself round the corner. It was all I could do to lift my head up.

A few hundred metres away, a group of people were stood around a jeep, loading up their bags and a few chickens. They looked as if they were ready to leave, and the sun had moved far over to the west. This surely had to be the last jeep of the day.

I forced out a pathetic little sound.

"Help!"

They couldn't hear me. I scrambled forward, trying to speed up, still maybe fifty metres away. I had to somehow force myself to stand, yelping and screaming as my stomach stretched out for the first time in days.

"Hello! Help. *Help!*" I almost shouted, stumbling over the rocks in a panic, trying to make myself as visible as possible, pushing myself up out of my hunchback position.

"*HELP!!*"

They turned and saw me: a mad man careering towards them, trying desperately to shout, arms flailing. White dust from the river bed covered my clothing, my boots, my big, curly hair. The ghost of the river bed; coming to get them.

The group all stopped whatever they were doing and just stared. I fell back down onto the rocks, totally broken. Two Nepali men began to run towards me.

I croaked up the only word that I needed.

"Pokhara… Pokhara."

"Yes yes, come come. Sick? You sick?"

I couldn't speak. I couldn't even cry - though I wanted to. A minute before, I'd thought I was going to have to turn round, which I knew would probably have been the end of me.

But now, look! There's people. There's the jeep. And the road.

Sarah and Lucy, I love you.

The two men half-carried me and my pack across the last few stones to the purple jeep. They laid me in the back and I curled up on the floor, clutching my heaving stomach. I really could not believe this was happening.

Let the pain come now; I don't care.

I'm bloody well safe.

I've made it.

The worst is behind me.

21

Paved Paradise

The engine spluttered to life. The last jeep of the day slammed into gear, jerked into action and bumped over the loose rocks and debris. As we followed the rocky river bed, each jolt made its way up through the worn out suspension system directly to my liver and surrounding organs. The Nepali passengers looked down at me as I contorted, screamed and writhed around on the dusty jeep floor, next to the chickens, in an effort to stave off the punches being delivered to my burning abdomen. No one spoke.

We eventually reached a tarmac road and the journey settled down. I looked back at the massive hills I'd just escaped from, leaving them behind at approximately forty miles per hour. After the past six days - plus the four days before that - it felt like warp speed. Trees shot past us, whole villages were gone in a flash, buffalos and carts overtaken with a little gurgle from the engine.

Man, what a machine. We were making ground like I couldn't imagine. I felt supersonic in this big, purple, half smashed up, filthy, brilliant jeep. The modern world never felt so good. And I'd soon be back in it at this rate, though I'd never thought that far ahead.

What was I going to do now? I had no idea. My guitar and other belongings were where I'd left them - locked up in a room at Charlie the Gurkha's lodge.

It was still light when we reached Pokhara. The driver jumped out and ran around to the back of the jeep.

"You want hospital?" he asked me.

"No," I said, surprising both the driver and myself, "Charlie the Gurkha's lodge please. You know it?"

"Yes, yes. We know Charlie." We took off again, away from the lake, towards Charlie's.

The driver and the remaining passengers helped bundle me out of the jeep and someone ran inside to call Charlie as I clung to the gate post. It seemed everyone knew this man. He had the same respected presence as a doctor in these parts.

He came running out.

"Oh… What has happened? Ohhhhhhhhhh…You look so ill! Your eyes! Yellow. Quick, come. Where is your friend?"

He helped me onto the bench on his front veranda, and I waved the magic jeep off.

"I don't feel well, Charlie. I need the toilet."

He helped me into the bathroom and gave me a towel. It was all I could manage to shuffle my old man shuffle towards the western style toilet. But I didn't quite make it that far, because some alien face in the mirror popped into view and shouted "AAAARRGGHHH!!!!" when it saw me. I clutched hold of the basin and leaned in for my first viewing of the incredible destruction of Mark.

My eyes were HUGE. Completely bloodshot. The whites had turned toilet-wall yellow.

Are they huge? Or has my head shrunk?

It had! Even skinnier than Sean's was during his pneumonia. My mouth was stretched open in a pained contortion; lips split and cracking, my tongue stuck to my lower lip like a dried out, trodden-on slug buried in a fur vest. My hair was wild and curly, and almost white from rolling around in the river dust. My neck was sunburnt and sucked-dry skinny, all pointy Adam's apple and straining tendons from trying to keep my screaming jaw in check. But it was the eyes that shocked me the most. They were absolutely terrified. Headlights from hell locked on full beam, as if the yellow bulbs could explode at any moment.

What's happening to me?

This is real, pal. You're in a bad, bad way.

God, Lucy and Sarah saw me only this morning!

No wonder they looked so shocked.

What if Mum and Dad saw me like this?!

Yellow eyes in this part of the world are a bad sign. Could easily be hepatitis.

The pain in my liver! Hepatitis! Of course - that's what I must have.

I was actually quite pleased with this self-diagnosis. Well, obviously hepatitis isn't brilliant, but there are other illnesses that are infinitely worse. Like spine bending, hydrophobic, make-it-into-the-newspapers rabies.

Then I remembered - Mick, who we'd travelled with the year before, had picked up hepatitis in Nepal. But he hadn't shown any of the symptoms I was displaying. He'd just felt a bit tired.

Maybe mine is a different kind of hep. The top of the range one that does this to you.

For the first time in a while, I tried to sit on a western toilet, but it really hurt my new scrawny bum. I then tried to have a wash in the sink, struggling to pull my foul, stained T-shirt over my head. My shoulders and chest were seriously shrunken - not an ounce of fat left on me. I looked infinitely worse than Sean had with his pneumonia. I wanted to look at my stomach for clues as to what might be going on, but I couldn't stand straight enough to see that far down. I washed as best as I could and yelped my way into a fresh T-shirt.

I had to get away from the bathroom mirror, so I limped, folded almost in half, back to the verandah. Being back at Charlie's, with all its clean surfaces, made me very aware of how disgusting I felt. All I could really manage to do was to grip hold of various items of furniture and hang on until another wave of sharp attacks hit my abdomen, or some inner fluid needed evacuating. Sitting was almost out of the question, and lying down brought its own problems – the main one being that I could hardly get up again – and I was too exhausted to stand. So I draped myself awkwardly over the back of the bench, with a cushion locked to my stomach, and waited for Charlie. There's something very embarrassing about being really visibly sick amongst strangers, especially in their own lovely home. I felt like I'd brought something monstrous and completely unexpected into their day - because I had.

"Come, come Mark. We must go to the hospital. You are very sick."

"Yes, Charlie. I think you're right."

The relief at being back in a familiar world that could provide help for me, or at least try and look after me, was huge. I was pretty much incapable of looking after myself any more, and had neither the strength nor the sanity to make any strong decisions. Maybe that's why I went back to Charlie's lodge, rather than straight to the hospital. It was now time for someone else to take over.

I was loaded into the back of a nice new motor, and we set off to the hospital. The luxury of the car was most welcome after the continuous jerky banging of the jeep. I was hoping that the Scottish doctor was there so I could give her the "See! I told you I didn't feel very well" line. It was the first mildly amusing thought to enter my head since Sean had left.

We parked up, and Charlie almost carried me into the hospital. I sat in the corridor for a while, bent over double, groaning, constantly shifting my position to alleviate the massive pressure building in my bowels, which I knew meant a 'run-for-cover' attack was imminent. Charlie went off in search of a doctor.

The corridors were still full of Nepalis in various stages of sickness - some extremely so - yet this time they didn't seem as shocking to me. I was easily as sick as the sickest looking person there.

No great comfort taken there.

Charlie must have used his influence, as I was soon able to skip the queue and was led into a small surgery - a room with a bed and a desk, behind which sat a young Nepali doctor. No sign of the Scottish doctor. Och well. Ne'er mind.

"Hello, you are English! I studied in London." The doctor seemed excited to meet me. That surely wouldn't last very long.

I folded myself half over the bed and looked along the thin mattress towards him. My eyes told him that I was really not up for a chat.

"Hmm, you have walked from Tatopani, I hear? You are like a local! Here, let me help you up." The poor man sort of half-pushed me backwards and bent to lift my legs. I screamed out as my abdomen was jolted around, which triggered the pending attack. Luckily there was not a lot left inside me, but what was ended up on his table.

He ran outside to fetch a bucket and a nurse.

Put me in a bed. Please put me in a bed. I'm exhausted.

My brain scrambled around, looking for a way to give the doctor some information that he might find helpful.

The clouds opened, the mountain popped out and I fell over. I think the Raksi...

We managed to clean me and the table down.

"OK Mark, I have to touch you around your stomach area. I think it's going to hurt. I'm very sorry."

Though I could tell his hands were barely touching my skin, it felt like they were reaching down inside me, playing squeezies with my organs, and firing off all the mousetraps in horrific, full powered unison. I was mainlining pure abdominal agony. I looked around wildly for something to gnaw on.

"I am sorry, Mark. But I have to feel higher, up under your ribs."

No, no no don't be doing that.

If you do, I'll...

FAAAAAAAAARRRRRKKKKKK'NNN NOOOOOOOOOOO!!!!!!

He did. He felt under my ribs. He poked his clever doctor's fingers right into THE SOURCE OF IT ALL... Which, as it turned out, was also my reset button. I blacked out, gathered some strength up, pinged my huge, blood-shot eyes open and screamed the kind of scream you should only ever hear when it's slaughter time in the jungle.

The doctor's tone was noticeably darker when he spoke again.

"Mark. You are very, very sick. It's your liver. It is very swollen. But also I think something else is wrong. You have to get to Kathmandu. Quickly. We cannot help you here. You must fly - tonight."

Hang on a minute. What is he saying?

The words weren't making sense.

"But this is a hospital. You have beds, don't you?"

"Yes, of course. But we do not have the equipment to help you. Or the doctors. You need a specialist. Or two."

This was not what I was expecting to hear. I thought I'd be put straight into a comfy bed and given some seriously strong pain killers and antibiotics. Maybe after a week of solid sleep I'd have a few scoops of pistachio ice cream.

Mmm. Lovely, smooth, cool, slightly nutty, green pistachio ice cream, in those little tubs we used to buy last year when...

"Do you understand, Mark?"

Oh shit.

"My liver? But what's wrong with it? I need to sleep."

"I don't know. But it's bad, I'm afraid."

"But, the pain? I can't move."

He shook his head. "I'm sorry. I don't think I should give you anything until you have blood tests. Any painkillers could put more strain on your liver and weaken you even further."

I tried to fight off the terrible fear and the disappointment that I wouldn't receive the help I was fully hoping for in Pokhara. I had to leave the hospital and drive back to the lodge with Charlie to sort out a flight to Kathmandu.

"We will get you there tonight, no problem. Do not worry. Charlie knows everyone." He grinned. "Only a one hour flight, then you are safe."

Charlie was now wise enough to not let me in the house – he'd seen the look on the doctor's face when he ran out to get a bucket. I repositioned myself across the wooden seat on his veranda as he made some calls to the travel agent.

I was in a state of constant movement. Every breath had to be helped through me with a turn to the left, a drop of the shoulder, a tiny twist to the right. No one position could fulfil what I had to achieve every few seconds.

Half bend, quick, straighten up, clench the jaw, turn the head, bring the back leg forward - NO - that was a mistake, back leg further back, that's better, oops - quick, bend it - now bring it forward, not that far you fool, that's going to lead to a WHOOPS - arm across stomach - NOOOO! Arm behind back...TOO MUCH....

I was a perpetual motion being. Twitching and wiggling, shifting, squeaking, grimacing, clenching.

I was also growing aware of my own aroma, now that I was back in pleasant, hygienic surroundings. All I can really say is that I actually smelt ill. Something foul was inside of me. And I was guessing that it had a lot to do with my reset button area.

Charlie returned, looking disappointed.

"All flights to Kathmandu are fully booked for days. I'm so sorry - I did try my best."

Recent rain had left many of the flights cancelled. There weren't that many flights a day even in good weather, and the backlog had to be cleared. Charlie had explained my predicament to the airline, but to no avail. His influence didn't stretch that far.

Shit.

This only left one other option: the bus.

Oh well, the bus isn't so bad. Twelve hours, a few stops - at least I'll be in a comfy seat. If I can walk for five or six days in this state, a twelve hour bus trip will be a doddle! Plus, the food stop in The Town With No Food won't seem so annoying now, as I'll surely sleep the whole way.

We gathered my belongings. Well, I lay across the bench watching Charlie gather my belongings: guitar, backpack. Filthy clothes were jettisoned. I was carefully helped back into the new motor to race over to the bus station on the other side of town.

By the time we hit the bus station, night had fallen. It was the usual mayhem. The rain had arrived, which just added to the chaos as water pooled around the buses, soaking everyone and their bags.

Charlie wedged me up on a bench in the ticket office and joined the queue for the Kathmandu Night Special. I watched his back as he eventually reached pole position. He waved his arms in the air and turned, pointing at me, almost shouting at the man behind the counter. I gave a stupid little wave, thinking that would help.

It didn't. He came over.

"Mark. Bad news. All buses to Kathmandu are full. They say to come back tomorrow. There might be a seat on the night bus."

Tomorrow? Fucking night bus? Tomorrow!?

I'll be dead by then. I will.

I'll have one final agonising scream and die on Charlie the Gurkha's front verandah. Dead in a half-drape.

I don't wanna die on a verandah. I don't wanna die in a half drape..

It was all starting to close in on me. Since I'd made it to Pokhara, things hadn't been going as smoothly as I'd hoped for, after my stupendous blast down from the mountains on buckling legs.

This was supposed to be the easy bit.

The doctor had scared me. He'd said I had to be in Kathmandu that night, and he really looked like he meant it.

But Charlie was nowhere near finished with the ticket man. I saw the old Charlie come out - the Charlie that had served as a Gurkha in the British Army. I remembered how Mum and Dad used to take us to London to see the sights when we were kids. We saw the Gurkhas at Buckingham Palace one day, marching past the big golden gates.

"They're from Nepal," Mum had told the four of us. "They say they're the most fearsome soldiers in the world. And they always carry a knife - a big, curved machete."

That's the kind of thing a young boy wants to hear.

Charlie turned on his heel and pushed his way back to the front of the queue. He banged his fists on the table, shouted - no, bellowed at the ticket man - and took out a wedge of rupees and hurled them onto the desk.

Then he came running over to me.

"Next bus, leaving in ten minutes. You must be quick!"

Of course, that meant that some poor bugger had been hoiked from his or her seat, but that didn't even cross my mind.

Charlie wouldn't take any money from me for the ticket, and I again didn't have the strength to argue. He passed my bag and guitar up to the baggage boy who tied it down under the tarpaulin, away from the bucketing rain, and then helped me up onto the bus. I could only take the smallest of steps. All my energy was spent trying to keep the pressure off my reset button.

I was loaded onto a window seat halfway up the bus, next a beautiful young Nepali woman in a stunning, bright yellow sari, who gave me such a look of horror that I actually felt ashamed for being so repulsively ill. I winced apologetically. Charlie spoke to her, and from her recoil, I don't think his words gave her any comfort.

"OK Mark, you must sleep now. Relax. Please, come and see me next time you are in Pokhara."

I thanked my Gurkha friend Charlie as much as I could between shallow breaths and racking pain.

Off he went. A lovely, lovely man. He turned and waved at me through the window, lifted his little cap and bowed in the rain, his grin never leaving his cheeky face. Then he stood to attention, saluted, turned on his heel and disappeared into the chaos of the bus station.

That was special.

My mum would be pleased to know I'd been helped by a Gurkha. Helped? He'd saved my life. I would've been lost without him.

I sank back into the welcome softness of my seat. This really was a Super Luxury Tourist Bus, in that the seats were intact, the springs seemed to be fully functioning; windows and roof appeared to be withstanding the rain. The final round of shouting and people hopping in and out of the bus began to settle as the driver climbed on board and powered up the big Mercedes engine that would carry me to Kathmandu, and safety.

The chatter in the bus quietened down, and it was then, for the first time since waving goodbye to Sean as he skipped round the mountain corner six days previously, that I actually relaxed.

I fashioned a pillow from my jacket, curled myself up on the seat and snuggled my head into the crevasse between backrest and window, feeling almost comfortable. All I had to do was to sit in this position, allowing for my perpetual motion of course, for the next twelve hours. That'd be easy after what I'd just been through. I just had to breathe. Tiny, shallow breaths. Maybe just enough air to keep a baby squirrel alive. That's all I'd need.

The interior lights were dimmed as the driver eased the bus out into the busy backstreets. We crawled through the traffic in near silence, trying to avoid the endless cyclists, cows and taxis.

My escape pod.

The driver hissed his way through the gearbox as we picked up speed, the engine settling into its cruising speed purr. The tarmac road was smooth beneath the wheels, the suspension cushioning me nicely from the gentle bumps in the road. My eyes nodded shut. I felt almost at peace. The exhaustion of the previous week flooded through me and I fell asleep, my head knocking slightly on the window, cushioned by my jacket. I dreamt I was back in England on a warm summer's day.

22

The Big Burp Theory

Imagine a ball of pain high in your abdomen - a burning pain so sharp, so excruciating that any movement is next to impossible. Everything inside you is swelling up, but at the same time being squeezed together, as if someone is pumping a huge amount of pressure up your inlet valve - like the poor old frog on the end of the schoolboy's pump. Then some ungodly bastard swings a baseball bat full bore and strikes you - BANG - right in the centre of that pain. Right in the liver.

That's how I woke up.

I didn't know what was happening. CRACK! Straight away, another equally vicious strike with equally devastating effects.

"ARGGGHHHHHHHHHH!" I screamed in pain and shock as I shot forward, clutching my stomach. Nothing on earth so far had prepared me for this level of agony - not even the previous week of drawn out torture in the mountains. It made the doctor's finger probe under my ribcage seem like a welcome titillation. The young woman beside me shrieked and leapt to her feet, looking down at me from behind her fingers, as I thrashed around on the seat like a soldier going down in a hail of bullets.

People were crawling over their seats to see who or what was making the unearthly racket. There was so much commotion that the driver stopped the bus. No one dared come too close until my hollering had calmed down, which took a few long minutes.

Then I realised what had happened.

The smooth tarmac road had come to an abrupt end a few kilometres out of town, taking my momentary reverie with it. The road had reverted to a potholed, pitted track, all but destroyed by the recent heavy rains, and was in a much worse state than when Sean and I had travelled along it to Pokhara.

We'd hit the first pothole at speed and the resulting bump had torn through me, exploding like a comet into my liver.

Bent double from the waist, I gripped hold of the seat in front and turned my skinny head upwards to shine my massive, scared, yellow eyes around the crowd of peering Nepali faces. All I could do was gibber and try not to breathe. Any movement of my chest was way too much. I was stuck.

I was the only westerner on the bus. A Nepali man leaned closer.

"You, Mister - you are very sick?"

I did my best to explain my situation, in tiny gasping words, as I hung from the seat in front. I told them I had to get to Kathmandu, and fast.

The pain had subsided a tad, but I was in a major state of shock. I was suddenly feeling extremely, violently ill. I felt a change inside, obviously for the worse. Surely, anything that painful had to have repercussions down the line. My fear-o-meter was red lining.

One of the men started an animated discussion with the other passengers. My spokesperson turned to me.

"The driver - he say you look too sick. He say we go back to Pokhara. He will drive to hospital."

"NO! No, no - you don't understa-AAARRRRGGGGHH!" The pain was still ricocheting around my liver. I half lifted myself from the seat and pressed my face against the back of the headrest I was hanging from, letting out low, animalistic groans.

I wasn't doing much to help my case, what with my perpetual contortions and endless grimacing. I couldn't have looked any more sick or smelt any worse.

"I - I HAVE to - to STAY on this bus. Please. I'll - I'll be OK. Please."

The discussion went on in the aisle for some time. Everyone seemed to have a say in the matter, apart from me.

If this bus turns round, I'm done for. What will I do? What can I do?

I saw the beautiful woman in the yellow sari talking to the driver. He nodded, shook his head, nodded. Then he went back to his seat, after giving the spokesperson a warning to pass on.

"He say he will drive, but if you get worse - maybe he will not take you back." I tried to smile to the beautiful woman, as she must have told the driver what Charlie the Gurkha had said to her. She may've smiled back, but she had her face hidden behind a hanky.

Thank God. For now, thank God.

Trouble was, we'd only just left Pokhara. I doubt I'd been asleep for longer than five minutes. Still twelve hours to go.

We drove off, and jolted through a pothole minefield. Every bump in the road, every big puddle we crashed through, was like the pain from the first blow that had woken me only minutes before. I could hardly breathe. Time became very slow and particular - measured not in seconds, but in gaps between potholes.

I sort of half sat, half hovered over my seat, like a man who had eaten way too much Christmas pudding and then swallowed a grenade. I clung to the headrest of the seat in front with one arm and clutched my jacket to my stomach with the other; my head down towards my knees.

My bruising liver became attuned to the state of the road, anticipating every impact and holding out for every few yards of smoothness, which were significantly reduced as the road ahead deteriorated. The constant banging from the bus had turned my stomach into one big ball of fire. My liver was Muhammad Ali's speedball, I was caught on the ropes and the ref wouldn't stop the fight. The Speedball in Nepal. I had no choice but to hang on and take it. I tried perching in a waterskiing pose. My knees, exhausted and worn out though they were from the trek, tried to act like shock absorbers to minimise the impact. The bus suspension wasn't built for this kind of off-road rally.

All the while I was desperately trying not to vomit, or worse. I presumed, quite rationally, that if I filled the seat with blood, which was more than likely - the driver would be well within his rights not to take me to Kathmandu. And the further on we travelled from Pokhara, the more worried I became that the driver also wouldn't want to take me back. Well, he'd said as much.

Which would leave me where?! The Town with No Food?

Or, more importantly, The Town with No Liver Specialist Department.

I desperately tried to keep my hollering and whimpering to a minimum, but this was impossible if we hit a big hole and I hadn't anticipated it correctly, or not recovered enough from the previous one that had just hammered through me - which happened approximately five or six times a minute, if I was lucky. Then I'd scream out, sending the poor girl next to me back to the furthest edge of her seat.

The video TV - the curse of Asian bus travel - was turned on at typical, obligatory full whack. The wailing of a melodramatic musical cut through my head, making the whole experience infinitely worse. The volume seemed to rise as the film played out, building to a crescendo of ridiculous proportions as the hero saved the girl, fought off the baddies, reinstated his family's honour and helped dig a new well for the impoverished village - all in song. I wasn't watching of course, but this was the usual plot.

After that, another video at full volume. I was starting to unravel mentally. I tried to rationalise with myself.

Mark, this journey is finite. You WILL get through this.

But it's TEN MORE HOURS.

Ten more hours of insufferable, torturous pain, with a soundtrack loud enough to pester the dead.

If I stayed perfectly still and anticipated all the bangs and jolts correctly, I could just about manage it. But the ones that did hit me were seriously hard, and would leave me open to a whole string of baseball bat hits, one after the other.

After many hours of what felt like a fairground ride gone hideously wrong, with music blaring through cheap, trashy speakers, we pulled into The Town With No Food.

Everyone left the bus except me - initially. But after a few minutes a vicious wave tore through me. I knew I had to find a toilet, or something that would do the job. A hole, a tree - the usual places.

I crawled on my hands and knees up the centre aisle and dragged myself down the two big metal steps that rolled me onto the side of the road. The effort dislodged something inside and I couldn't go any further. The violent gurglings that had been building inside were on the move. The inflated frog was about to speak.

I lay in the gutter, looking up at the night sky. The Milky Way spread through the gaps in the clouds, and shooting stars traced across the black. I lay my head on the broken pavement near the front wheel, pulled my trousers down and exploded everywhere.

At the same time I started vomiting. But this time it wasn't your usual murky, yellowish vomit: thick, black fluids poured out of my dry, hoarse throat. In all my travels, I'd never seen or heard anything like it.

More and more gushed out of me from both ends as my stomach somersaulted over and over, shrinking to the size of a pea before swelling back up to a prizewinning pumpkin. I couldn't move but I knew I had to clean myself up somehow from this internal assault. There was no way they would let me back on the bus - not in that state. I dragged myself to a toilet without a toilet behind a food stall with no food, and did my very best to wash myself down in the dark. All the while, more and more of the black stuff was shooting out of me.

For a moment I thought I might actually die in that stinking hole beside the road, somewhere between Kathmandu and Pokhara. I thought of the hell that I'd be putting Mum and Dad through, once the locals found me and cleaned my passport up enough to pull an ID.

I tried to banish those sort of thoughts from my mind, and crawled out of the toilet, back across the road to the bus - luckily it was still empty - when I collapsed into the gutter again.

It was there, under the Milky Way and the shooting stars, puking up unknown black fluids and sobbing with pain and pure fear, terrified of the next leg of the journey, that I had an epiphany. I truly did.

A flash of pure clarity.

I suddenly, beyond all doubt, with complete certainty, knew what was wrong with me. It all became fantastically clear.

... I've got a terrible case of wind!

There's air trapped in my digestive system, which is pushing my liver up into my lungs - causing this massive pain!

Air - or wind. It was laughable. I couldn't believe I hadn't realised before.

That's all this is! It'll shift soon, probably with one huge belter of a burp.

I lay in the gutter, almost chuckling between tiny breaths.

You're a human sheep on windy-grass, Mark. You don't need a doctor - all you need is the bloke with his pointy deflating stick to bring relief to a troubled man.

It all made perfect sense, and it was all going to be OK. I was, sometime in the next ten hours or so, going to do the biggest burp that any human had ever passed, and then I would be perfectly alright, if a little surprised.

It'll be like an echo of the big bang, and it will give me my life back. Hallelujah.

This thing started with the burps, and it's going to end with the mother of all belches.

I might blow the windows out of the bus doing it, I might blow the teeth out from my gums, maybe even the hair from the back of the driver's head. And God help the people all around me when I blow – because there'll be very little warning – but that doesn't matter. I'll try and warn the lady in the yellow sari.

The idea was absolutely hilarious to me, though I couldn't actually physically laugh.

The world's biggest burp, and I'd be doing it.

That epiphany was how I found the strength to heave myself back up the two big metal steps of the bus, and inch along the centre aisle to take up my place for round two. Ding ding. I'd conveniently set aside the doctor's words: "There's something seriously wrong with your liver, and you have to get to Kathmandu - fast."

The bus filled up, but - understandably - the young woman in the yellow sari did not return to the seat next to me. No one took up the empty seat. I saw her later, squeezed onto her friend's seat further up the bus. The spare seat was a blessing though, for it enabled me to contort myself into new positions, should I need them.

And I did, within seconds of the bus starting up again.

Bang - first pothole. Boom - next one. Here we go again. Eight more hours of concentrated, teeth clenching agony; eight more hours of whimpering and crying. The night dragged on. My legs were beyond exhausted, as I was almost in a ski crouch much of the time, pothole surfing across Nepal. More stops. More lying in gutters, more black fluid from either end. All that kept me going was the big burp theory, the impending boom that would clear my system and make headlines in the Kathmandu Post, before Reuters picked the story up.

Come on baby! Out you come. Don't be shy, the world awaits you.

When daylight came, I looked and felt like I'd been in a cage fight with the devil. So he had been in town - not only that, but he'd caught the same bus out as me. We stopped in a cold roadside town a few hours after dawn. The black fluid looked even more horrific in the cold light of day. Though the stops were a relief for me physically, they were killing me mentally. I just wanted us to reach Kathmandu - preferably whilst I was still alive. We'd been on the road now for almost twelve hours. By my reckoning, we should have been almost there. But this little town, way up on a winding mountain road, was clearly nowhere near Kathmandu. It was nowhere near anywhere.

From my kerbside curl up, I managed to ask the Spokesman where we were.

"We will be in Kathmandu soon."

"Ohh. Good - how soon?"

"Maybe seven hours."

I pulled a very disturbing version of the "What, you carry pigs?" face.

"No… Not seven hours…" I just about managed to whimper, in a pathetic attempt at redirecting reality. "Not seven. No."

"Yes. Seven hours. Soon."

Obviously, the terrible condition of the road had slowed us, often to a crawl.

I hadn't factored in even the merest hint of the possibility that the journey would take longer than twelve hours. I slumped further into the gutter, not fully able to process this mind-warping piece of information.

The bus would have to go without me. I just couldn't physically face any more banging, shrieking, pothole surfing madness. This was what the word 'unendurable' was created for. This precise moment.

But that town would have been my grave. I had to make it to Kathmandu. I was thinking more and more of the terrible phone call Mum and Dad would soon be getting if I gave up. But this was no time to start feeling sad.

Come on, Mark.

You were about to get back on the bus until he said the seven hour thing. Nothing has changed, really. You can do it.

So with virtually every nerve in my body screaming "Noooooooooooo!" I dragged myself back out of the gutter, up the steps and onto the bus. The driver gave me the universal look of "I've got my eye on you, son," as I writhed my way past him and folded myself up into my corner, nowhere near ready for the next stretch as the bus pulled away.

I had no idea what damage the constant impacts were doing to my insides - reducing them to a mushy liquid was my best guess.

Oh god. Maybe that's what I'm puking up. My liquidised liver.

That was a disturbing thought. My liquidised liver notion smothered and completely deflated my beautiful burping epiphany.

The wind fantasy was over.

The big burp was never going to be.

23

End Of The Line

For the next seven hours, the sweat somehow continued to pour out of me, though I couldn't understand how any liquids were being produced inside my parched body, which was now only a few steps up from the mummified Egyptian remains I used to gloat over in books as a kid. Ramesses IV of Woking, now holidaying in Nepal. All I could do was to just about hang on, as the seconds and minutes banged along.

The roads narrowed as we neared Kathmandu, mid afternoon. But rather than head straight for the bus station, we crawled through the outer city backstreets for at least another hour, stopping every five minutes or so to drop passengers off at random intersections and marketplaces. The wait between stops and starts was driving me absolutely crazy, as baggage was unloaded from above and passed down to waiting arms. My perpetual motion had intensified to full body spasms that first flipped me one way then another across my seat.

Stick my legs out, bring my legs in, head against the window, head onto the seat rest in front - FLIP!

JUST! BLOODY! DRIVE!

The last time I'd had that thought, I was fighting fit - even up for fighting the bus driver! How the mighty fall, Ramesses.

I hung on by the thinnest filament imaginable to whatever sanity I could muster - which wasn't much, seeing as I'd convinced myself that I was puking up the first of my major organs. I hadn't fully worked out the mechanics of how the mushed up liver made it into the stomach - was there a pipe connecting the two? Would it have to squeeze through the gallbladder first? Had it found another route into my oesophagus, bypassing my stomach entirely? One thing I was sure of though, was that nothing on earth could be worse than the night I'd just had.

Unless I coughed up my heart. That wouldn't be good.

When we eventually trundled into Kathmandu bus station, I let the bus empty out before I crawled my way to the front and down the two big metal steps for the last time. Many of the remaining passengers bowed and Namaste'd to me as they took their baggage and left. One old lady leant down and squeezed my hand. That in itself would've brought the tears on, if I could've made any. I felt a very long way from home, and a very long way from help. I was completely alone, and in a really dangerous mess. I didn't know what to do, and kind of curled up on the pavement, folded up, as the pain from my insides ripped through me. This was all way beyond my comprehension.

But someone brought my bag and guitar and helped me to my feet - kind of - and before I knew it a rickshaw pulled up beside me and I climbed in the back; my bag and guitar taking up valuable space, pushing me into the corner.

"Where to, Mister?"

There was only one place that came to my mind. And once again, there'd be no doctors there.

"Everest Lodge, Thamel, please." The guest house where Sean and I had stayed only a few weeks before - where Sean had fought off his pneumonia and almost boot-boxed a false confession out of the Red Man.

As soon as I uttered the word 'Thamel', the driver yanked back on his throttle, and the little two-stroke bastard shot forward, accelerating to full speed in a gut-wrenching split second, the tiny wheels crashing down into the first of a thousand potholes on the terrible, washed out city street. No Mercedes suspension or cushioned seats on this baby. The dead springs bottomed out, my head hit the roof and I banged down onto the several millimetres of padding covering the metal seat. We took off like a banshee into the traffic.

"ARGGHHHHHH!!!"

I screamed for mercy, trying to cover my mouth, as black fluid was already squirting out between my fingers.

"PLEASE, STOP!!!!"

He sped up. Maybe one of the bus passengers had warned him to make this fare a quickie. We banged through the backstreets, as he forced his machine around impossible corners, undercutting cars, bikes and buses. I nearly passed out as I hung desperately to the framework.

Half an hour later, we ring-a-dinged, gurgled and shrieked into Thamel. The driver slammed his brakes on, stopping outside the guest house. I fell straight out onto the street, feeling like I'd emerged from a nineteen-and-a-half hour car crash, with the world spinning one way and me spinning the other. I handed some rupees over, took my guitar and bag and sideways-crabbed my way into the concrete reception area.

The two same youths were there, manning the barebones desk. They recognised me from before, back when I'd had flesh on my body and normal sized eyes in my normal shaped head; back when I didn't look like I'd been gorging on an octopus' ink sack for breakfast.

"Oh. Mr Guitar Man! You are… Oh, what happened?" They looked to the empty space beside me. "Where is your friend?" They'd seen Sean when he was sick. Now they had this apparition in front of them. God knows what they thought had happened to Sean.

I leant myself up against the desk, in absolute shock from the rickshaw ride, which had almost completely turned me inside out. These two young men were all that was between me and what I craved more than anything - a bed to lie on.

"Room… Please." How I managed it makes no sense, but I proceeded to fill in the required form, passport number, length of stay - HA! - address in England… All that nonsense.

I could feel them staring at me as I winced and buckled and groaned in front of the desk. They exchanged confused looks.

"OK, room on the second floor." They flicked me the keys.

Obviously not that worried then.

I somehow pulled my bag and guitar up two flights of dark, concrete stairs and all the way down to the end of the corridor to unlock the door to a small, even darker room. I dragged my pack and guitar just inside the door, and was about to lurch onto the bed when a stomach cramp signalled the inevitable. I crawled back along the corridor again and into the toilets. Then, almost vomiting just from my smell alone, I tried to have a wash in the shower block. I stunk. I really needed a shower, but that wasn't going to happen. There's no way I could've taken my clothes off - the movement would've been impossible. I also needed air lifting out of Nepal, but that wasn't going to happen either.

I saw myself in the mirror, and the dry tears welled up behind my eyes. Those extra seven hours had almost finished me off. The face that I'd seen only yesterday at Charlie the Gurkha's house had taken a terrible dive.

Every mile of the trek, every bump in the road, every terrified thought - all of it was etched into my thin, young face. Every day without water or food, every vomiting attack, every bowel explosion, every sleepless night - it was all there, screaming for help right back at me. I'd gone from looking like a healthy canary on holiday to looking like a dead man on holiday. It was the saddest thing. I crawled back to my room, whimpering, not even attempting a wash - a crap-encrusted, brain busted, saggy ruin of a boy.

I pulled the door shut behind me and crawled onto the bed.

This is it.

Journey's end. I'd made it this far, but no further. Not even to a hospital. I don't think I even thought about what the doctor had said about urgently getting to a hospital. The bus journey had totally obliterated me.

The room was as cold as the crypt we used to dare each other to run through as kids back in Derbyshire - but no one was going to run home to fetch my mum. I felt so ill and beaten down that I just wanted it all to end. I wasn't thinking of dying - I was just so far beyond exhaustion and so far into pain that I couldn't actually face having to do anything about it.

Lying straight wasn't an option because of the fire in my abdomen, so I curled onto my side, knees pulled up, feeling rotten deep inside. I lay there for the remainder of the afternoon in quiet shock, not quite understanding how I'd survived those nineteen hours on the bus. Never mind the trek. Or the rickshaw.

OK. No more movement.

The light from the window faded depressingly into the evening as I lay very still, very cold, trying to work out how I'd got myself into this situation. But things weren't making much sense, and I was never far from utter confusion.

In my clearer moments I thought of England, and leaving Maria behind – God, I hadn't thought of her for days. But there was little room for her in my scuppered brain. I thought of my poor Mum and Dad, and what it would do to them to think of me in this state. I thought about the whole ridiculous trip that looked like it was coming to an end in this shit-box of a room.

I wonder how Sean is.

He's probably in Muk-tin-ath, making people laugh.

"Hey-up - you enjoyin' Muk-tin-ath?"

I bet he's not wearing his brain muzzle. I hope he never puts it on again. God, he was brilliant on that bus journey - he made all that happen. Those monks won't be forgetting him in a hurry - there'll be some monastery up on

The Tibetan Plateau singing Hava, Nagila Hava after lights out. Lucky we never taught them The Gulmarg Shuffle...

What about the Speed Bump Himalayas! Only he'd ever think of that. He'll be fit as a bastard by now... Oh Christ, Sean, why couldn't you have hung around a few extra minutes. Things would be very different now. Or would they? Maybe not.

But he would've stuck by me.

The room swam.

Hang on. Where am I? Up in the hills?

Shit. If I'm up in the hills, that means I've still got the bus journey ahead of me.

No no no...

But haven't I just been on the bus? Yeah, that's right, Charlie The Gurkha from Buckingham Palace. Yellow sari. The phantom burp. Or did I do the burp? No, I liquidised my liver instead. I remember now. The black goo. I wonder what colour my kidneys will come up as? Condensed oxtail soup colour, I'd say.

I used to have that when I'd be home from school with asthma...

My brain muzzle was well and truly off. My thoughts jumped around like a frog trying to cross a pond on flaming lily pads.

As the evening drew in, I could hardly move a muscle. My breathing was just tiny little gulps. If my lungs inflated even slightly, the pressure downwards onto my liver and stomach area was unbearable. I mastered the art of breathing without breathing. I'd just imagine the air going in and out, ever so slightly, sort of dancing around in my wind pipe, just above my lung flap.

I was totally stuck, and there was nothing I could do about it.

I couldn't close my eyes because as soon as I did the ghosts were back, skittering around the room, nipping at my heels, pulling me down to that terrifying place I'd been to in the mountains. It felt like something malevolent was lurking just beneath the surface, and this time it knew how to get me for sure. But directly in my vision, dangling from an old, black wire from the ceiling was a pathetic thirty watt bulb of luminous pain, searing its way into my head. The light sent aching beams into the back of my eyes, up through my nerves to my shot, confused brain.

Sounds from the hotel drifted in and out of my consciousness. Voices. Footsteps. Doors banging. I wrestled with the ghosts versus the jagged shards of light. I wanted so desperately to sleep. Things became very, very still. It was just me and the thirty watt bulb, which I could do nothing about.

And then, through the thin wall right next to my head, some huge bloke with a beer belly and big seventies sideburns started pounding the drums with sticks made from whole tree trunks, and some skinny dude with a mane of black hair and slim white fingers ripped into the mother of all guitar riffs as the bass erupted like a wall of Himalayan thunder, and Robert Plant suddenly screamed about how long it had been since he'd rock and rolled... woman... dun un dun un.

The music seemed to be blasting directly into me - 1000 watts of amplified rock 'n' roll straight up a pipe to the middle of my head, where it exploded with the thirty watt bulb laser show - a psychedelic nightmare which normally I would've paid good money for.

Oh, Jesus. Please. Not now.

I wanted it to stop - more than anything, I really wanted it to stop. And I wanted the light to go out. So I tried to shout through the wall, using the tiny pocket of air in my lungs.

"Please... turn it down."

Jimmy Page bent into his solo as John Bonham attacked the drums with all the controlled fury of the rhythmically insane...

"Pleeaase - turn it down!"

The volume dropped this time, and a no-frills Englishman's voice came back to me through the wall, muffled but definitely miffed.

"Yeah, OK, but it wasn't exactly loud - is that any better?"

I froze. My head stopped spinning. The room righted itself and the ghosts dived for cover.

That voice.

Can I get batteries for my Walkman in India?

Have you ever seen a tiger?

What happens if you get sick?

"... Craig? Craig Dunbar?! Is that you?"

There was a slight pause.

"... Err, yeah. Who's that?!"

For the first time in hours I tried to move - not far - just a bit closer to the wall.

"It's Mark - Mark from Tesco! Craig, listen - I need help... I'm not well."

Hang on, this isn't real either.

What, you reckon you're gonna be saved by rock 'n' roll via some bloke you used to-

The door rattled open and there he was, towering in the corridor on his size thirteen feet, a massive grin plastered across his tanned, healthy face: Craig from Tesco, with his endless India questions and love of Led Zeppelin. He'd obviously bought some Walkman speakers.

Unfortunately the effort of shouting through the wall had wobbled my stomach, and just as Craig sprung into the room I vomited a long plume of black fluid onto the floor in front of him. That slowed him down a bit.

When I'd finished spluttering, I had to work out if Craig really was standing there in the room. He appeared to be, and I didn't really know what else I could go on. Check his passport?

"Craig, Craig... shit."

"Bloody hell, Mark! What's happened to you?"

This really was happening. I'd just been converted into the most beautiful cliche imaginable - I'd been saved by rock 'n' roll.

Taking little shallow breaths, I tried to explain to Craig what had happened.

"I started burping... With Sarah and Lucy. Went trekking. Sean was too strong. The mountain popped out... I turned back... Blood. Walked back on my own... Sarah and Lucy again. Charlie the Gurkha bought me a ticket. Got bus here - shit, the bus... I'm sick, Craig. I'm really sick."

There. Wrapped that up nicely. All the information he'd need to take over from here on out.

Craig - my fellow nightshift dweller, the man that I'd almost scoffed at about coming to India - was nothing short of fantastic from that moment on. He immediately ran to the shop for some fresh water - which clearly, to anyone with a healthily functioning brain, was high on my 'to do' list.

I was being saved. In my vile state I could hardly think of myself as being lucky - but at the same time, I was one lucky bastard.

He made me drink, which made me vomit - but he persisted until I at least had some good fluids in me. He handled the vomiting and the smell without a blink. I think he'd quickly realised that he'd found me just in time. I would have died in that room that night, because I had no physical or mental strength left in me to ever move again. Whatever was inside me was rampaging after the bus journey and rickshaw ride, and I had a terrible rising fever.

"What the hell were you doing lying here? Waiting to get saved?"

Well, it worked, didn't it?

"I can't believe you were just lying there. We have to get you to a hospital, straight away."

Yes. Of course we do. Hospital.

I remembered the American clinic where Sean had been treated for his pneumonia.

"Please - just no rickshaws."

He helped me downstairs and past reception. The two lads peered at us strangely as I shuffled past them; Craig just about keeping my head from dropping below my knees.

Out in the tiny back streets of Thamel, the noise was even louder than Craig's tinny speakers. There weren't many taxis around the back lanes, but Craig went off to to find one while I crouched on all fours by the kerb. I couldn't tell where the stench of the gutter finished and the stench from me began. I vomited onto the road as we climbed into the back of a taxi and took off again across the city. I tried to brace myself for the inevitable crashes and bumps. At least I wasn't in a rickshaw. But the driver managed to slam down hard over the holes and lumps in the mashed up roads. I jerked forward, screaming, and tried to curl into a ball.

"God Mark, try to hang on." The only reason I survived that taxi ride was because Craig was there, beside me. I was no longer alone.

After another agonising thirty minutes we rolled up to the American clinic, and Craig helped carry me into the reception. A few tourists were sitting around, obviously waiting to see a doctor. Their waiting time was about to grow a whole lot longer as I crawled, heaving and groaning, past their shocked faces.

24

The Lips Say it All

The young American receptionist rushed from behind her desk as Craig hastily called out for help. That triggered her to shout out, "Doctor James, please come quickly."

A white-coated doctor, not that many years older than myself, ran out of a side room and the three of them carried me into a small, clean surgery room and lifted me onto the bed.

"OK, can you tell me what's wrong with him?" the doctor asked Craig. I didn't recognise him from the pneumonia days with Sean.

"Well, basically, he's sick. I found him in the room next to me in Thamel. He's been trekking, as far as I can tell. His name's Mark. I'm Craig. We used to work together in Tesco. It's his stomach I think, he keeps vomiting black stuff. And screaming."

The doctor leaned over me as I shrieked myself into my 'at ease' position: on my side, legs curled up, head down to my chest, all movement banned. I still wore the filthy clothes from the trek: jeans and T-shirt crusted in the white riverbed dust and remnants of umpteen visceral outbursts. I was one filthy mess, curled up in the lovely clean and shiny private American clinic in the ambassadorial suburbs of Kathmandu.

"Hello Mark, I'm Doctor James. I'm going to help you. I need to look at your stomach. Can you roll onto your back please, Mark?"

This was all happening very fast for me. From a place of delusions and skittering ghosts, where time was almost stopping - or overtaking me and leaving me behind - to suddenly having a Led Zep gig in the middle of my brain; Jimmy Page bending his uber amplified strings into life-saving rock 'n' roll riffs straight from the gods, Plant's voice oooooohh yeah-ing and telling me it's been a long and lonely time; Craig from Tesco with the size thirteen feet appearing in my doorway, then a screamer of a taxi ride and suddenly there's a doctor about to help me.

So I couldn't really say very much.

"Mark, can you please try and lie on your back. We need to get your clothes off. I'm going to fetch a nurse. OK Mark?"

A nurse came in, and together they peeled my T-shirt up and over my head. Craig sat in the corner, taking it all in.

I had to endure the hands on stomach thing again, only this time it was so bad I *couldn't* black out. Or maybe the reset button only works once. The bus trip had tenderised me, beaten me, liquified and mashed me, chopped me, overheated me, pulverised and smashed me. And now I had Doctor James's hands roving all over me, searching, probing, and worst of all, poking. Up under my ribs. Poking and feeling around.

"OK Mark, we're going to get you out of these clothes. Then we'll put you on a drip and take some blood. I can't give you anything for the pain yet, I'm afraid."

The nurse stuck a needle in my arm and drained me of a good few vials of my thick, dark blood.

I was soon wearing a hospital gown - clean, white and sterile like the room - and it felt perfect. Light, not tight, hardly touching me, not restricting me. The nurse stuck a drip in my arm and the saline flowed up the pipe and into my vein and I could feel my body suck the cold fluid out of the bag and right down into my core, and from there spread out to all the billions of parched, dying cells shouting out for a sip. The first good feeling I'd had for quite a while.

The nurse washed my face, which was the second good feeling. Water! I still liked water. So I didn't have rabies then. That was three good things.

Doctor James returned.

"Mark, I can't yet give you a definite diagnosis, but I can tell you this is very serious. Most likely, there's a tropical abscess on your liver - a large one. How long have you been in Asia?"

"Not long… Six weeks."

"Oh? Well in that case… No, it doesn't fit. These abscesses usually grow about a centimetre a year. And yours is dangerously big."

Thankfully Craig helped out here.

"He was in India last year, and spent almost a year between here and Turkey. So that would be over two years ago, I think."

"Hmm. That still doesn't add up. Mark, your liver is very swollen, so much so that it is pressing onto your diaphragm. When you breathe in, your lungs expand and push your diaphragm down onto your liver, and the abscess. That is why it is causing you so much pain."

Yes, that makes sense. My baby squirrel breaths.

Shit, this is worse than I thought.

Why the hell didn't I explode on the bus?

My knowledge of abscess stress limits was, unsurprisingly, minimal.

Abscess? Why the hell would I have a tropical abscess on my liver?

How did I manage to get one of those?

Was it something that I ate?

Or drank? Much more likely. I bet it was that shit Israeli vodka we used to neck every night in The Bottle Of Vodka Supporters Club near Tel Aviv... Serves me right for being club president...

The doctor's serious voice snapped me back from my leap-frogging brain.

"Also, you have an infection battling inside you. Your white blood count is very high, so I'm going to give you a big shot of penicillin to help you. But you need to fill some forms in. The nurse will help. Then we'll get you settled for the night, and discuss options in the morning."

Oh, that sounded good. Settled for the night. At last, I was getting real help, though I was definitely worried about my liver prognosis. But I had people on my side. A really good forklift driver and a nice, caring doctor not long out of medical school. And a clean clinic. I could be a lot worse off. I could be a Nepali, sick and curled up on the waiting room floor at the hospital back in Pokhara, with no chance of any major help, no friends to take me to fancy clinics, no one to think of options for me. Or I could be back in that horrible room at the hotel. Help was happening because I wasn't from the local area. I was so relieved.

Or at least I was until the nurse asked for my insurance papers.

"Errrrrrrrrrrrrr... what insurance?"

"Mark, you can't stay here without health cover. Unless you can pay in cash. Can you?" The nurse looked worried.

Do I look like the kind of bloke that can pay in cash?!

I haven't even got a credit card.

I had my eight hundred pounds in travellers cheques left, and that was it. That would've lasted me for the best part of a year in and around India and South East Asia, with the last cheque saved for a boat or flight from Bali to Perth. But that eight hundred pounds wouldn't go far in the world of private health payments to an American clinic.

"I'm very sorry, Mark," the nurse continued, "but you won't be able to stay the night here unless you can pay. There's nothing we can do about it. You'd need a nurse all night, maybe even the doctor. Plus payment for the room. And any treatment you'll need. It's very expensive." In the hour or so I'd been there, I'd already spent about a month's worth of travel money. Doctor James was looking embarrassed.

"I'm afraid she's right, Mark. If it was up to me I'd keep you here, but I only work here. This place is a private clinic."

Craig stepped in again. "But what can we do?! You said yourself he's really sick. Look at him! You can't turn him out like that."

He may not have said it, but I bet he was also thinking "What the fuck am I supposed to do with him!?"

"I understand. I do." Doctor James was pondering. "Well, you can stay here 'till I leave in about two hours. We won't charge you. Stay on the drip, you still need fluids. Then go back to your hotel, and come back in the morning. We can see how the penicillin is working on the infection. I'm really sorry, but that's the best I can offer."

I lay on my comfy bed, stunned. Even the frog had stopped jumping about. It sat on a flaming lily pad, the fire licking around its bulging eyes and warty skin, waiting for the inevitable: the seemingly unavoidable.

So the nurse and Doctor James had to squeeze me back into my disgustingly filthy and uncomfortable jeans and T-shirt, and Craig had to help me back into a taxi and take me back to the glorious hotel we were staying in. The bangs as we hit the potholes were much worse now that I knew what was actually happening. I could almost see my diaphragm battering against the abscess, pushing the disgusting, pussey mass down onto my tenderised pork chop of a liver. If I'd known that was happening on the bus journey, there's no way I could've handled it. I'd still be lying on the roadside in The Town With No Food. Dead, I presume.

My fever burnt all night. Craig sat with me as I drifted around varying states of consciousness. Like earlier, before Craig found me, time sort of stopped. All memories seemed to overlap and occur *right now*. I was operating like a lucky dip machine, sending a hook down to pick up some random occurrence from my subconscious, which I'd mix with some variation of this trip. I thought Sean and I were cow trekking across Switzerland, retracing Hannibal's crossing of the Alps on a couple of saddled-up Friesians. I thought Charlie the Gurkha had waved to us when we were kids at Buckingham Palace, and shouted out "Don't worry,

Mrs Giblin, Charlie will be there when you need him!" Then Craig would swim back into view and I'd be back in Tesco, loading boxes of saline fluid onto hairy yaks, saving up my money for the trip of a lifetime - only there was a nagging feeling that maybe I shouldn't go, and spend the money on something a bit safer, like swimming with crocodiles. Or shark tickling.

Morning came, and I was shattered from the night's feverish delirium, having hardly slept. Craig helped dress me in cleaner clothes and half carried me to a taxi for our date with Doctor James. I was in an even worse state than the day before when I was eventually rolled onto the doctor's bed, clutching at my heaving guts.

No time was wasted with any "And how are we today?" kind of chat. My temperature was taken - officially burning up - and more blood was taken for more tests.

After a couple of hours on the drip, Doctor James came and sat by the bed. It's fair to say that he wore what is recognised as 'a severely worried expression' on his young face. He was chewing on his upper lip.

"I've just got your blood test results back - and this isn't good I'm afraid Mark - you're white cell count has increased hugely since yesterday. The infection is winning. The penicillin doesn't appear to have had any effect. I'm afraid you're in severe danger."

I lay there, stunned. Craig wasn't saying anything either. Doctor James hadn't finished yet though.

"I don't think there's much I can do for you, Mark. You're in need of some serious medical attention, and you need it now! But you're not going to get it here."

Craig stepped in again.

"Well does that mean we have to go to a bigger hospital? That's OK, we can do that."

"Sorry. I didn't make myself clear. I meant in Nepal. There's nowhere in Nepal that can help you, Mark."

It's strange when you hear that your ray of hope has just vanished - out the window. Just like that. Gone. I had a massive feeling of being caught; trapped; boxed in. Not unlike on the glacier, when I realised I was stuck. Or when I had flown through the air, having just ripped the speed-o-meter from my motorbike with my stomach - though that was obviously a lot quicker. But the feeling was the same: this is it. You've gone too far. The scales have just tipped against you.

"Mark, if you stay in Kathmandu, you're going to die. Your only option is to fly to Singapore with a nurse, and book into a private hospital where they might have the correct equipment to help you."

The last time I'd heard a silence like the one that followed was when I'd told the opium man that the quality of his produce was below par.

Doctor James continued.

"And I honestly can't promise you that they'll have the equipment. Or the medical skill that you need."

"That would cost thousands! He can't afford that. He told you yesterday." Craig was doing the talking for me. I was busy trying to understand the implications of all these unpleasant words being dished out on me, whilst at the same time trying not to breathe, trying not to scream out from the incredible ball of fire emanating from my beaten liver, trying not to vomit the black stuff or explode blood out of my arse, and trying to mentally remain in the room and not wander back to the saddled-up Friesians taking Sean and I over the Alps - which I'd much rather have done, of course.

"Mark, what about asking your family for help?" asked the doctor.

"No. No money. Parents in Turkey." Of course, reason would dictate that this would be the obvious thing to do. In fact, why hadn't it been mentioned before? But the thought hadn't even crossed my mind. There was never much cash flying round in our family, and I knew my parents had taken the little they had and just flown to Turkey - their first holiday for years - and, I had no idea how to get hold of them. My brother Eric was in England when I left, but was talking of clearing off somewhere. And what were Amanda and Alison, my sisters, going to do about it?

Jesus! As if I can even think, or come up with any answers.

"I'm not sure what to suggest then, I'm afraid. You will die if you stay in Nepal. I don't think you have a lot of time. Singapore is your only option, but you have to go - now! And you will need a nurse to fly with you. You cannot be on your own, Mark."

I couldn't believe it. I'd trekked for six days with barely any water, survived the bumpy nineteen hour bus journey, dumped myself into a hotel and almost died right there on the bed before I was miraculously found by Craig via Led Zeppelin, and I'd finally made it to a proper clinic - only to be told that this was as far as I could go.

So rock' n' roll hadn't actually saved my life - it had just prolonged it for a few days. Which doesn't have quite the same ring to it, and would look shit on a T-shirt.

Fuck.

"I'll go to England. Fly."

"That's a long trip, Mark." Doctor James thought for a moment. "I'm not sure you'll make it. You'll definitely need a nurse."

"How much would that cost?"

"More than you have, I'm afraid. The insurance companies usually cover this kind of thing, but I know it's expensive. And you have to pay for the flight to get them back here."

Time was running out.

"I'll go on my own. I have to. That's all we can do."

And please, don't make me talk anymore. It's agony.

Doctor James scratched his head and chased his lips around.

"OK Mark. I'll ring some travel agents. We have to get you on a flight today. Try and rest, and try not to worry. We'll find a flight - it's not exactly peak season, is it?"

Doctor James went off to his office to make the calls, leaving Craig and I to ponder in silence. I knew I had to try and rest, but my brain was so wired, exhausted, and stressed from all the pain over the past ten days, and I'd hardly slept in a week. And if I wasn't worried before, I certainly was now.

Relax Mark. You're getting a flight sorted out.

You'll be home by tomorrow. God, I can't believe it...

The doctor returned.

Oh, shit. He's chewing his top lip again.

And tapping his bottom lip with his finger.

He blew out a long breath before speaking.

"Not good news I'm afraid. Everything is booked up for days. I can get you to Delhi, but that's about it."

I felt myself slip closer to the edge. Delhi?

Kathmandu in 1987 only had a small airport that didn't handle the big jets. You could fly to Delhi or Rangoon and possibly Bangkok, but not much further. So my only option was to find a flight from Kathmandu to Delhi, then a connecting flight from Delhi to London.

I bleated useless words out between tiny non-breaths, which did no-one any good. "But... Can't... Isn't... So... But... Are..?"

"This is crazy!" Craig butted in, "there has to be a flight to London. I read in the Lonely Planet that sometimes travellers sell their tickets in hostels. How about I go to all the hostels and hotels, check the notice boards."

Good man! Yes, Craig, go. Quick.

Off he went. The doctor carried on with his phone calls, leaving me to try and rest again. But it's hard to rest when you've been strapped to a ticking bomb. I lay there for hours, feeling steadily more sick and depressed. Doctor James came and sat with me between rounds of phone calls, all of which led nowhere.

Craig returned mid afternoon. He didn't need to say anything, as he'd borrowed the doctor's 'chewed top lip' approach to delivering bad news.

"Nothing. I went to loads of travel agencies too. They all said the same thing. Nothing to London for nearly a week." Doctor James didn't need to say the obvious - in a week I'd just be a memory. Or maybe only in a day...

Oh shit. My poor parents...

Come evening, I was sent back to the hotel for the night with Craig again.

"Come back here first thing, but please try and drink water, Mark." Doctor James was looking very concerned as I was helped out of the clinic.

Taxi. Shriek. Vomit. Diarrhoea. Sweat. Thirty minutes of pothole pressure abscess torture.

We made it back to my dingy, stinky, thirty watt room, and I curled up on the bed to suffer through another night. I'd pretty much turned entirely yellow.

Sleeping wasn't an option. There was definitely something waiting for me when I started to drift off. Something grabbing at me, but I couldn't quite see it. If it had been more welcoming, I might've gone - just shut my eyes and let it take me - which would've been a much easier option than trying to fight against it.

Craig sat with me for the whole night, helping me to the toilet when needed, which was often - and forcing water into me, when I'd let him.

When morning came, I didn't have the energy to get up. I was as good as dead - as much from the depressing series of events the day before as anything else.

I could be almost home by now if there'd been a flight last night.

Shit, I can't get in a taxi again...

I lay in bed as Craig fetched more water and I concentrated on my new version of breathing - I was terrified of exploding my liver entirely. I lay there clenching my fists, gripping at the side of the bed. My fingers dug deep into the sodden old foam mattress.

"Mark, you have to get up. We can be at the clinic soon - we can't just stay here."

"Yes... but I can't." Poor old Craig - why the hell did he have to walk in on this? But he remained calm throughout.

Just then, I heard a stomping coming down the corridor, heading this way.

God, now what?

Are they going to kick me out of this room?

I bet they bloody are.

Then what?

A loud knocking on the door made us both start and sent me into a squirming fit of panic, convulsing around again, trying to find that magic position in which it didn't feel like a vital organ was going to blow.

But before Craig could answer the door it burst open, slamming against the wall.

"I made it, Mark!" Sean stood in the doorway, looking fit and strong, radiating a healthy glow that had replaced his post-pneumonia pallor.

I reached for my bucket, retching up gushing black liquid; my abdominal muscles squeezing and tightening around my stomach and liver.

After I'd finished, I looked up at him with my yellow eyes and shrunken yellow face. His features were rearranging themselves as he tried to make sense of things.

"'Allo Sean… I'm not very well."

25

A Salty Tear

The last time Sean had seen me, we'd had a hug and a hearty, hungover wave goodbye on the track just outside Tatopani. Sure, I'd not been particularly well, but I hadn't displayed symptoms that would have left him too concerned for my wellbeing as he trekked away on strong legs and high spirits.

He'd hardly have given me a thought. Striding solo through the mountains, fit and well, looking forward to a final blow-out in Kathmandu or wherever.

Sean's jaw was now hanging open as he watched me writhing and buckling around the bed, guarded over by Craig, whom he'd never met.

"You're Sean, I take it," Craig said. "He's in a bad way. I'm Craig - I found him like this a couple of days ago. We used to work together in Tesco."

"What? You just found him... How?! What the fu..."

Craig filled him in on the doctor's ominous diagnosis. It was not just the vomiting and diarrhoea that was so awful to witness - it was the wriggling time in between the attacks. When the black volcano erupted, it was actually a release from what had been building up inside.

It was so good to see Sean again. He knelt down at a safe distance from the bed, looking intently at my shrunken, yellow face.

"You poor bastard. We're going to get you home, Mark." He said firmly.

"That... would be... ideal. Thanks, Sean."

Sean knew my mum and dad, my brother and sisters, my house, my record player, my fantastic punk albums, Crispin our fat cat, my guitar twanging... If possible, having Sean there made it all seem even more real. If I was to die, he'd be the one that would be sitting with my distraught parents, explaining how I'd spiralled down so quickly from a fit and healthy twenty-four year old to a shrivelled, terrified, screaming yellow shell in a couple of weeks, so far from home. Maybe he'd have to fly home with my coffin. I didn't want that to happen.

But having him there gave me a glimmer of hope, so I found the energy to allow myself to be lifted into a taxi, and off we went to the clinic again. Sean then had the pleasure of seeing me buckle and scream and holler and beg for mercy, as we drove across the city.

"I thought I was in agony with my arse boils. You had to go and trump me, didn't you Mark?"

"Always, Sean... always."

"How was your trek, Sean?" Craig was probably eager for a distraction after two days with me. And any distraction was a blessing.

"It was great, thanks. After you turned back, Mark, the clouds all cleared to the north."

Funny, I hadn't even noticed.

"I had an incredible week of walking. You're right, it's bloody amazing up there. I didn't get to Muk-tin-ath. I just hung around Jomson, and flew back to Pokhara. That Charlie bloke told me you were sick, but he didn't say you were... *that* sick. Then I got the bus back here. Took bloody ages. The road was shit."

We made it to the clinic. My white blood count was even worse than the day before. I felt like I was starting to fade. All I wanted to do was lie on the doctor's couch and never have to move again. I felt I was rotting inside, and the black, tar-like liquid was the rotten parts of me coming up.

Sean and Craig took off into Kathmandu again to try and get me a flight, whilst the doctor hassled his mates in the small expat community, as well as acquaintances in the embassies around town, to see if they could pull any strings. I lay on the hospital bed, trying to cling to the tiny bit of hope that seeing Sean had brought me. But that feeling was fading as the morning ticked away, and I would've happily shut my eyes and drifted off, if either my body or the terror had let me. The fever was obviously adding fuel to the fire; rational thoughts were a fleeting reality.

I lay on my side, watching the drip drip of the saline dribble down the tube into my skinny, yellow arm.

Drip drop.
Tick tock.

Drip drop.

I heard a commotion from the reception area, and then the door to my room banged open.

Doctor James ran in, and his lips weren't eating each other.

"Mark!! Mark!"

Please. Say something good.

You have to. I wanna see my parents again.

Please.

"You're going home, Mark! Tonight. I've got you a flight. My friend in the British Embassy, she pulled some strings…"

I didn't hear the next bit. I was bobbing up to the surface, swimming up from the bleak depths I'd been wallowing in. One big, salty tear left my eye and rolled down my nose onto the bed.

"Will you look at that," smiled Doctor James, "the saline is working. You must be full to the brim."

I smiled. First time in a while.

Sean and Craig came back soon after, looking glum. But not for long. They listened with grinning heads as the doctor filled us all in on the details.

"The flight is late tonight. It's not perfect, but it's the best we can do. Fly to Delhi, then it's a six hour stopover. In the morning fly to Amsterdam. Another four hour stopover. Then onto London."

"You lucky, lucky bastard!" Sean shouted.

I smiled, trying to ignore the hard facts. Stopovers? How the hell was I supposed to deal with them? I chose to put these thoughts out of my mind, and take things step by step. Well, crawl by crawl.

"OK," the doctor took over. "So you haven't got a nurse to accompany you, you're going to have to be really strong, Mark. It won't be easy."

Oh, really?

"I'm going to give you another shot of penicillin. That might help the infection… I hope. I advise getting to the airport early. Obviously, your friends here will be taking you."

We had to get moving. The penicillin was shoved up my vein - hopefully to start a war with the abscess, or the infection, or whatever the hell was taking place inside me. Doctor James wrote me a note to take with me - something along the lines of:

Please help this man. He is very, very sick.

That letter was my nurse. I thanked the doctor as best I could. Even though I could hardly speak, I'm sure he saw the gratitude in the massive, yellow, bloodshot balls that had taken the place of my eyes.

"I just hope you make it home safe. Please, will you write and let me know what happens. And of course let me know what is actually wrong with you, because you've got me stumped!"

He was a good man, that young American doctor, and he'd tried his best to help me.

Then Sean, Craig and I left the clinic for the last time. All the nurses and staff waved me off as I was lifted into the cab. I was touched.

Just two more cab rides to go.

I huddled up in the back seat, clenching my stomach as usual.

Once more up the stairs to my tiny, dark room.

Four more hours on this horrid, stinking bed.

Craig went off with my passport to pay for my ticket. He had a hard time convincing them that there was no way that I'd make it in person to pay the cash. But he got it all sorted and hot tailed it back to the room.

"All done Mark. Here's your ticket - don't lose it."

I smiled. "We should celebrate," I said, half joking.

"Yes - we should!" said Sean.

So we did. Well, Sean and Craig did. They brought some beers back to the room and they had a party around my bed. It was the best thing they could've done for me, and I loved them for it.

"You know what, Mark, if you'd stayed with me on the trek, you could've flown back to Kathmandu from Jomson. Bet you never thought of that, eh?"

What, and miss out on all the fun I've been having?

"You're a bastard, Sean."

Sean and Craig did a great job of distracting me from worrying about the flight, cracking up over some of our pre-sickness stories from the trip.

"... and then the stooooooopid git just stepped off the bloody rowboat, and sent me into the FILTHY toilet-stew of-a-lake. I wanted to belt him, but he wouldn't stop laughing."

I lay there happily listening, in between the usual rounds of unpleasantries from within, occasionally ruining the party vibe with a black spew attack.

"Jesus Christ, Mark," Sean asked, stroking my back as I heaved and spluttered. "Looks like you've been drinking condensed Guinness."

The attacks seemed to be getting more extreme, more violent. But my spirits were much better. I was finally going home, and having Sean and Craig laughing around me made me feel half normal again. I'd probably not laughed for ten days, apart from the little giggle I'd had after convincing myself that I just had wind. That in itself was enough to make a young man miserable. *God bless you, Sean and Craig.*

They packed my bag up for me and we readied for the airport, and cleaned my face. Over a few panting minutes, I managed to get some sentences out.

"My guitar, keep it. Go sell it in Freak Street. It's worth about a hundred quid. Get what you can for it, convert the money into beer and have a night out on me."

"What a noble man. My mate Mark! We'll drink to your health."

Once more down the stairs, back out into the stinky, dog-ridden, filthy streets of Kathmandu in 1987, and clamber into one more taxi. I was so glad to be leaving. All I had to do was cope with one more bumpy ride to the airport.

"Did you see that, Craig?" said Sean, as we pulled away. "The sneaky bastard just did a runner from the hotel! You did! You didn't pay. They saw you leave with your bag, and they didn't say a word. You're a pro, Giblin."

The taxi took what felt like hours, even with Sean laughing and carrying on. He was paying me back for all the laughs we'd had round his bed when he was ill. I'd recommend it to even the sickest patient.

The airport was small, with only a few check-in counters scattered around, and the familiar chaotic feel of a place that just about manages to function. It felt like the bosses had gone away and left volunteers in charge who weren't exactly sure how an airport was supposed to work. People were everywhere; some looked like they'd been camped for days. Whole families spread out on blankets, cooking food.

Craig and Sean settled me into a chair and took it in turns to queue up for me as my flight number clacked into place above one of the desks. The queue was the usual scramble of pulling, shoving and shouting.

Sean was a changed man to the young lad who had been overwhelmed by the chaos of Delhi seven weeks before. And he was a bit pissed. He elbowed his way through the surges, looking like he was enjoying himself.

"Reminds me of being at Chelsea! Wahey!" he shouted back over the pushing heads.

But I wasn't doing very well after my last taxi journey. I writhed around on the chair, desperately searching for respite from the pains in my abdomen. I doubt the Nepali people had seen many westerners as sick as the yellow, wild haired madman squirming around in front of them, and many of them were grouping around me for a stare.

Sean made it to the front of the queue, and I saw him gesticulating towards me. He spent a few minutes there, leaning over the desk, occasionally turning round to point, holding my passport up and pointing at me.

Oh God, don't make me get up.

Please. I can't walk over there.

I watched Sean elbow his way back through the crowd.

"Mark, this is fucking unbelievable. They're saying you can't get on this flight. It's fully booked. Your name isn't even on the list. Come on, let's get you over to the counter so they can see you. Don't worry, we'll sort it out."

They dragged me to my feet and took me over to the man who'd been left in charge, so he could see for himself why I desperately needed to get on that plane. I hung onto the front of the counter, as close to passing out as is humanly possible, after being pushed through the swarms of hopeful passengers.

"Look. Here's the ticket. Here's his passport. See? This flight, this ticket, this man. Well, it is him, promise."

The Nepali man behind the desk looked at my passport, and pulled the hugest double take when he compared it to the limp, skinny wreck being held up in front of him. He checked the list, made a phone call, barked into the phone. I hung onto the edge of the planet as he hung up.

"I am very, very sorry. No seat. All taken. Nothing we can do. I think big mistake."

I was going nowhere.

I collapsed in a heap onto a chair, feeling everything spin away, just out of reach. I was fully conscious, but I could feel myself letting go. It had taken everything I had in me to make it this far, to end up at a check-in counter at the only international airport in the country, with a worthless ticket. A ticket to nowhere. A ticket out of here in a box. There was nowhere else for me to go. No more taxi journeys, no more American clinics, no more nights in dark, dingy hotel rooms.

I was completely, utterly - not a shred of resolve left in me - done in.

This is it. I'm going to die here.

I'm not going to see my mum and dad ever again.

I wasn't even going to die in No Man's Land.

Place of death: airport check-in desk.

Sean and Craig knelt on the floor beside me, suddenly very, very sober. Sean stroked my back. They were having just as hard a time processing this major fucking nightmare balls-up as I was. Things began to feel very quiet and strangely still, like I'd felt just before Led Zeppelin had prolonged my life for a few days. My last drops of hope drained away, and an utterly bleak, cold feeling took over.

No one had anything to say.

Sean looked at me, watched me go down. He saw my face crumple, and my body slump, like an animal accepting the lion's jaws clamping onto its hind quarters. He stood there for a moment, eyes wide.

And then he flipped.

He lunged back towards the desk - all six foot and a bit of flailing limbs, madly pushing people out of his way - and boomed over the desk:

"THERE IS *NO WAY* MY SICK FRIEND IS NOT GETTING ON THAT FLIGHT. SO YOU - SORT IT OUT! *NOW!!!!*"

He banged my passport and ticket down on the desk, staring intensely at the startled ticket man behind the counter.

"… But Mister, very sorry, the flight is full-"

They tried to argue back, flustered. But Sean would just bat them down every time, banging his fists on the desk.

"I'M NOT MOVING UNTIL YOU LET HIM ON *THAT* PLANE."

He can be a formidable bastard. Thank God.

Five minutes later, he pushed back through the crowd, waving a boarding pass in the air.

"Mark, my friend, you are going home."

I just stared up at him from my slump. Craig jumped up and grabbed the ticket.

"That was incredible, Sean. That bloke was shitting himself!"

"That's what I told them Mark was going to do, if they didn't let him on that flight! Told him he'd sit in front of this counter all night, shitting."

They were laughing. I was just wrestling myself back up from the deep again. If the abscess didn't kill me, these ups and downs surely would.

"Sean… you're a bloody star," I squeaked.

From then on it was a flurry of activity. I'd been put on another flight that was leaving even earlier, and I had to hurry. Sean and Craig checked me in, I had my passport stamped, and they attempted to rush me through the departure gate.

We couldn't hug - too painful. I could hardly speak, as that was too painful as well.

"Sean, Craig… you've been… I don't…" If I'd said any more, I would've collapsed in tears.

Sean stepped in. "It's going to be OK, Mark. Don't forget the doctor's note. Show everyone. I'll be home soon myself."

"Get yourself fixed up, Mark, and come to Australia. I'll be there next year," Craig said.

"Just think," Sean had a cheery thought, "by the time you get home we'll have converted your guitar into beer!"

I'll never forget saying goodbye to them.

But saying goodbye also meant I was on my own again, which was terrifying. I knew that whatever was to come next wouldn't be easy. Not by a long shot.

As I disappeared through the departure doors, hunched over, almost crawling - I looked round and saw them staring back at me. I had a horrible feeling that I wouldn't be seeing them again.

Sean shouted over to me.

"I'll call your sister to meet you at Heathrow. Good luck, tiger."

Of course. I'd never thought of doing that.

26

Handed Over

I staggered, bent double, step by tiny step, through the departure doors onto the runway; a steady stream of upright, healthy people gliding past me - all of them staring, mostly in horror. I made a constant "argh-argh-argh-argh" staccato noise to try and alleviate the pressure inside.

I had about as much chance of climbing the north face of Everest unassisted as I did of climbing the dozen or so steps into the tiny propellor plane. There was no way I could lift my knees high enough to take a step - one: because I was so weak, and two: because the movement would've squeezed my stomach up into my liver. The two hostesses ran down the stairs just as I was starting to sway. I pulled my 'Please help this man' note out for the first time, and between us we managed to hoik my useless body up the steps - mostly screaming on all fours - and into the cabin.

I was tipped onto a clean seat in the cramped little plane next to an Indian businessman, who shuffled as far away from me as his narrow seat would allow. I looked like a cross between a badly stuffed scarecrow and a retired crash test dummy, and the rotting smell from my insides was several degrees worse than merely rank. I tried to apologise, but he squeezed his face against the window, holding a hanky to his mouth. A hostess said something to him - sorry about the stink, maybe? - but he didn't respond to her either. Maybe he was trying to shut his senses down.

The propellors raced and we jolted to a start, which made me cry out and reach for the sick bag. Most heads in the small plane turned around to look.

Shit, what about take off? I hadn't thought of that.

The acceleration!

Oh no, no no…

No long taxiing to distant runways at this airport. It was chocks away, line up the nose with the runway lights, flick the power to full and aim for the nearest star.

I hadn't prepared myself at all. Within seconds the little plane was bumping and bouncing down the runway, the pressure from the acceleration wrapping my liver around my spine like a speeding car smashing into a line of lamp posts.

I tried desperately to find the best position for my raging organs, and finally settled on the 'hanging off the seat in front' position I'd adopted on the bus.

The air lifted the plane from the tarmac, as I provided ridiculous sound effects, and we were off - climbing high and smoothing out, allowing me to relax slightly from my 'high alert' position. I eased back in my seat, closed my eyes and tried to return to 'baby squirrel breath' mode.

Mark, you're leaving Nepal. You're on your way home, just try to relax. You lucky bastard.

That always gave me a hint of a smile.

Just as I was settling myself down, a stewardess appeared at the top of the aisle with a loaded trolley. The last food I'd been near was the boiled egg I'd attempted to nibble on before the rope bridge - but now a strong, sweet, fish curry aroma filled the cabin. My hair trigger stomach flipped with nausea. I rolled from my seat and crawled to the toilet at the back of the plane, where I spent the whole flight curled around the metal bowl as the tiny aeroplane flew south towards Delhi, occasionally being smashed around as the turbulence from the receding Himalayas tossed the little plane about, and tossed me around the cubicle like a gerbil in a tumble dryer.

Forty minutes or so later, there was a banging on the door.

"Excuse me sir, we are about to land. Please, go back to your seat."

I unlocked the door, and the poor woman recoiled as she pulled the door open. She managed to recover enough to help lift me from the heap I'd ended up in beside the toilet. They'd be getting the cleaners in not long after touchdown for sure.

I was helped to my seat, which sent the businessman back into his corner, and I hollered for mercy as the stewardess tried to tighten the seat belt around my waist. I braced myself as best as I could, awaiting the inevitable BANG as the wheels touched down. Gibbering seemed to help.

So I gibbered and gibbered.

The businessman left his seat and legged it for the door a split second after the seat belts light had gone off - he'd probably held his breath for the last five minutes. I was helped down the stairs and left on the runway to shuffle towards the terminal. I lumbered over to retrieve my bag from the pile of luggage that was being offloaded from the flight.

Why the hell did I bring my bag with me? What would I be needing? A change of socks?

You crazy bastard, Mark.

Six hours until my flight to Amsterdam; four until I could check in. I rolled into a corner, trying to escape the commotion of the hectic Delhi airport crowds, and lay down, half propped up on my backpack, feeling my abdomen fighting itself, like I'd swallowed a live python.

The turbulence of the flight had not only battered and bruised my external parts, but had stirred something within. I could feel the sickness rising again as sweat covered my hot skin. The warm Delhi night air was doing nothing to help my fever. I lay on the hard terminal floor, hazily peering up at all the people running back and forth. The noise was like cannon fire in my head, with the glaring airport lights firing directly to the middle of my aching brain. Thousands of sandalled feet slapped around me as I gurgled, spluttered and gibbered the minutes away, mostly in front of a crowd of twenty or thirty Indians, none of whom came within a few metres of me.

A couple of hours passed by. Still I couldn't move, but the pain was building again. The python was angry. Or hungry. I writhed around in my corner, frantically squirming and crying out, flipping onto all fours; onto my side; back onto all fours.

I started to retch, croaking through my parched throat.

At least I won't make a mess. There's nothing left inside me.

Unless any more blood or black stuff comes up.

Which it did, of course.

I crawled into a toilet in a frenzy, past the long urinal and into a hole-in-the-ground squat cubicle - oblivious to the turning heads and the legs I had to push past to get there. The convulsions from expelling the black goo almost forced my face right into the stinking squat, which I had to rest my head next to for at least the next five minutes until I'd recovered enough to move.

You don't have to be an experienced traveller to know that you do not ever want to be crawling around a toilet floor in India - even in the airport.

I crawled back to my bag, washed my face from my water bottle, and lay there for a long, long time, dreading another attack and growing ever more worried, as I was just starting to feel something else going on inside me, in my chest.

It's your imagination, Mark. You're spinning out from that squat attack. Be calm.

You've just had your face down a shitter. That's bound to get your imagination going...

But I knew it wasn't my imagination - that is, unless my imagination was seated in the base of my right lung. I could feel it when I closed my eyes and concentrated: something dark and putrid. I could smell it when I shrieked out after a convulsion, like the air had touched something rotten.

This was bad. Another organ on the way out.

How many does that leave?

I had to find the KLM check in desk and queue up. But that would mean standing up and fighting through a mob of pushing, shouting, elbowing people. I didn't know what to do. The toilet attack had almost finished me off. I could not see how I was going to manage this crucial step - the one that would take me back to Europe. Time ticked away, again, as I just managed to go from tiny breath to breath.

I kept passing out and snapping awake, first of all not sure where I was, and then horrified at where I was.

Then a heavily accented Indian voice was in my ear.

"Excuse me. Hello. Mister, are you OK?"

I opened my eyes to see a dark, south Indian face peering down at me.

"No... I'm not... Here." I thrust him the letter that the American doctor had written for me.

Please help this man, he's very, very sick.

He looked down at it, and wobbled his head.

"Please, where are you going?" he asked.

"Amsterdam... KLM." I pulled my ticket from my jeans for him to see. He looked at it for ages, and then turned it the right way up.

"OK. Please, do not move," he said, squatting beside my head. For some reason, I handed him my passport as well. He stood, turned on his sandals and disappeared into the crowd.

I slumped against the wall, confused by my own actions.

Now what?

That bloke obviously didn't work at the airport. And he didn't have any luggage himself.

You fucking idiot Mark, you've just handed your ticket AND your passport over to an airport scammer.

I lay down on my back again and closed my eyes to try and block out the bright airport lights.

For the second time that day, I stopped caring. I was just too far gone, too exhausted, too physically defeated to even move, let alone alert someone to the theft of my ticket. But can you even call it theft if you've voluntarily handed over your stuff?

Arrest that man, I gave him all my valuables!

It's easy to slip into a sort of trance when you've hardly slept for a week. For a while there, like on the first afternoon in the room in Kathmandu before Led Zeppelin saved me, I couldn't work out if I was still on the trek, lying in the gutter beside the bus, or back at the guest house with Sean and Craig. Time ticked on, and I ticked along beside it. Just.

"Mister, Mister, wake up. Show this man your face!"

I snapped out of where I'd disappeared to.

WHOAH, I DON'T BELIEVE THIS!

He was back, along with an official looking gent with an ID badge dangling from his fawn shirt. They checked my face against my passport. The young, fresh faced, short-haired lad looking back from the page barely resembled the huge-eyed, yellow-skinned, emaciated creature that was sprawled on the airport floor. He certainly looked at me for considerably longer than it normally takes to check a passport.

"OK, OK," said the official. "You wait here. I will make sure your luggage is on. One hour to boarding, Mister." He smiled down at me. "You are a very lucky man."

So everyone keeps telling me.

The kind man with the dark south Indian features sat down with me, as he tried to get me to drink some water and gently rubbed my back. I don't know if he was a passenger, a taxi driver or an airport worker. Whoever he was, he stayed with me and hardly said another word, but just smiled, whenever I focused enough to look him in the eye.

The queue for the flight eventually began to shift, and he went off in search of a wheelchair, but to no avail. He helped me up and supported me as I clung to his arm and helped me towards the desk. My boarding pass was swiftly checked, and I was able to head through to the departure gate. Before he left I shook his hand, and tried to thank him. He shushed me, gave a little bow, a head wobble and a "Namaste", then turned and disappeared back into the lively chaos of Delhi airport.

That huge blessing was my final contact with India.

I was passed into the hands of a Dutch stewardess, who helped me onto the packed plane. I tried to explain my predicament, and handed her my precious note.

"OK, Mr Giblin. You try and relax. We'll have you home soon."

We readied for take-off, which obviously meant I had to somehow put my seat belt on. As I tried to pull the belt around myself I found that my abdomen had swollen; there was a clearly defined lump sticking up under my rib cage. The pain spread out from there, up into my chest, across to my newly warped right lung, and down to my lower bowel.

Shit. What's going on?

At the end of the runway I braced myself for the dreaded acceleration, which under normal circumstances would have me grinning like a big kid. Accelerating aeroplane equals adventure. But as soon as the big Rolls Royce engines kicked in and hurtled us forward, I was a bona fide mess.

I screamed over the roar of the engines as the rapid little bumps from the huge plane belting over the tarmac ripped up through me. I couldn't sit upright, even with all the pressure from the acceleration pushing me back into the chair, and I once again hung from the seat in front. I was vaguely aware of the other passengers, but I was locked in my own painful world now. The nose tipped up and we rose into the air, as I wailed and cried into my balled fist.

Eight hours to Amsterdam. This is the last really big hurdle, Mark. Just hang on.

But even the low, endless drone of the engines seemed to be hitting me in the solar plexus; spreading over my new, worrying lump.

The stewardess returned.

"Mr Giblin, we have made some space for you at the back of the plane. You might be better off there." Maybe there'd been complaints - I wouldn't blame them.

I crawled up to the back of the plane, near the toilets, where the four empty seats were. I couldn't get comfortable, so I lay on the floor and weaved my limbs around the metal chair legs. Anchoring myself to something solid seemed like a good move.

I had a stack of pillows and blankets pressed to my stomach and clutched at a bottle of water. Drinking made me vomit - which would mean an awful trip to the toilet - but I knew I seriously needed water inside me. If only I kept a drop down, that would surely be something.

Every now and then, a worried looking KLM face would lean down and talk to me. But I couldn't really speak.

It's OK. You're going home. You've nearly made it, Mark.

For hours the subsonic drone of the engines seemed to envelop me in a low frequency trance as I stared at the back panels under the seat, too scared to sleep, too worried to relax. I batted away dark thoughts which carried plenty of weight: am I going home to die? Will I even make it home?

Place of death: Row 52, Seats D-G.

I was deeply scared of what was coming next. But mostly I just tried to make it from minute to minute without an inflight implosion. I don't think I slept for even a moment.

Eight hours later, we entered Dutch airspace. Obviously I couldn't stay on the floor for the landing. The air hostesses coaxed me up and helped me onto the seat. I shielded my abdomen in pillows and blankets, but unfortunately the touchdown was baseball bat gentle, and the reverse thrust of the four big jet engines burned straight through me.

Once the plane finished braking, I unclipped my seat belt and fell back onto the floor in a heap, grovelling. I lay there as we slowly taxied to a stop at the terminal, and carried on laying there as the flight emptied.

I'd made it to Europe, alive.

27

The West is Not an Illusion

"Mark, I've called for a wheelchair. Can you sit up?" The stewardess helped me from the floor onto the back seats and sat down beside me. "You're almost home, just hang on."

I sort of nodded with my eyes. One blink for "Yes", two blinks for "Shit, I'm dying, help me for god's sake, I'm turning black inside." A supremely healthy-looking Dutch boy about my age arrived with the wheelchair, and helped lift me up.

A wheelchair! For sick people to be wheeled around in when they have to be moved! Incredible.

I whispered my thanks to the stewardess who'd had the unfortunate job of helping me back and forth to the toilet during the flight - she'd be running for the hotel shower for sure.

God, how long has it been since I had a proper wash? Over two weeks?

And how many hours have I walked in that time? How many terrible explosive accidents have I had?

How many toilet floors have I crawled around on? And I had my head almost down an Indian squat hole only twelve hours ago. Not to mention the smell from my insides...

The giant Dutch boy wheeled me into the terminal and parked me up in a corner. He was a tall boy amongst a sea of giants.

"OK, you stay here, I will get someone here in one moment. Are you OK?"

Two blinks.

Don't leave me alone here. I know I smell. Please don't run away...

But he was gone, springing away on his fit, giant legs. They'd be great for going trekking on. I wished I'd had them to walk back on last week.

The airport was the busiest, cleanest, shiniest, glassiest, most fully-functioning hub of light and space and KLM blue on the planet - and everyone seemed to just take it for granted.

You lot have no idea what's out there, do you?

There's people lying in hospital corridors in Pokhara, vomiting up blood, hoping to maybe see a nurse, let alone a doctor.

And we're all here - amongst all this health and efficiency.

Everything just felt so rich. People strode around gnawing on neat-looking sandwiches and Danish pastries, sipping coffee, reading newspapers, clutching briefcases and funky handbags. Blonde hair, tanned faces, big breasts, short skirts, leather shoes, designer suits, sportswear, Walkmans, cool shades, clean air, water bubblers... It was like being in a Modern World Expo. The heat and noise, the hustle and bustle of India was gone, just like that. I'd emerged into a completely different world again, via a tunnel through the air. It was almost as shocking as arriving in India seven weeks ago. Not everyone comes back from India looking as shocked as I did though. I was a bad advert for the place. I was a bad advert for travel, full stop.

As my huge, bloodshot eyes marvelled over this shiny clean world from my hunched up heap, a little blue electric airport cart pulled up in front of me, driven by a blonde woman decked out in KLM blue, looking like she'd just left the film set of Thunderbirds.

"Hello! You are going to England. You're Mr Giblin, yes?"

"Yes... I am."

"You look like you need help, sir."

Bloody hell, the long legged lad really HAD gone to fetch someone!

How could all this be working so perfectly?

She helped me onto the back of the blue cart, and I lay across two seats, facing backwards, as she shwooshed me the across the length and breadth of Schiphol Airport. No bumps, no bangs, no yanking back on the throttle, no head-snapping two stroke acceleration. I looked up at all the faces gliding by - mostly European.

She delivered me to a chair at the British Airways check in desk, and was gone with a beep-beep.

This could easily be a dream.

Time could easily come and steal me back to that room in the mountains, the alien autopsy room, with those snakes under the...

"Oh, hello, sir." A British Airways woman knelt down beside me. Loads of make-up, southern accent. Big airline lipstick smile. "Someone from your KLM flight phoned ahead. You don't need to do anything. Your bags have been checked through. Can I just see your passport, and then you can wait here for your flight."

"OK," I managed, snapping back from my feverish thoughts. I handed over my sweat stained passport with the evidence that I was once a fully functioning human.

Her lipstick smile didn't even falter when she saw what I was supposed to look like.

"That's fine, Mr Giblin. Can I get you some water?"

I nodded.

"How long...'till flight?" Blink blink.

"Four hours, sir." Smile smile.

Four hours to concentrate on my lump, my liver and my lung. And I thought 'hell' only had two 'L's.

Four hours.

I learnt just how slowly a clock can tick. It felt slower than the clock at Delhi airport. Infinitely slower than the ka-thunking grandmother clock in Abdul's houseboat on Dal Lake.

Maybe time is slower in Europe... Further from the equator...

Shit, I swear that second hand has stopped moving... I should tell someone...

I tried to raise my spirits with the thought that I'd be seeing my family in a few hours. Not my parents - I knew they were in Turkey, but my sisters - and maybe my brother, if he hadn't already cleared off somewhere - would be there at Heathrow to meet me. And help me.

Almost home.

I writhed and groaned the hours away, battling the python, tasting the putrid air seeping up from my lung, and tried to imagine my white blood cells running around with tiny buckets of water to cool my fever and stamping out the hideous sickness I was feeling. I tried NOT to imagine what the doctors were going to do with their mauling hands and bony fingers when they took charge of me. I'd done all I could for myself - it was almost time for the doctors to have their turn - plug me into the special equipment that doesn't exist in Nepal, and hope they know how to use it.

On the other hand, things were definitely looking up. The perfectly tiled and grouted toilet floor was a much better place to be grovelling around than the ones I'd become accustomed to, though the chemical fumes rising from the pristine metal throne burnt into my sore eyes and throat. The handy roll of soft paper conveniently placed at seat height was a great touch, as I could use it as a head rest between vomiting attacks.

Finally, it was time to board. I'd washed my hands and face as best as I could after my last stint on the toilet floor, and was as ready as I'd ever be for the last hop to safety. I was wheel-chaired up the ramp by a tall Dutch girl, and helped into a cramped seat by a Dutch British Airways steward.

"I'll be back in a moment, Mark. You OK there?"

I managed a nod and the smallest "Thank you." An English businessman in a suit approached to sit down next to me, but drew back in horror when he saw the shaking, almost retching gonk sharing his row. I tried to make myself as small as possible, embarrassed by the smell of my own rotting body. But at least I wasn't spraying blood, or putrid black vomit, or having another toilet explosion. I squirmed and pressed my face against the cold of the window and watched the European clouds move across the morning sky.

The steward returned, and I held out my magic note, but he waved it away with a smile.

"Don't worry, sir. I'm aware of the situation. Just try and relax, and you'll be home very soon. You poor thing, you look like you've had quite a trip." Then he took the weight right off my skinny shoulders with just a few simple words. "There'll be an ambulance waiting for you at Heathrow."

Another moment worthy of tears.

A British ambulance. Black leather bed. Blankets. Nurse.

Saline!!! Oxygen tank, dials, needles. SIREN!!

You lucky, lucky, lucky...

The business man looked even more perturbed as he listened in. I turned my arse to face him again, and pressed myself back into the window.

Only fifty minutes more and I'll be on English soil.

I can make it. Relax, relax...

But of course I couldn't relax, because I was facing another take-off. The engines roared, and we began the hurtle down the runway with me piercing the air with my staccato "arghh-arghh-arghh", as I hurled up my fetid lung air. I kept my eyes clenched shut and my pillow pressed against my stomach as we climbed higher. An air hostess came round with drinks and snacks. I noticed that the man beside me didn't touch his sandwich. He had his back to me, and seemed to be cupping his hand around his mouth. After a while, he turned round to face me.

"Excuse me... are you alright there?"

Nice of you to ask.

Speaking was too much of a strain, so I thrust him my note. He read it and raised his eyebrows, looking quite disgusted, as if he thought I might die sitting next to him, or cover him in some foul fluid. Both were definitely possible. He very unsubtly shuffled as close as he could towards the aisle, away from my sickly unpleasantness.

We flew over East Anglia and on towards London, as the green fields of England gave way to the sprawl that sprung from the Thames. It was a long fifty minutes, in which all I could do was focus on my next breath.

We came in to land over the ugly factories and warehouses surrounding Heathrow. The sky was blue. The sheds gave way to roads and then runways. I braced and clutched my pillow and held on for dear life. My dear life. The wheels touched down and I screamed into my open hand as the engines braked us to a crawl and the ailerons tucked themselves back into the wings as we trundled along to our waiting gate number.

Gate 17. Awaiting ambulance and a chance of life.

I'd made it home.

The relief flooded up through me.

Like the Nepali businessman before him, his English counterpart was out of his seat and running down the aisle for fresh air as soon as he could.

Once again, the plane emptied around me. I sat there quivering and clutching my cherished note, waiting for the ambulance man.

I'll accept a stretcher, happily…

I watched the last passenger leave the plane as the steward from earlier approached me.

"We've landed, sir."

Well yes, I had actually noticed.

I grimaced and tapped my note, mouthing the word "Ambulance" at him.

"What ambulance?" He looked at me awkwardly.

I looked at him *very* awkwardly.

"The… the one you told me… had been radioed for."

Christ, please stop making me speak.

He mouthed the Dutch word for "Oops!" and his lips had a little wrestle.

Uh Oh.

"Hold on sir - I'll be right back."

No! I can't wait any longer, I'm done!

I was about to get onto a stretcher, you healthy-livered freak. Come back!!

The steward reappeared a few minutes later looking very apologetic.

"So sorry sir - terrible mix up. The ambulance hadn't been called. Please wait, we're sorting something out for you now."

But you told me, you lying, fit, tanned-faced bastard, you said there was an ambulance waiting...

Sorting out what? A fucking helicopter??

Sorting yourself a gin and tonic more like...

If I'd had the ability, I would've ranted and raved, screamed and cried, accused and insulted. Instead I sunk back into a groaning ball and waited. After about ten minutes, an Indian porter arrived with a wheelchair. I was wheeled out of the plane and into a packed and bustling Heathrow, which looked nowhere near as efficient and well thought out as Schiphol.

I was wheeled up to the arrivals desk, and I handed my passport up to the immigration officer.

"India, eh? Ooo, drink the water, did we? You'll be more careful next time, won't ya!" He peered more closely at my passport picture. "Blimey, son. You wanna get yourself to a doctor. NEXT!"

The porter pushed me through to the baggage carousel and virtually tipped me out of the wheelchair, turned around, and left me grovelling by a bench. Perhaps his shift had just finished. I had to limp over and retrieve my bag from the carousel, and no-one helped.

I dragged my bag through customs and towards the arrival lounge, trying to lift my head up so I'd be ready to see Amanda and Alison. If there were any tears in me, they'd be coming out in a minute, for sure.

Shit, Mark, keep upright, don't collapse... Don't start snivelling just yet... Be strong, just one more minute....One more minute...

I inched along the railings that funnelled me through to arrivals, peering up from my chest at all the faces waiting to greet their friends and relatives, expecting at any moment to hear my sisters call "Maaaaarrrrkkkkk!"

They weren't at the front of the waiting crowd, so I pushed through the hugging, laughing, crying reunions, looking for my own family, my sisters - I was about to see my sisters!

But I didn't.

Because they weren't there.

It made no sense. I knew Sean would have phoned them - it's not something that would have slipped his mind. But then maybe he never got through to them? I hadn't considered that possibility. I looked around in a panic.

Now what? What the hell should I do now?

I couldn't think straight. My brain seemed to float just beyond my grasp;

all I could feel was a complete sense of confusion and worry. And pain. Of course the best thing would be to go and speak to an official looking person, show them my saviour note and wait for an ambulance to come. This would obviously happen because I was back in the UK; safe under the huge, reliable and comforting umbrella of the NHS.

But I didn't do that. I never even considered it.

I did the most ludicrous thing imaginable. For some reason, I left the terminal, sideways-crabbed over the slip road and crawled past the taxi stand to where the buses for Woking departed from. A young couple were already standing there, watching me as I reeled towards them, clutching the railings and bollards.

"You alright mate?" the boy asked.

I seemed to have slipped back into escaping-the-trek mode, batting off any notion of help.

"Fine…When's the bus?"

"Just missed one. Another one in about an hour… You sure you're OK?"

I gurgled a "Bleurgh."

I curled up on the pavement beside the railing, and I waited. No packs of roaming dogs, no stench of rubbish, no screaming rickshaws belting out thick, black smoke or loud Hindi music. It was mid morning in England, and the sun was shining. India and Nepal were long gone.

A few more pairs of feet arrived for the bus, but I didn't even look up. I was in Mark Zone, hanging on by the merest thread to reality. Somewhere inside I knew what I was doing… I was rescuing myself.

The bus came. The same voice from before asked me if I wanted a hand, but I waved him away. I pulled myself to my feet with the railings and somehow lifted my legs up the HUGE steps. Bigger than the steps to the tiny plane in Nepal, but I still managed it.

"Bloody hell, son, I don't think I should be letting you on here, I'm not a bloody ambulance driver. This is a bus!" The driver stared at me as I pulled myself past him.

I fell into the first seat and said "Please… Woking… I'm OK." The dirt from the trek and the white dust from the riverbed were still on my boots. Worse - the smell of my illness was wafting all around me. I had brought a little piece of Nepal back to Woking.

No one sat beside me. The driver never asked for money, and drove away smoothly without even practicing his revving.

The roads and fields grew more familiar as we neared Woking forty minutes later. This was my old stomping ground: where I'd cycled for miles on my paper rounds in the snow, fished in the streams, raced my motorbikes, been chased by groups of drunken youths; picked magic mushrooms in the muddy grass on beautiful Autumn afternoons. I felt like a knackered old salmon, flapping up the last shallow stretch to its home.

When we arrived at Woking station, I had to crawl out of the bus. As I was on my hands and knees, the driver fetched my bag.

"You wanna get yourself to hospital, son."

Now there's a thought.

I managed to crawl into the backseat of a waiting cab before the cabbie had a chance to reject me.

"Where to, Mister?"

"St Peter's Hospital... please."

Ahhh, so I did have a plan.

Or did I only say that 'cos the bus driver mentioned it?

As we pulled away from the train station, I peered out the taxi window. I watched the crowds of people; their faces flying past.

And then - I swear to God, I saw one face I knew.

Maria, standing on the side of the road.

I could have sworn she saw me too. She seemed to be staring right at my taxi. I went to raise my arm, but we were already gone. I spent the next fifteen minutes replaying that in my extremely stressed brain, trying to work out if I was hallucinating.

The taxi pulled up to the plastic doors of the emergency entrance of the hospital. I paid and thanked the driver with a travellers cheque, before staggering towards the building that I knew so well from my youth.

You bloody did it!

You can let go now, Mark...

From Tattapani, western Nepal, to St Peter's Hospital, Chertsey, in eleven days. And every bloody moment of that journey was etched into my brain.

I'd made it. But only just.

I looked deranged. My hair was curling in all directions and my huge, terrified eyes were bulging out of my thin face, which was shrunken and somewhere between a sickly yellow and burning fever red. I was as thin as a rake, nowhere near upright, and totally, utterly debilitated. I grasped the doctor's note in my pocket and stumbled through the plastic doors, where I collapsed onto the cold, hard floor, my arm outstretched, holding my note.

I managed the tiniest baby squirrel request:

"Help."

28

Isolation

My collapse and subsequent writhing around on the floor was pretty dramatic, even for an Accident and Emergency room. A couple of nurses sprang into action and bundled me onto a trolley.

"What's wrong love? Where are you hurting?" Their voices were like music to my ears.

I handed over my precious note, though the last thing they needed was a piece of paper to tell them what kind of condition I was in, as my misshapen body had that well covered. 'Please help this man, he is very, very sick' wasn't what caught their attention. It was the American clinic's headed paper that sparked them up.

"Kathmandu? Isn't that near Mount Everest? Have you just flown back from Kathmandu?!"

Just flown back from Kathmandu? Just flown back from Kathmandu?! Are you ready?!!

"I…"

The fever, the relief, the pain, the stress, my diaphragm and my three 'L's: Lung, Liver and Lump - hadn't enhanced my story telling ability.

"But - how did you get *here*, to this hospital?"

"Taxi… from Woking Station."

They looked at me like I was completely mad, and I looked back at them like I was completely mad.

"I… I don't feel good."

That was all I managed to say before I expelled my thick, black, Nepali pancake onto the floor around the trolley.

Story time was over.

The first thing they did was to cut the disgusting clothes from my body with a good pair of English scissors. Out popped my skinny, swollen, yellow abdomen: my very own pain container. I couldn't let the nurses touch my stomach or chest; the pain inside was just so vicious, like a burning hot coal searing its way through my liver at one millimetre per hour.

The reek of decay coming from inside me was impossible to ignore. Human skin is good, but I needed the hide of a rhino to hold in the fumes I was creating.

A young doctor was onto me almost immediately, ready for a poke. A drip was attached to my arm and, like in the Kathmandu clinic, I swear I could feel the cold saline moving up through my veins and around my body.

"You've come from Kathmandu? Were you in hospital there? Did they do any tests on you?"

"No… Maybe abscess… Liver."

"Hmmm, unlikely. They can take years to form." He smiled at his knowledge.

I know! I know all about that.

"You're very swollen. Does it hurt if I…Whoa!" He jumped back as if a gun had gone off in his hand as his finger tickled my hot coal, leaving me convulsing and howling and curling into a protective ball like a prodded hedgehog. This was clearly no burst appendix crisis.

"Oh, yes, you're very sore, aren't you." He looked stumped, and then, very serious.

I lay on the trolley, covered by a thin sheet - thankfully not over my face, though I couldn't have been far from it - as the nurses ran around me, taking blood, keeping up the patter, readying me for admission.

"You've put a rocket up this place, haven't you love? Don't worry, you're safe now. Bet it's nice getting out of those clothes. Good to be home, eh? Did you have a nice flight?"

A porter was called to take me to wherever they needed me to be - hopefully to plug me into that special equipment that was nowhere to be seen in Nepal - and just as I was about to be moved, I heard a voice I knew: my eldest sister, Amanda, using her polite voice, which was about an octave higher than her "Wat-dya-think-yor-lookin-at?" voice.

"Excuse me, I'm looking for my brother, he's just arrived from Nepal. His name is… OH GOD, MAAAARK!!" Amanda could always be shocked into a yelp, even as a little girl. She was a grown woman of twenty seven, but she screamed at the sight of me on my trolley, looking like a stretched out tortoise without a shell. I'm surprised she recognised me.

She was standing just inside the plastic flap doorway, shaking. I couldn't understand how she was there - not even I knew I was coming to St Peter's Hospital. Maybe she'd followed the smell out of the airport and down the M3.

She rushed over and grabbed my hand; tears streaming down her face. "Oh Mark, what's happened? Sean phoned me…" But she couldn't talk, and the nurses quickly stepped in.

"I'm sorry, I know this is emotional for you, but we really need to get Mark settled - he's in a terrible way. We're going to put him in an isolation ward," the nurse said to Amanda, "and then you can come through and sit with him."

A what? Isolation ward? Why?

What?!

And then I was wheeled away, as Amanda shook and tried to stop the tears.

This was all way too much for me. I didn't want her to see what I was going through, or understand what I'd been through. Not because I didn't think she could take it, but because she'd have to tell my parents how bad I was at my worst - and this was surely my worst. My brain was overloaded with stress, fear and emotion, and even though it was just the two of us there, I don't think I'd ever felt as much a part of my family as I did just then.

And this might just be the end of it.

I'm sure she felt it too. We'd all grown up into complete individuals, but I felt we were all together again; young, with our mum's worry and love inside, and protected by our dad with his big forearms and Scotland Forever tattoo.

I was wheeled away and placed in a small isolation room, which had a long window facing out to the corridor.

Shit, is that where people come and view me?

Another prospect I hadn't anticipated - isolation.

I was surrounded by masked strangers in gowns, masks and gloves, who went into action on what was left of me - peering into my headlight eyes, listening to my chest, and gradually honing in on my abdomen with their killer fingers.

No way.

You ain't touching me there…

My screams were too much, and they backed off. The general feeling that I was getting from the doctors and nurses was by no means encouraging. I began to feel a different kind of scared.

What if they can't help me?

What if I'm just too far gone?

Could that really happen? All from travelling?

The masked prodding gang left me, muttering to each other.

"You gave me a fright, you little bugger." Amanda smiled down at me, putting on a brave face. "Sean phoned last night. It was a terrible line. He said you were bad - but, bloody hell, Mark! It had to be you, didn't it?"

I held onto her hands.

"I was at the airport, Mark. I couldn't find you. I got them to call out over the tannoy, but you must've gone."

My God, I must've just missed her.

"I raced home, thinking you were there. I didn't know what to do. Then I phoned here, and you'd just arrived." She was crying, but really trying not to.

She probably overtook the bus I was on... Oh, Amanda...

But a nurse came in with a medical orderly, and stopped any more chatting.

"Mark, we're taking you for an ultrasound, do you understand?"

Uh-oh.

"We have to find out what's happening in your body, and this is the best way. They'll have to press against your tummy though."

NO NO NO NO NO...

Amanda had to leave, and the orderlies, safely wrapped up from head to toe, wheeled my bed down the endless corridors of the hospital that I knew well from my countless trips there in the past for my asthma, and from my stay after my nasty motorbike crash a few years before. The well-thumbed folder with my name on it in the records department of St Peter's Hospital was about to grow considerably fatter.

I was wheeled into the ultrasound room, which looked harmless enough, and almost as modern as Schiphol Airport, though nowhere near as busy or blue. My gown was lifted and a cold jelly spread across my swollen upper abdomen, which forced me to grip hold of my skinny, yelping head in pain; my big eyes peeping out from behind bony fingers. The operator, a young woman with a very cautious look on her face, leaned over me.

"I'll be as gentle as I can, Mark. OK?" She then pressed the wide-nosed plastic wave gun down and rolled it back and forth across my bulging stomach lump, forcing the hot coal to burn deeper into my bruised, battered and liquidised liver. The world turned black as she slithered the gun back and forth, back and forth, as I tried to fall through the table, or grow more ribs to protect myself; my mouth stuck open in a silent, airless scream as all the individual bangs from the bus journey joined hands and formed one continuous line of unbearable pressure on my mashed liver.

There weren't any words in my head; just a huge, echoing nothing as the wave of pain separated me first from the room, and then from myself.

I knew I was right on the point of dying. And I hadn't had the chance to see my mum again.

29

Visitors From Below

I heard the ultrasound operator's voice trembling from somewhere above me.

"I've finished Mark," she said. "You've been very brave."

Then I heard small squeaking noises, which sounded familiar. I felt myself almost breathe again, and the squeaks became little yelps in my windpipe.

I hadn't been very brave; I was actually petrified, because I'd almost run into the ghouls that I'd first encountered up in that dingy room on the trek. Dark shapes had come rushing at me, and I'd tried to scamper away, but I couldn't seem to escape and I was falling towards them. They were almost wrapping around me when the operator spoke and I heard myself squeaking.

When I came to enough, they wheeled me back to my strange little room. The sheets felt clean and cool - the complete opposite of what I felt inside. I didn't want to tell anyone, but I thought I'd died.

"Any idea what's wrong with him, Doctor?" Amanda asked, in the corridor outside my room. She could see me through the window, having just watched me being trundled back from the ultrasound, struggling for every tiny breath, my skinny chest hardly moving under the thin sheet, my eyes wide open. "You know he's been in India, don't you?"

"Yes, he had a note from Kathmandu." The doctor was looking very grave. "We have no idea what's wrong, Miss Giblin, but he's very weak, and he should've been in hospital weeks ago by the looks of him. We're running tests. We want to transfer him to a London hospital, but quite honestly, we don't think he'd survive the journey."

Amanda looked stunned.

"I think you should test for AIDS. Look at him. He's skin and bone. He was fine six weeks ago. Oh God, what am I going to tell Mum?"

"We are testing for AIDS, yes. And I think you should get your parents here, as soon as possible. I'm afraid things aren't looking good. We'll try him on some antibiotics, but we're not holding out much hope. Whatever is inside him has caused a lot of damage."

"But he's only twenty four... What shall I do? I'll have to go home and try to find Mum's hotel in Turkey. But I can't leave him... What if he... dies? All alone..?" She held her shaking hand over her mouth, and waved through the glass to me.

"Is there anyone else you can call that should be with him? Brothers or sisters?"

"Eric's in France, Alison's in Greece... I could contact his old girlfriend?"

I watched Amanda talking to a doctor out in the corridor, then she came and sat with me as the room span and I concentrated on trying to get some air in my lungs without moving.

I grabbed her hand. "Where's Mum?" I asked.

"She's in Turkey, Mark. I'm trying to call them. Just relax." After the ultrasound experience, I knew I was a whisker away from going for good.

"I want to see Mum."

Amanda did her best not to look too scared.

"I know, Mark. I know you do."

A nurse came in with some bags of fluids.

"Mark, we're putting you on these antibiotics, which will fight the infection. OK?" Another catheter was poked into my right wrist, and a couple more bags were dangled above me. Amanda smiled at me.

"That's good, Mark - they're starting treatment. They think this will work."

"I'd like some soup... Not oxtail, though. And tea."

And then I was all on my own again, apart from the nurses who ran in every few minutes to take my pulse and blood pressure.

Amanda ran out of the hospital, jumped into her banged-up white Mini and raced the five miles back to Woking towards Maria's flat, where she'd once paid me a visit. She rang the doorbell, and Maria opened up, wrapped in a towel.

"Maria, I've got some bad news. It's Mark - he's in hospital."

"No. He's in India."

"No he's not. He's in St Peter's, Chertsey. He's really sick. You should come and see him."

"Oh. But I'm running a bath."

"There really isn't time for that…"

"Oh, OK. Come in…"

Amanda waited in the living room, staring at the huge Swatch clock on the wall for twenty long minutes, as Maria fussed around upstairs.

"Maria," Amanda called, "We have to get back. Mark is really, really bad." She was certain I wouldn't be alive for much longer.

"OK, I'm nearly finished," Maria called down the stairs, "I've lost my stoopid eyeliner."

Amanda stood gaping at the bottom of the stairs. *Who is this woman?*

When Maria finally emerged she was fully made up, looking like she was going down the wine bar for Ladies' Night. She'd curled her hair, squeezed into a little black top and denim mini skirt, and was just clicking her big hooped earrings into place.

"Look, I've chipped my nails," she said, holding out her little tanned fingers. "He won't mind, will he?"

Amanda pondered the same question again: *Who IS this woman?*

They jumped into the Mini and drove back to St Peter's: two twenty-seven year old women with curly black hair; one with a face smudged by tears, and one with chipped red nail varnish. Amanda took the time to explain to Maria what she knew so far, which wasn't much. Maria fiddled with her finger nails and looked out the window, humming.

Either two minutes or two hours later, someone else entered the room and approached my bed very cautiously.

I flicked my eyes around, trying to understand.

Maria? No one had mentioned Maria coming - or had they?

Had Amanda just told me she was going to pick her up? Shit, I'm losing my grasp on things.

But there she was - Maria, standing beside my bed.

"Oh, Mark, hello my darling. How was your holiday?" she asked, as if I'd just got home from two weeks in Spain.

Amanda came back in.

"He's not really with it, Maria. You won't get much out of him."

"Do you think he'd like some ice cream? He used to like mint choc chip - in bed. Naughty boy."

"Erm, I don't think so Maria. Look at him!" Amanda had only met Maria once before, and appeared very confused by her inability to take on board what was happening to me. "I'll leave you two alone for a while."

For some reason, Maria being there completely threw me. Without even thinking, I said:

"Maria… what have you done?"

She pulled back, managing to look everywhere but directly at me.

"I have done nothing, Mark, I promise. What do you mean?"

I didn't know what I meant. Rational thinking was the last thing I was capable of. But she could not look me in the eye. From where I was lying, she just looked so *guilty*, and somehow unsurprised. I slowly, slowly tried to quiz her further.

"Maria… is there anything I should know about… Anything I could tell the doctors, to try to help me? This… is… serious."

"No Mark, nothing. Promise. Why are you saying this?"

I put the remaining brain power I had to work, trying to make sense of everything.

Had she been shagging around when we were together and passed on something horrific?

But then, wouldn't she be sick too?

I looked her up and down, puzzled. Figure still looked perfect, even through the NHS issue hospital gown. No obvious abominable abdominal grotesqueness, and she didn't scream when anyone touched her. Her eyes weren't yellow and her odour didn't seem to be repellant. Her breathing was neither too shallow, nor stilted. She was walking upright, like a fully functioning human - not lurching and stumbling like something from a Boris Karloff movie, gripping her sides and howling, dropping to one knee every few paces.

I had to conclude that she was totally fine. Or at the very least, she didn't have what I had.

In 1987 HIV and AIDS had just hit the headlines in the UK. Ignorance and fear were rife. Maria had told me once before that she'd heard you could catch AIDS from kissing. She wanted to go and live in Scotland, in a caravan, far away from other people, so that she would be safe. Maybe she thought that people didn't kiss in Scotland, or at least not if they lived in caravans.

She'd also been no stranger to the needle before I'd met her, but she'd promised me that was all in the past, and over well before we'd lived together.

But the way she wouldn't look at me - just looking down at her fidgeting fingers, humming, was plain weird.

And that's when I started to think that she'd hexed me.

It all made sense to my addled brain. The stories she always told about her witchy aunt... my mind was spinning. I thought about the peculiar way she had acted in the weeks before I'd left to go to India, her silences, and my endless night time walks around the lake as I tried to work out what the hell was happening.

Was that all part of the spell? I thought she'd just been keeping me keen... It had certainly worked.

She'd never been too far from my thoughts in India. I'd even ended up asking her to come and meet me in Australia. That hadn't been part of my plan when I left. And how weird that I'd seen her face - her of all people - from the taxi window at Woking station that morning. I was positive that she had been looking straight at me from the crowd of faces.

It was all way too much for my exhausted, obliterated young self to contemplate.

She fidgeted nervously with her hospital gown as I lay, grotesque, yellow, scared and skinny, staring up at her with my suspicious horror-show eyes.

"Maria... tell me..."

"I don't know what you mean, Mark. I should go. You need to sleep. I'll come back tomorrow."

And she left. Couldn't get out of there quick enough.

She did! She put a bloody spell on me! And it's gone wrong. That's why she's looking so guilty.

If the hospital had offered a ducking stool service, I would've had her strapped in straight away.

Now my head was really spinning. I thought it'd be best to keep my discovery to myself for a while, until I got used to things. I'd only been in the hospital a couple of hours and I'd already been surprised by my sister turning up, been thrown into an isolation ward, taken on a quick trip to the other side after a hellishly painful ultra-sound ordeal, and unearthed a secret coven of one in Woking. And I still hadn't slept.

Amanda returned, and took a hold of my hand.

"Where's Mum?" I asked. Again and again.

"I'm phoning the hotel, Mark. Try and relax. She's a one, that girlfriend of yours. Bloody hell, Mark."

She's not my girlfriend. I left her to go to India.

But I couldn't forget her... Because she hexed me... I even asked her to come and meet me in Australia...

A doctor soon came back with the ultrasound pictures.

"OK Mark. As suspected, there's a big abscess on the front of your liver. Big as in bigger than a golf ball. And there's also a smaller one on the back of your liver."

He traced his fingers over the grainy black and white image on the plate.

"And this dark area here, at the base of your right lung - we think that's also an abscess."

No wonder I feel like shit.

"What happens next? Do you cut them out?" asked Amanda, which saved me the effort of asking, and allowed me to carry on flitting my scared eyes around the strange little room.

I just walked out from the middle of the Himalayas. And caught that bus... You've no idea what I've just...

"We have discussed your situation and we feel that the best way forward is to try to counter these abscesses with drugs, rather than to operate. For the moment."

My eyes widened even further. This did not sound like a good plan to me. I wanted those things removed from my insides fast, and I didn't think drugs would even touch the sides of the vicious, not-so-little bastards.

I tried to say as much, for what it was worth.

"No... you have to operate..."

"Mark," the doctor said, "you have to rest."

But in the safety and comfort of the hospital, the horrible reality of my journey was beginning to hit me hard. Just the three plane journeys from Kathmandu to Delhi, Amsterdam and Heathrow would've been enough to severely traumatise anyone in my condition. Add all that had gone before - plus the recent witchcraft bombshell that no-one but myself and Maria knew about, and my other little secret that I thought I'd just died and somehow come back - and you had one seriously disturbed, entirely drained young man.

I closed my eyes and tried to ignore the silence in the room, which was hard, because it was *everywhere*. My body was silent. My sister was silent. The drips were silent. The sheets were silent. I didn't trust it - something was going on. My thoughts were like a runaway train, hammering down a messed up timeline - I was up in the mountains again, in that eerie room; I was on the bus; in the clinic; on the toilet floor in Delhi; at the airport with Craig and Sean. I snapped my eyes open with a horror-stricken shriek.

"Shhhh. Sleep Mark. I'm here." Amanda was looking down at me, obviously extremely worried.

I was terrified of sleeping, after what had happened during the ultrasound. I knew there was something waiting for me just below the surface. I struggled and struggled to stay awake, but eventually the absolute exhaustion won, and I nodded off, still holding Amanda's hand.

And I got the biggest fright of my life.

The dark shapes rushed in straight away and turned into big, black, shiny, heavy horses that stomped around in the corner of the room, frothing at the mouth. All I had to do was drift off for a split second and there they were, stamping and braying, trying to drag me away with them. I'd never liked horses anyway, and these evil-faced bastards scared the hell out of me, with their thick black manes and flaring nostrils and pulled back, frothing lips. I would have been much happier with a couple of Friesian cows.

But worse than that was what was under my bed. A giant, disembodied hand was down there - much bigger than me - and it would rise up to grab me the second I dipped into sleep. Up it would come, closing its humungous, cold, bloodless fingers over me, and I'd jolt awake, screaming.

Christ almighty, what have I done to deserve this?

Surely the Gulmarg Shuffle hadn't been that bad?!

Shit. I'd better get word to Sean.

I clutched madly at my sister's hand, begging her not to let me sleep.

"Where's Mum? Is Mum here?" Then I'd calm down a notch, and nod off. And every time those big, black, horsey bastards were there, doing horse wheelies at me.

And the hand. Grab, grab, grabbing at me. It wasn't just a mindless hand though, it knew what it was doing. And it was devious. I could almost feel it daring me to sleep. If I could've scrambled out of that bed and run up the corridor in my nightie, I would've done.

If I slept, I'd wake up thinking I was back in the Himalayas and that I had a full day's walking ahead of me, which was the most terrible feeling. Amanda did her best to calm me down. Travelling between Woking and Old Delhi in one day is too much to take - Sean will attest to that. You wanna try Kathmandu to the isolation ward, St Peter's Hospital in a day, with a stopover rolling around on a mushy toilet floor at Delhi airport.

My sister sat with me for my first night in hospital. Every time I woke up I'd have to work out where I was and what was going on, and every time I'd ask where Mum was.

"She's coming, Mark. They'll be here, don't worry."

30

Edge Of The World

The next day, I was still wild-eyed and crazed, still surviving on the baby squirrel breathing technique I'd mastered. I'd spent the night flitting between the two worlds I was straddling, with fleeting visits to various places in Nepal that confused me even more. Amanda was still sitting beside the bed, holding my hand.

Then she was gone again, and Maria was back. She busied herself around the bed as I lay there, unnerving her as I followed her with my huge, yellow eyes. By now I was fully convinced that she'd bewitched me and was sending me down to hell with a kiss.

"Maria, are you... sure you..?"

"Mark, shhhh. You can't talk. Your tummy is sore. And you are making me nervous."

She fussed around my bed, still avoiding my eyes and doing peculiar things, like cleaning my feet. That sounds like a loving thing to do for someone who'd been through what I had, but I'd already had a bed bath - probably more for everyone else's sake than mine - and my feet were just fine.

"Maria...they're clean..."

"No they're not. They are smelly, and I know how to clean your feet, Mark." She'd hum away as she busied herself between my toes, and I tried to calm my brain down.

She's preparing you, Mark. This is all part of it... Like Egyptian burial rites, they pull your brain out through your nose... But she'd never get away with that here...

No, hang on, you have to be dead for that - shut up - she's just keeping herself busy... You know that's what she does, fiddles with things... She's a fiddler... She'd better not fiddle my brain out of my nostrils... that'd be another organ gone...

But after a while, her careful attentions did help me to relax slightly and stop seeing everything she did as part of the curse. Well - as relaxed as anyone could be with the devil's giant hand living under their bed and a couple of black, frothing shire horses snottering and hoofing around in the corner.

Amanda returned and spent the next several hours batting off my never-ending pleas to fetch Mum. I couldn't get it straight in my head that my parents weren't just about to drop by. Later that afternoon, after Maria had shaved me, cleaned my fingernails, stuck a warm flannel into my ears and headed home for a bath, Amanda tried explaining things to me.

"I spoke to the hotel in Turkey, and Mum and Dad have gone on a three day trip, and - typical Mum - they did it away from the Tour Operator. So no one knows where they are. But don't worry Mark, I'll speak to them soon."

I nodded, dipping below the surface again.

Then my eyes snapped awake.

"Where's Mum? Is she here yet?"

The tears were bubbling up behind Amanda's eyes again, and she ran from the room. I drifted around the world, from awful bus journey to Passu Glacier to the trek to the Led Zep room, and generally became weaker and weaker, with no respite in my frantic grabs at sleep - they were the mental equivalent of the bus journey.

Amanda was distraught and exhausted. She still hadn't heard a word from our parents, Eric and Alison weren't contactable, and she was having a hard time pinning a doctor down for information. She finally managed to corner one as he swept past my room early evening.

"Doctor, I think he's deteriorating. He can hardly sleep, he's ranting, and he just looks so... weak."

"Miss Giblin, there doesn't seem to be much we can do for your brother. We are trying - but we've never seen anything like this. You really have to get hold of your parents. I'm very sorry, but we very much doubt that Mark is going to make it."

She looked through the window at me in my room - fidgeting, drifting off, snapping awake. Endlessly.

God, Mark - don't die. I can't handle this on my own.
She had a good cry and then came back to sit with me, prepared for another long night.

I jolted awake.
"Is that you, Mum?"
"It's Amanda. Mum's in Turkey, Mark. I'm here."
"Oh. I thought Mum was here. She's coming though, isn't she?"
I went on like that all night.
Somehow I hung on, though Amanda thought each of my massive attacks from the inside would be my last. She always seemed to be beside my bed, holding my hand, stroking my head, holding up the flask of tea or soup - though I was only taking the tiniest of sips. Maria drifted in and out, and whenever possible I'd keep an eye out for any signs of witchery.

On about the fourth day, Amanda heard from Mum and Dad in Turkey. She explained the situation and told them they had to get home very quickly. They had to wait a further twenty four hours for the insurance company to talk to the hospital and make sure all was legitimate. Amanda and the doctors were absolutely convinced I wouldn't be alive long enough to see them.

They flew into Gatwick at six o'clock in the morning, and Amanda went to pick them up through an incredible pea soup fog. Half an hour from the airport there'd been a massive car crash on the motorway, and six army trucks had stopped to help clear the debris. Amanda jumped out of her Mini and asked the soldiers if there was any way they could get her through the carnage, crying as she explained why. They shifted smashed up cars out of the way and cleared a path for her to nip through. She picked up a very anxious Mum and Dad from the airport and whizzed back to St. Peter's - about an hour's drive.

"They won't let us in to visit at this time of the morning, hen," my mum said.

"Mum," Amanda almost smiled, "I don't think they'll mind. You wait 'till you see him. Then you'll understand. He hasn't stopped asking for you. He keeps thinking I'm you."
Please let him be alive.

I was awake when my door opened and Mum, Dad and Amanda almost ran into my room. I saw their faces drain of blood, and their tears came straight away.

"It's OK now, son. I'm here." Mum's warm Scottish voice flowed all around me and I gave her the biggest smile that could come out of my skinny, death-like head as I struggled desperately to avoid any muscle movement that could ruin the moment. I tried to apologise for disturbing their holiday. Dad leaned over and kissed me on the brow.

"Nothing matters more than this, kid," he said with a wobbling voice. I hung onto them both: one on either side of me. Mum looked about a decade older than when I'd said goodbye to her, only weeks before. I hate to think what she thought of how I looked.

All I could do was pass out again, but this time I had my mum to hang onto as the big hand pawed and roamed around under the bed. I drifted around all afternoon, sometimes hearing quiet conversations between my parents and my sister.

"He's hardly breathing. I'm scared to take my eyes away."

"If he breathes, he screams. It's best when he's asleep."

"He's skin and bone. I cannae understand it. He looks like he's been through hell."

"Imagine if he hadnae had Sean to help him!"

"I'm still not sure what happened. I think he walked back from the trek on his own."

"In that state? He couldnae have done. Look at him! Oh hen, he phoned me just before he went trekking - you don't think he was calling to say he felt ill, do you?"

"Have you noticed he keeps looking at that corner, Mum?" asked Amanda, from what sounded like a mile away.

"Aye, I have. Why's that, hen?"

"I'm not sure. But he's not very happy about it. Nor will you be when he crushes your hand to a pulp."

"God help the poor boy, he looks terrified."

Amanda still thought it was likely that I'd die very soon, but she was also relieved that she wouldn't have to deal with it on her own. A doctor came by to fill Mum and Dad in on the latest news, which wasn't good.

"Mr and Mrs Giblin, your son is dangerously ill. We still don't know what is wrong with him, just that he has abscesses on his liver and lung, but we think the only chance he has is for us to operate - tomorrow. I don't think we can leave it any longer. He's very weak, as you can see - and it'll be a major operation. We have to get to his liver and his lung, and find out what else has happened. It's going to be extremely dangerous for him, and you really should prepare for the worst."

Dad and Amanda held onto Mum, as they all wept.

"Can I stay here the night with him? He wants his mum - he wants me with him."

"Of course you can stay - we'll be operating first thing."

Dad and Amanda went home late that night. Mum sat by the bed, stroking my hand.

"Mark, they're going to operate on you in the morning."

I smiled. "Good. That'll help."

"Yes. They think so too. You'll be OK, son. I won't be far - I'll never leave you. You know that, don't you Mark?"

"Yes. I do. You're the best Mum."

"Och son..."

"Tell me about Turkey."

"Ohhh, son, you were right. It's beautiful. We went to Bodrum - didn't you and Gareth work there or something? And we went to Ephesus. I can now say I've been to one of the Seven Wonders of the World. Oh I loved it. I sat on the hill and just imagined all the things that happened there - the plays, the parties, the battles..."

I lay with my eyes shut, listening to her lovely voice drifting in and out all night.

And then it was morning. I was barely in the room, though I knew the doctors were fussing around me.

Amanda and Dad came back early in the morning to be with me and Mum before they took me to the theatre. They joined Mum in the corridor.

"They've been in there for a while. I don't know, but they're not looking hopeful. Oh, God, this is awful. Oh, please, don't let my wee boy die." They watched me as the doctors and surgeons stood around my bed. Finally a doctor came and spoke to them.

"I'm sorry, but we cannot operate. In the condition he is in, there's no way he'll survive the operation. He's deteriorated even more. His blood pressure is too low. All we can do is carry on with the antibiotics, and, well, hope for the best. I'm very sorry."

Amanda collapsed into Mum's arms, and she collapsed into Dad's arms.

For the rest of the day and the next, they sat watching me, holding my hands, to make sure I wasn't alone when I eventually died.

31

Bedside Fiesta

I felt like I was permanently awake for those two days, looking at Mum or Dad or Amanda, and sometimes Maria. Occasionally I'd catch Mum staring at Maria as she twittered on with her inane chattering.

"I paid thirty pounds for these shoes, and the manager of shop said: 'You should stand there all day in them, and I'll pay you the thirty pounds back!' Can you believe he said that, Margaret? I'm not gonna stand in his stooopid shop, to let people I don't even know look at my feet!"

Mum was far too polite to yell "Shut up, you awful, shallow girl!" But her expressions were conveying her feelings quite clearly. Of course Maria didn't even notice, and jumped onto the next bit of tattle that appeared in her head.

"Someone told me they use monkeys to sew shirt buttons on in China... Ha! Bloody stooopid, innit? As if a monkey could thread a needle."

I was still alive the next day. And slowly, I was growing more alert. Everything was in focus.

"Hello, son. You look a wee bit better." My mum was smiling down at me, holding the soup flask to my lips.

"I thought I was having an operation, Mum?"

"Well, Mark - they, err, thought they'd just leave it a wee while - because you seemed to be doing really well!"

"Oh. So those things are still inside me?"

But I did feel slightly better - not as distant. I'd been battling the horses and the hand almost constantly, but for the previous few hours I'd actually kept them at bay. My fidgeting had dropped a few notches, and so long as I didn't take any big breaths in, I could stave off the huge abdominal attacks.

I had more tests and another ultrasound on my ultra sensitive abdomen. The drips were constantly being refilled with bags of industrial strength drugs, and sent down a pipe into the very sore pipe hole in my wrist to take up the fight raging inside me.

The ultrasound was as painful as before, but at least I didn't stick my head into the void this time. I just screamed and screamed.

I must be getting stronger.

The antibiotics seemed to be containing the abscesses, which apparently hadn't grown since the first ultrasound. My white blood count was down to a slightly less astronomical number, indicating that I was still fighting whatever was going on inside me.

Samples from a range of my bodily fluids had been sent to London for testing at the Hospital for Tropical Diseases, but nothing came back as a hit. The main thing though was that I was alive and still fighting. Maybe we would get a name for the illness later. Or maybe I'd be the name for it: Gibboscess of the liver - my very own disease. Symptoms include: desire to head as far from safety as possible, a strange attraction to foreign toilets, inability to ask for help when needed, ability to drink right up to the moment you nearly explode, ability to conjure up otherworldly visions, ability to stink like a sun-roasted cadaver, and, it seemed - an incredible ability to not quite die, over and over again.

Then, on about the eighth day in my strange little room, the doctors gathered around to deliver some good news.

"Well Mark, we are happy with the blood tests, and we no longer think what you have is contagious. So tomorrow you'll be transferred to a general ward, and we'll carry on with the antibiotics. How does that sound to you?"

The doctors looked pleased. Surprised, but pleased. My family were ecstatic. I was relieved. Not convinced, but relieved. A general ward had to be a step in the right direction. The thought of going in the wrong direction from an isolation ward doesn't sound good.

So my bed was moved, along with my drip stand, down a mile long corridor into a men's ward which, to me, seemed full of life. After the silence of the past eight days, it felt like being rolled into a funfair on a Friday evening. Newspapers were ruffling. Someone was doing a crossword. Tea was being sipped; biscuits dunked.

Turn it down lads, I thought we were supposed to be ill.

I liked it already, though I was the youngest in there by at least twenty years, and I looked the closest to death. I gave my mum another huge smile.

"Oh son, I think you're getting better."

"I do too, Mum. Where's Eric and Alison?"

"Alison is still in Crete on holiday - we don't know where though, but she's back next week. Eric - well, your guess is as good as mine. Somewhere in France."

Maria dropped by in the afternoon, free from the NHS gown that everyone had to wear in the isolation ward. She can't have been wearing that much underneath it, if her new outfit was anything to go by. A tiny black skirt was stretched over her wiggling little bum; her black stockinged legs tapered down to a pair of high heels, and her breasts were pushing up and out of her lacy little top. Her curly black hair was pinned up to show her tanned neck and shoulders. She planted a juicy lipstick kiss on my cheek, bending over the bed as I tried hard not to trigger ANY muscle reactions.

Is this still part of the bewitching?

"Hallo my darling. How is my travelling boy?"

Newspapers and crosswords were put aside, arms were folded over hospital gown chests, and a line of grinning men's faces followed her every move as she wiggled up and down the ward. She covered more ground than the nurses as she fussed around the bed, straightening the sheets, filling the water jug, dipping out for a cigarette, popping out to make phone calls.

Having space around my bed brought a new problem, in that Maria thought the space should be filled by her large, noisy Spanish family. She came in on the second day with a round, happy-looking blonde woman with super big glasses.

"Mrs. Giblin, this is my mama."

"Oh, hello. How are you?" smiled Mum, polite as ever.

"Hallo! I leeeetle English. Hallo!"

"Esto es Mark, mi novio…"

"Ohhhhhhhhh!" She came at me with arms out and hands open to grab my face and administer a dozen little double-sided pats to my gaunt cheeks. Then she turned and almost chased Mum round the bed for a hug.

"Ohhhhhhhhhhhhhhhhhh!"

She brought with her a bag of food, which she spread out on the trolley table - salmon, salads, cakes, fruit, and gesticulated how it should really all be in my belly within the hour, to fatten me up and make me all well again.

Maria explained to her mum what was wrong with me in Spanish, which sent her into a swift series of Hail Marys, chest crossing, anguished hand-wringing and gasping.

Apparently it was my "Higado inflamado masivamente que le hacia oler", which sounds a lot more intriguing than "It's his massively swollen liver that's making him stink."

Mum had a polite, slightly awkward smile on her face, which faded when the ward door swung open again and a flock of people came scurrying towards us.

"And here's my dad... my sister... her boyfriend... cousin... cousin... cousin..."

Cousins I'd never even heard of were soon telling me in Spanish accented, lager-speak English about their new cars and what they paid for them: "What a mug they were, man, I tell ya, it's worth twice that. Wanna see a picture?"

Arrrrggggghhhhh!

It was like a swat team: "Right, you go in first, butter him up. Get the food out. Then we come in. No one - and I mean NO ONE - give Mark a minute to think. Keep talking. Pablo, you take the first hour. Tell him about your Ford Cortina. He'll like that. What did you pay for that again? Fuckin' mugs."

Mum would be forced to the back as the Spanish entourage bustled around and crowded around my bed, talking loudly at a rat-a-tat million miles an hour, waving, shouting, laughing, pinching my cheeks, hoovering up the picnic. No one in our family had ever spoken as fast as this lot - not even the cursing Delhi rickshaw driver had spoken as fast as this lot, and he was quick.

I tried to catch Mum's eye in a weak attempt to cry for help as the quick-fire Spanish words ricocheted around the bed, but the party continued on. It was a Spanish family version of our sick bed parties in Nepal, only they don't work as well when you can't speak the language and have no interest in cars, kettles, shoes or absolute bollocks.

All Mum would say was "Och well, son. They don't mean any harm." But the look on her face was like we'd *all* died and gone to hell.

The second week wore on. Blood tests, ultrasounds, metal tubes passed up into my rectum, readings, mutterings, doctors' visits, endless drips. But after the initial buzz of me not dying and then moving into the general ward, things began to turn sour.

Every night at seven o'clock, after the Spanish mob had all left, I'd be hit with a fever, which would last a couple of very uncomfortable hours. The nurses would let Mum and Dad stay well beyond visiting hours - I was less fidgety when they were around. My dad would come straight after work at 6.45pm exactly, with a "Hiya pal, how you doing?" Mum would go outside for a cigarette, and when she returned my temperature would rocket.

I'd lie there panting, the sweat pouring off me, fearful of the night ahead. A fever meant the return of the demon horses, and worst of all, the devil's hand under my bed. I could actually hear it down there, scuttling about, scratching. I'd hang onto Mum and Dad's hands with tears in my eyes, until finally they'd have to leave for the night, about nine o'clock.

All the doctors prescribed for my fever were bigger and stronger electric fans, which were set up around the bed, all aimed at my roasting head. After a few nights of this burning fever I told my parents I was sure I was deteriorating again, rapidly. They were really starting to worry now - but what could they do?

I was sick of the drugs, and tried to tell the doctors that they weren't doing me any good.

"Well Mark, trust us, they are working. They might take a while longer than we thought, but you are very sick."

The result of this was that the doctors ramped up my drug intake, which only made me feel a whole lot worse, if that was possible - as if the drugs were increasingly poisoning my already poisoned system. I actually began to feel worse than when I'd arrived. I was still hardly eating anything, and taking most of my fluids in through my drip.

Towards the end of the week my parents were exhausted with worry, and took things into their own hands.

"Now son, we've talked this through: we're going to remortgage the house and put you in a private hospital in London. Not enough is being done to help you here. Dad is going to the bank tomorrow. So don't you worry, it's going to be OK."

I was horrified. I couldn't see what difference it would make, and the thought of being moved really wasn't appealing. I was still knackered from Nepal.

We argued. I was at an obvious disadvantage because of my giant liver and the pain from my diaphragm pressing on it, but I slowly managed to get my point across.

"No… There's no way… I'm going to be… responsible for you… losing the house."

Mum leaned over, with the saddest look in her eyes. "No son. There's no way we're going to lose YOU over this."

Whoa. What?

Shit.

They think I'm going to die.

The mentality that had helped me walk those six days over the mountains in Nepal hadn't really left me. I'd relaxed a lot since then, of course, but I still hadn't really entertained the idea for too long that this *would* actually *kill* me. I just knew it *could* kill me, and I'd been very close. And maybe I'd had one little tiny death - but even *that* hadn't killed me.

I began to think about dying. What would it be like? Well, I knew I wouldn't just slip away. It was going to be very painful, and probably very messy. And scary. Because something awful was waiting for me; that was very apparent. Would I pass through into a new world of agony? Was I going straight to hell? For what, though? Fighting too much during the punk rock years? Not giving a shit about getting a career? Having too much fun? Stealing the effects pedal that did absolutely nothing? Christ, if I fit the criteria for going to hell, it was going to be very busy down there.

It was all too much for my brain. I just knew I didn't want to die. And I didn't want my parents to have to live through that.

One of Dad's customers at the garage in Ashford was a doctor, so Dad sought advice on which private hospital would be my best bet, but the word came back that St Peter's Hospital actually had the best liver specialists at that time, and I couldn't be assured of any better treatment elsewhere. It would just cost more money than we'd ever seen.

So they didn't remortgage the house, and I was hugely relieved. I couldn't bear the thought of them giving up everything for me. Their whole lives had been a struggle. If I was going to die, being even deeper in debt certainly wasn't going to help them.

So they sat by my bed holding my hands, tears just behind their eyes, as I clung on.

32

Dough Boy Sinking

In an endeavour to either get me up and moving, or because of my exotic fragrance - probably both - a nurse insisted I have a real bath, rather than a bed bath. But I could hardly move without doubling over from the ball of fire in my guts. The diarrhoea had also returned with a vengeance. The night fevers left me cold, shivering and weak in the mornings. Worst of all, I felt like the doctors and nurses thought I was being soft, which was really annoying me.

"Come on Mark, up you get, time for a proper bath now. Come on, it's not that bad - you can do it."

I'll be doing it all over your feet in a minute, you upright freak.

I was helped into the bathroom by a couple of hefty male nurses, who helped me off with my gown and left me hunched over in front of the mirror. I saw myself naked for the first time in weeks. I had begun to retain the fluids that I was taking in via the constant drip, which had a disturbing effect on me.

I was bloody hideous - infinitely worse than the poor boy I'd seen looking back at me in Charlie the Gurkha's bathroom mirror. That face had not even been on the bus journey yet, or the rickshaw, or the multiple taxis and flights. Or been stuck down an Indian bog hole. Or given up hope, several times. Or been chased around for nearly two weeks by a giant, sinister hand and a pair of black hoofing shire horses. My eyes were almost squeezed from their sockets, like they were trying to make a break for it; my face sunken to the bone, exhausted and badly spooked. My face, I discovered, has a naturally inbuilt banana shape that curves to the right, and is only noticeable when there's no meat left on me. My wild, curly mass of hair did nothing to help my skinny banana face along, and my fever-burn glowed under a sickly yellow pallor.

My shoulders and chest were just skin over bone, and I had an old man's hunch from the weeks of abdominal pain pulling me forwards. My arms had no muscle left and my elbows and hands looked massive and bony in comparison.

But my stomach and thighs were, bizarrely, an entirely different matter - this was where the fluids had gathered. They were horribly swollen: great, doughy, white masses that hung over my hips and knees. I pushed my finger deep into my marshmallow thigh, and watched, horrified, as the dent that was left behind slowly disappeared as the fluids reclaimed the space.

It was revolting; I couldn't believe what was happening to my young body. I'd been fitter than I'd ever been only two months previously, after six months of working my arse off every night in Tesco. Or at least, I thought I had been.

Not anymore. I'd been catapulted out of the Himalayas, straight into the body of a very peculiar old man.

My knobbly knees were particularly unattractive, sitting on top of bony white shins, which disappeared into fat, doughy ankles and feet. I stared at myself in the mirror, wondering what the hell could be destroying me so rapidly, from the inside out.

In the bath I looked down at my elephantine thighs wobbling in the water, my groin hidden under the big fold of tummy dough. I sat there, wallowing in self-pity and lukewarm water, until the nurses came back and hoisted me out.

I felt physically and mentally drained when I finally lay back on my bed. I asked the nurses to pull the curtains so I could try and have a sleep, but the horses were only just out of sight, and the hand under the bed was gearing up for something big.

The fevers and the diarrhoea intensified over the next day or two, but the doctors would never deviate from the line: "The drugs are working."

NO THEY'RE FUCKING NOT!

Mum and Dad sat with me as much as they could, as did Amanda. Maria and her extended family were still swarming around my bed, but their parties were just getting too much for me to handle.

"Maria... please... no more family... I'm too sick."

I'd been worrying for a few days about telling her, but she didn't give a toss.

"OK my darling, you funny boy, Mark."

Why? Why am I funny? Please don't hex me anymore.

So Maria would arrive on her own, still managing to raise the average temperature of the ward by a few degrees with her stockings, miniskirts and low tops, or white vest over skin tight jeans and sneakers. She really wasn't helping my fever.

St Peter's Hospital, which was probably built in the fifties, was an excellent homage to the extraordinarily long, ugly corridor. Plastic doors did little to keep out the cool, late September air.

On a breezy morning, after an awful, sweaty, wide-awake night, I was wheeled along endless corridors in a cronky old NHS wheelchair for yet another ultrasound. Through plastic doors into more corridors, out across the car park and past Accident and Emergency, down into more corridors. Twice round the roundabout...

Jesus, this is killing me.

I had a pillow pressed against my abdomen, which did little to cushion me from the vibrations travelling up and into my liver. The orderly left me in a particularly dark and cold corridor outside the ultrasound room. I was dreading the test - the smear of the tummy jelly, the rolling pressure of the sound gun over my liver.

The worst thing was that I knew exactly what the results from the test were going to be, as I'd felt the abscesses growing inside me. I'd told the doctors this repeatedly and I didn't need another sound graph to prove it.

But of course, they did.

Sure enough, the grey and white lines on the ultrasound screen built up to show clearly the expanding abscesses. To me, they were like putrid eggs of stinking pus, about to hatch monsters inside me.

After the hideous test, I was plonked back into my wheelchair and rolled out into the dark, miserable corridor to await the orderly to trundle me back to my bed. That was all I wanted - my bed. Even with the hand underneath it. I could feel the cold autumn air wafting up through my thin, backless hospital gown. I was freezing.

I wriggled and writhed, trying to find some peace for my liver, which felt like it was pumping in pain after the ultrasound onslaught. But no one came for me. I sat there for an hour, cramping badly, nauseous, going through my range of pathetic whimpers and kicked-dog moans.

Then I saw someone I knew: Angela, my old travelling mate Gareth's sister, weaving down the corridor, looking like a drunken cheese-clothed hippy. Her face was half-swollen, and she held a cloth to her mouth, looking pretty sorry for herself under her long, curly hair.

"Angela!"

"Wudy 'ell... 'ark?... Oh shit..." She stared at me, obviously stunned at my transformation. I'd seen no one apart from my family, Maria, and half the Spanish population of Woking. But of course, everyone knew I was ill. She sat with me, gawping, as I recovered enough to look her way again.

She pointed to her swollen mouth and spoke in that post-dentist way; thinking she was actually moving her numbed lips and jaw.

"Wisdmmm 'eeth. Ow!"

"Oooohh," I managed, my head falling back onto my chest.

Shit, this is gonna be a good conversation.

"You 'ook 'reezing, you 'oor hing," she mumbled through her cupped hand.

I was. I was shivering. And shivering means muscles moving. I was shivering, writhing, contorting, squeaking; pulling banana faces of pain.

"Why arrr uuu in the 'orridor?! This is mmmental!" Her lips fumbled, eyes still fogged from her anaesthetic. I pointed to the ultrasound door.

"Finished... an hour ago."

"Aye? Anower a'ohh? 'Idicuous!! I'm 'oing to ffffind a nurse, OK? - uuuu carn shhhay here liiike 'is."

I nodded, not quite knowing what she was on about. It was hard to concentrate, and she had a mouth full of anaesthetic, wadding, stitches and uncontainable dribble.

She returned a few minutes later.

"'Omeone 'ummin." She dribbled, nodding like a mad woman; blood and spittle flecking her lips.

"Someone's coming?"

"...'Es. 'Omeone 'ummin... 'oon."

"Soon?"

"...'Es."

No one did. There was no way I could pretend that I wasn't suffering badly, and getting worse the colder I got. My big skinny knees stuck out from my gown, shaking and knocking together, my swollen ankles sloshing, as Angela tried to keep me calm, in drooling mumbles.

"Uddy 'ell, 'ark. I'm 'oin to 'ell 'em I'll fush uuu 'iyselffff."

"You'll push me?"

"'Es. I'll fush uuu."

She came back a few minutes later, up in arms, in a muffled kind of way.

"'Ey shed nooo! Uneeonschh 'ont 'et 'ee."

Fuck, this was like trying to get a story out of Lassie.

"Pardon, Ange? Uneeoschh?"

"'OONEEEONCHHH."

"Ohhhh! The unions won't let you?"

"'Es."

Well, I think that's what she said.

I was so desperate to lie down, to help straighten my abdomen and take some pressure off my increasingly raging liver. Sitting up, folded over was the worst position I could be in. But I was in that corridor for two horrendous hours. Ange sat with me the whole time in mumbling, dribbling disbelief that no-one was coming to my aid.

"It's a 'ucking 'isshhrace."

"Fucking disgrace?"

"'Es."

When an orderly finally came I was shivering uncontrollably with cold in my bones. I waved goodbye to Ange, as she berated the porter for the agony he'd helped rain down on me. I think.

"What did she say?" he asked, as I was pushed back up the long, cold corridor.

Mum and Dad sat with me that evening, as usual. I was feeling really low - the worst I'd felt since arriving at the hospital. A doctor hadn't even been to see me since my ultrasound. My parents looked so worried for me, but I couldn't even give them a brave, reassuring grin.

Dad talked to the nurses to try to understand what was going on, but still no-one was very forthcoming. My fever arrived bang on seven o'clock as usual, and even worse than before.

Three large fans were set up beside the bed, which only depressed me further.

Is this seriously all they're going to do for me? Fan me down?

I could have stayed in India and employed an army of punkah wallahs, and been no worse off. I was positive that the doctors were definitely avoiding us. I felt abandoned by them, like they knew they'd made mistakes with me. I could see the fear in my parents' eyes as they dabbed the sweat from my forehead.

The nurses allowed them to stay until lights out on the ward. I was very teary when they left. My mum hadn't cried in my presence since the first day, though whenever she came back from a cigarette I could often tell she had been.

She was such a good mum. And my dad, for all his faults, would do anything for us. They were wracked with worry when they kissed me goodnight.

"We'll see you in the morning, son."

I wasn't so sure. I didn't trust myself to speak, as I had a terrible feeling that I might be saying goodbye to them.

They waved me goodnight from the end of the ward, and I watched them leave as the fans buzzed hard around me. I knew I was in for a bad night.

It was a Thursday.

33

This Is It

I lay sweating until the early hours, when the cramping pains shooting violently around my abdomen intensified to an alarming level. They were similar to the pains on the bus journey, except that by this point my temperature was immense and I felt much, much sicker. I buzzed for a nurse, and she sat with me until dawn. Not much was said.

The day began, as always, with the breakfast trolley clattering up and down the ward. The noise was penetrating straight into the depths of my brain, like Led Zeppelin had done through the wall in Kathmandu. My brain was on fire from it, and I wanted so much to cry out for the ward to *JUST SHUT UP!!*

Breakfast, for whoever was well enough to have any, thankfully finished after an hour and the clattering noise of the plates and bowls settled into the morning fuss of nurses changing the beds.

I lay on my side watching it all, hardly moving.

Then a huge, deep spasm erupted in me. I'd been strategically put in a bed next to a toilet, and I don't know how I managed it, but I rolled out of bed and dragged myself there just in time.

That was when my body let us all know that enough was enough.

All kinds of fluids shot out of me from both ends. Green bile, black water... and then came the blood. Bright red gushing blood; an inconceivable amount of it. I almost passed out on the clean toilet, and frantically clung to the bar beside the basin. When the attack finished I crawled the few feet back to my bed and cried out for help.

My skin had turned grey - presumably not a brilliant sign either. The other patients all joined in, shouting for help for me.

"Doctor, quick!"

"Nurse, nurse, NURSE! Something's happened to Mark."

"Quick! There's blood!"

Everything sounded very distant.

Nurses arrived, calling into their pagers, and trying to steady me.

"Mark! Can you hear me? Mark, look at me. Can you... Oh god... DOCTOR!"

I felt the eggs hatch, explode, implode, erupt... I had to be helped to the toilet again, and more blood poured out from between my legs as I collapsed beside the bowl.

From there, everything moved a lot more quickly. I knew I was on my way out. I felt things were now well and truly beyond my control, but I also knew this had been coming. And no one had listened - apart from Mum and Dad.

I was helped back onto my bed and the nurses swiftly pulled the screens around. One ran off and - finally - returned with a doctor; one that I'd never seen before. He took my pulse, ran off again, and returned clutching bags of blood.

"OK Mark, I need you to grip the bed now and try not to move too much."

My eyes were locked to his.

"I'm going to cut a hole in your neck to get some blood into you. OK?"

His hand came up holding a scalpel. His free hand felt around for a few seconds to the left of my Adam's apple, his fingers choosing the spot, before the scalpel sliced into my neck. He pushed down with a twist to prise through the gristle, which I felt open up. A pipe was then forced down my fresh neck hole and attached to a bag of blood. I was fully aware of what he was doing, but frozen in shock - probably a good thing under the circumstances.

"Right Mark, we have to get you to surgery straight away. They're preparing now, so we'll go in as soon as possible. Do you understand?"

Oh yeah. I understand alright. I'm dying...

"What... time ... is... it?" I breathed. I could barely talk with a pipe sticking out of my throat.

Ten thirty. Mum would be here soon - she was never late.

She mustn't see me like this.

I lay on my back as they stabilised me as best they could, before rushing me through the ward on my bed. The looks on the other patients' faces weren't encouraging, but they all shouted for me, wishing me luck, telling me to hang on. Their voices followed me out of the ward. I dug my fingers deep into the sides of the mattress.

Here it comes. After all this, I'm about to die.

I was scared, in incredible pain, and definitely drifting...

And then, there she was: Mum, coming round the corner in her fawn coloured raincoat, still wet from the morning drizzle.

What an elegant, beautiful woman she was. I watched her take it all in; this commotion all centred around her son being rushed from the ward, grey from head to toe, with a tube of blood sticking out of his neck.

On seeing the blood from my neck hole splattered across my chest, Mum almost dropped to the floor. But she saw the look of terror in my eyes and knew she couldn't. She ran to me and took my hands, telling me that she loved me, that everything would be OK; she'd be waiting for me, everything would be fine.

"Och son, I'm here. I'm here, Mark."

Her voice was stalling; I could tell she was close to breaking.

"Don't cry Mum... Please, don't cry."

"I won't son, I won't cry. I won't." But the tears were rolling down her cheeks.

"I'm sorry Mum... I'm so sorry Mum," I kept repeating this, over and over. I felt terrible for the trauma I'd put her through, and so sad that I'd be leaving her behind. But she just gently shushed me, intent on calming me down.

Every breath was killing me and I couldn't stop crying out from the hideous fire that had exploded inside me.

But I'd run out of time.

"'Bye Mum. I love you," I managed to whisper as she kissed me on the forehead, and then I was rushed away down the corridor. I watched her grow smaller, standing in her fawn raincoat.

Completely alone.

34

Fire and Ice

The pain hit me before the voices did. A previously inconceivable pain, obliterating the place where my abdomen used to be. This was worse - much worse - than the sudden baseball bat thwack to my liver that woke me on the bus to Kathmandu. Deeper, sharper, and infinitely more serious.

I thought that the pain alone was going to kill me, there and then. Killed by pain - I didn't even know it was possible. The doctor who had cut a hole in my neck had now been replaced by a tiger straddling my chest, ripping me apart with vicious swipes, sticking its claws into fresh, raw wounds; twisting, pulling and slicing deeper through bundles of fired up nerves.

"Mark, wake up. Can you hear me? Mark, you *have* to wake up."

My eyes snapped open and I tried to scream, but I couldn't even breathe. I tried to look around, but any movement was now a thousand times beyond excruciating. Inhaling even the tiniest little breath was almost impossible.

Nothing made sense, but I knew something major had happened. And I was one hundred percent alert - I hadn't forgotten anything; I knew I'd been in crisis, and I knew I'd just said goodbye to Mum.

A nurse leaned over me.

"Mark, you've had a very big operation. We're just going to keep you here for a little while. Do you understand?"

I can't breathe. I can't breathe.

Masked faces were flitting around above me.

"Mark, you have to stay awake. Keep your eyes open."

I can't. I can't breathe.

I had to concentrate. I had to get an angle on the pain, because as the seconds ticked on I grew more convinced that it would kill me.

I'd had plenty of practice with handling pain in various situations and degrees over the past month, but this was a whole new, undiscovered planet of the stuff. The first obvious problem was that I couldn't breathe, which I'd thought I was already used to. But now I *really* couldn't breathe. A baby squirrel breath would be a luxury. I'd kill for one of those minuscule pockets of air to dance around in my wind pipe. I now had to learn to live on the lung capacity of a resting mole. I couldn't scream, but at the same time I couldn't *not* scream - this pain had to have a voice, but a voice needs air. My body had me in a Catch 22 headlock. Plus, I was shaking with cold right down to my icy bones, and the shivering was making the pain worse.

Then, I felt the tingling precursor of a sneeze inching into place.

Oh God, no. Not now, NO...

But I couldn't help it. My chest expanded, my organs squeezed together, my lungs sucked in all the cold air they could, and I sneezed it out again at a thousand feet per second.

And almost died.

My body jerked up and my abdomen went into spasms. The baseball bat was now being swung by the huge, vicious hand. That's what the bastard was waiting for. *He* was going to be the one to finish me off.

I hung on as the tiger buried its jaws under my ribcage and scraped and scraped 'till my eyes were rolling in my head. I desperately looked for any signs of reassurance in the faces of the young nurses. But their pained expressions told me that there was nothing they could do.

You're on your own, Mark.

Minutes passed and the pain didn't subside, not one jot - it was only getting worse. It seemed to be adding to itself, accumulating. It was no longer coming from just my reset button area - my hot coal; my bursting eggs - it was spread from my lower bowels up to my lungs. My mind jumped around, searching frantically for some kind of logical reasoning.

Why are they keeping me awake?

Why won't they give me any painkillers?

What the hell is going on?

Here's what had happened in the fourteen hours since I'd said goodbye to Mum, which had felt like only a few minutes ago:

I'd been cut open from my ribs to just below my belly button, and once inside they'd found a bacterial crime scene of destruction. The huge abscess on the front of my liver, which had burst, they burnt off with acid. They then had to reach in and roll my liver forward to burn off the smaller abscess on the rear, which apparently wasn't so small any more.

And, apparently, I died.

With my belly wide open, prised apart with metal clamps, under the brilliant lights of the operating theatre. It was all just too much for a human body to live through.

But somehow they brought me round again, sent me back under and continued the operation.

They cut out my gallbladder, and dealt with the abscess on my right lung by chopping off the bottom part of the lung. A thick pipe was then fed through my ribs into my lung. Drain pipes were inserted into my liver and gallbladder area, and throughout my abdomen.

And I died again.

Belly still open.

Again they managed to kickstart me, but decided not to continue with the operation this time.

In a mad panic they'd had to tidy up and zip me up with thirty odd stitches and eight deep stomach stitches that pierced through all the muscles of my gut. Then they'd had to take away the anaesthetic and wake me up - quickly. The only way I could survive would be to remain conscious.

That was why I was in such an agonising state. It also explained why the operating staff were huddled around me when I had first woken up.

But of course I didn't know any of this as I lay there trying not to breathe, yet simultaneously trying to remain alive.

I clung onto the nurse's hand, trying my hardest to control my breathing.

"Pain...kill...ers." *Please.*

"Soon, Mark, soon. Just keep breathing."

I had to build on my previous skill of breathing without breathing. The trouble with learning to breathe is that you don't have long to master it - like a bird learning to fly, pushed from its nest on the walls of a tall cliff. I tried to imagine the air flowing into my lungs like air through an open window, floating round the room and flowing out again. I wiggled my toes and fingers, like imaginary fans, wafting tiny currents of air up to my mouth. It was like trying to reach a state of calm whilst the tigers fight the hyenas over who gets to rip your heart out the next time it dared to beat.

Without my previously learnt skills, I'd be dead for sure. But over the next several minutes, I managed to skim the air in and out of my lungs, and, very cleverly, not die again.

Once I'd stumbled over that major hurdle, I was wheeled into a side room, which to me felt like a narrow corridor. The nurse didn't let go of my hand - not that I'd have let her. I squeezed and squeezed as every whisper of breath ripped through me, like the world's smallest cyclone. I begged her for painkillers and water. She assured me they'd be coming soon.

Keep skimming that air in, Mark…

I felt some people moving down the corridor at speed towards me, slowing as they neared my bed.

"Och, Mark…" Mum and Dad were beside me.

"Oh son, what have they done…" Tears were rolling down their drained faces, their eyes flitting around, trying to comprehend their son in that freezing cold corridor in the middle of the night, lying outside an operating theatre, attached to pipes and machines, and obviously in big, big trouble.

The hospital had phoned them, and told them to come and say goodbye to me. Told them I'd already died twice. Their twenty minute drive must've felt about as long as my Kathmandu bus journey.

My mum was my mum: the most wonderful mum a boy could wish for. She could barely speak, but she didn't need words. She was with me all the way.

They took hold of my hands, which gave the nurse a break, and gently stroked my hair. My eyes jumped between the two of them, desperately looking for help.

My dad leaned down to kiss my brow. As he did, he lightly brushed against the thin sheet that was doing nothing to keep me warm, and sent me into a hideous cycle of pain-scream-pain-scream. He jumped back, terrified that he'd killed me. There was so little of me left to kill after the abscesses and the incredible surgeons had finished with me.

Shortly after this, the nurses ushered them out to leave. It was clearly too distressing for me, and I needed every ounce of strength and concentration just to try and handle the pain and my breathing. And to pray that I didn't bloody sneeze again.

They never did get to say goodbye to me.

So began the new longest night of my life. It knocked all the others for six.

When every tiny breath has to be controlled, time goes very, very slowly. My one and only aim was to not let my diaphragm move. In the small hours I was given the tiniest slither of ice to hold in my mouth and wet my lips. It was like a tiny, cool oasis in a huge desert of fire, and I held it on my tongue and swabbed it around until it melted away to nothing. I gripped the nurse's hand for the next six hours as she sat with me until morning, trying to keep me calm, talking to me, telling me stories of her own life, as my abdomen writhed and summersaulted and burned from the scalpels and acids and manhandling. I never let go of her for a minute. I begged over and over for water and painkillers, and it was her job to keep deflecting me. She couldn't just say: "If we give you any medication it will kill you."

The inferno in my abdomen never receded all night, but morning did come, and I was still alive, and still in what I believed to be a corridor. My nurse was incredible. She probably had to spend the next day in surgery herself, after what I'd put her hand through.

After another visit from a doctor, a nurse finally rocked up with the only thing I wanted to see: a morphine drip. I was hooked up and the taps were turned on, and maybe eight hours after being zipped up and woken up, I felt a small trickle of relief.

But it was only just enough morphine to take the edge off. I was too weak for a full whack of the glorious stuff, though that was what I craved most. But at least I could breathe a tiny bit better now, which was hopefully all the help I'd need to see me through.

I asked for my parents, and when they arrived I even managed a small smile. Mum's hands were shaking; her face almost as grey as my skin had turned when I exploded. Her night was probably worse than mine. They sat with me for another hour, no one saying anything, but it was still too distracting for me. I had to concentrate on breathing and surviving.

Then, after a couple more hours, I was told that I'd soon be moved into intensive care. This involved trundling through the corridors on my trolley.

I clung onto the sides of the trolley, and my poor nurse's hand, and onto each tiny pocket of air I could manage to inhale for as long as possible, as the bumps travelled around my freshly ripped apart tummy.

Once installed in my corner in the intensive care ward, I was again hooked up to a bank of monitoring machines. Only then did I get a handle on how desperate my situation was, as the nurses settled me in and arranged the various multi-coloured bags attached to multiple tubes that all emerged from different parts of me.

I eventually managed to tilt my head enough to look down, and wished I hadn't.

Ten pipes were snaking out from under my gown, each carrying a different coloured fluid. Green, black, red... all the different types of unidentifiable goo I'd been passing since my time in the Himalayas.

The neck pipe was still in place, but to compliment it a thick piece of hose now also drained out between my ribs from my right lung, several smaller pipes emerged from various hot spots around my abdomen, one emerged from each arm, and for good measure, one came out of my penis.

Oh God, no wonder Mum and Dad looked shocked. What the hell have they done to me?

But I had no time to ponder. Even with the small dose of morphine, movement remained virtually impossible. I still had to concentrate on my shallow breathing. One breath out of place and it could easily be curtains.

My family and Maria all came to the ward later that morning. Everything was terrible enough from where I was lying, but they all had to look at my failing body; my new set of pipes, the monitors bleeping, with the aftermath of the operation and the shock of the previous night quite clearly reflected back up at them. It wasn't a good day for anyone.

I drifted in and out of consciousness, but mostly just lay as quiet and still as I could, trying to move the air in and out of my lungs without moving. No one could help; they could only sit quietly and watch.

Maria couldn't handle it for more than a few minutes. She stared at the bags with complete confusion and horror, and sat silently fidgeting, barely looking at me, gnawing at her bright red nails.

But my family sat beside my bed until night came.

The surgeon, an Egyptian fellow, and his entourage came to see me mid afternoon. He was incredibly curt.

"Aha! He lives! You are a very lucky young man." He paraded around the bed, not really looking at me, which I thought was odd. Maybe that comes with the territory - he'd seen what was inside me. But he had an unpleasant manner, and a dismissive way of answering my parents' questions.

"What was wrong, Doctor?" Mum asked.

"Wrong? Everything was wrong! You don't need the details. Just be thankful you've still got a son."

Tell me what bloody happened, you rude man. And don't speak to my mum like that.

"Uh huh. But what can we expect now?" Dad asked.

"Well we'll just have to wait and see, won't we?" He said this in an arrogant, almost sarcastic way, like it was the dumbest question he'd ever heard.

I couldn't believe it. I was in awe of him - he had saved my life, and

I wanted to thank him. There was absolutely no need for him to be so brusque. Maybe I'd ruined his dinner party or something.

When he cleared off, his assistant hung back for a chat. She could see that I was shocked by the surgeon's manner. She was a young English doctor, and happy to tell us what she could about what they'd found upon opening me up.

She said that the smell had been unbelievable, which didn't surprise me in the least; I knew I was rotting inside. And of course, this was all very sudden and unplanned, so they had no idea what had really happened. From what they could tell, the main abscess had burst and drained into my bile duct, which hangs off the liver and heads into the gallbladder. That would've been the blood I was passing the previous morning. They burnt off the remainder of the abscess with acid, and did the same to the smaller one at the back, which, in her opinion, would've burst very soon too. They dealt with the abscess on my lung by slicing the bottom of my lung off. They quickly removed my badly diseased gallbladder. That was the last thing they did before tucking everything else back in place and quickly stitching me up.

She never mentioned the double dying. Probably best to save that for later.

"You know, Mark, it's a miracle you're alive today. The surgeon was incredible. And we didn't think you would survive the aftermath. You've done amazingly well."

Bloody hell. I should be dead. This is incredible.

The only part that made me feel really uncomfortable was the use of acid on my liver. That really got into my imagination - hissing, smoking, bubbling, searing away at the flesh. I thought I could still feel it burning away inside, taking the place of the burning coal. All the other surgical procedures I was fine with. More than fine - I was fascinated. And more than anything, I was relieved. Because this fantastic woman was telling me that the things that were killing me were gone from my body.

My mum and dad looked horrified.

"And what happens now, Doctor?" Dad managed, in a shaky voice.

"Well, we'll just keep monitoring him, and hope everything is OK."

Oh shit, I'm not living on hope now, am I?

It was obvious that I wasn't out of the woods yet. I still thought the pain might kill me, especially if I had to scream out - which I did, often. And my breathing problem was ongoing. And I could tell I was very, very weak.

What else can happen to you when you've hit rock bottom?

35

Invaded and Inflated

Evening was always my worst time in hospital, but that night my morphine drip was increased a notch. Another slight edge was shaved off the pain ball.

The lovely morphine just about detached me slightly from what was going on down below. I would have happily taken a triple dosage and spent the night on Planet Oblivio, but that wasn't going to happen.

A couple of days went by in intensive care, slowly, with my family almost constantly by my side. I woke once and my younger sister Alison was by the bed, staring at me with the as-to-be-expected look of shocked anxiety. I whispered her a hello, and drifted off. She'd returned from her holiday to be met by Mum and Dad at the airport with the news that I was in a bad way.

Unfortunately, I wasn't doing very well. I was freezing cold, deep inside. Heaters were brought to my bed, but they did nothing to help. I needed bone heaters in my marrow - or an electric blanket turned up to 'slow cook.' I lay shivering under my thin sheet for hours on end. Even with the morphine coursing through me, the shivering was hugely painful on my traumatised innards.

Doctors were constantly prodding and poking me with their fingers, and sticking really long metal pipes up my bum. The distress of being turned over was always the worst part. All my tubes and drips had to be rearranged to flip me onto my left side. Then the doctor would line up his metal pipe with my worried little round target: whumph. And I'd be rolled back over again.

"17 cm! A new record!" One doctor exclaimed - a little too enthusiastically for my liking - after withdrawing a pipe from deep inside me.

Maria was acting peculiar, as usual. My parents were finding it very difficult to tolerate her silent fidgeting, or worse, her crazy chattering, so whenever she arrived they'd wander outside and leave us for an hour. She never stayed long though - the intensive care situation made her edgy, which is understandable. I don't know why I didn't tell her to stop coming. Her visits didn't relax me, I didn't look forward to them - if anything, they stressed me. I knew she was leaving soon to go back to the Canary Islands to live, and so I should just have let it all fizzle away. But intensive care units are a really bad place for a breakup - far too much beeping, humming and near-death experiences going on. I was still convinced she was feeling guilty about something, and it had to do with her curse. I'd had a lot of time to think, though very little time to think clearly. I'd concluded that she probably put a spell on me to return to her from India. But she hadn't really been specific enough, and I had returned, but almost in a box. Which was why she was feeling guilty. Be careful what you wish for - or rather, be careful what you hex for.

I still thought it best to keep this to myself.

Every day, there she would be: teetering around, clacking up and down the intensive care ward in her heels, skirt flicking around her tiny waist.

"Who dresses like that to come to a hospital, son?" asked my mum.

Christ, not many dress like that to go out to the pub!

One afternoon, Maria pulled the curtains all around my bed, sat down and began to run her hands up and down my leg, under the sheet.

What are you doing? Bloody hell, I can barely breathe!

I tried to convey a warning with my eyes, but she carried on with her hands, leaning over me, rubbing herself against my arm.

"Is that good, my darling?" she whispered into my ear in her sexy Spanish accent.

Yes? No? I don't know. Help!

It was kind of like the opposite of joining the mile-high club: I was in the rock-bottom club. The recently crash-landed club.

Her hand was well on its way now, raising my heart beat and need for more oxygen than the mole-at-rest breathing could provide. I was starting to panic.

Suddenly, the curtains flung open and a young Aussie nurse came bowling in. Maria sprang away from the bed, leaving me in a very obvious state of excitement.

"What are you doing to him?! For God's sake girl, he can hardly breathe! Leave him alone, or you'll kill him!" she barked furiously, pulling the sheets over me.

Maria acted dumb, turned on her heel and click-clacked back down the corridor; every nurse, doctor and patient's eyes were on her as she wiggled out of sight.

"Wow, what is going on with that girlfriend of yours?" the Aussie nurse asked me, shaking her head. "That *has* to be a first."

Blink blink blink.

She bewitched me and feels guilty. Only I know.

Maybe she's trying to kill me before anyone finds out.

"Oh well," she nodded at my sheets, "at least one part of you is still working."

The next morning I was lying in bed, cold and shivery as usual, just about getting over the long, lonely night. I was resting, eyes shut, concentrating as ever on my breaths.

"Here you go, mate! I think he might be sleeping though." The Aussie nurse was at the foot of my bed. I opened my eyes.

Sean!

"Bloody hell, Mark..." His mouth hung open as he surveyed the calamity stretched out in front of him, attached to numerous revolting bags and drips and bleeping machines.

"You poor bastard. Shit." He had his bag over his shoulders and was looking fit and well, with a bit of weight back on his bones.

"I just got in... called your mum from the airport..." He could hardly get any words out. It'd been two and a half weeks since they bundled me through the airport at Kathmandu. I could see his brain trying to compute what might've gone on.

"Hello Sean," I whispered.

"God, they've had a go at you, haven't they? Did you say something to annoy them?"

I smiled.

"Did you ... sell the guitar?"

"Yeah! We did." His eyes roamed all over my tubes and bags - I looked like I was being emptied out; drained off.

"Your neck... did they cut a hole in your neck?"

"Yes. Tell me about the guitar."

"Well we sold it the next day, got about twenty quid for it. Gavin turned up! Craig's mate from Tesco - Greebo. We all bought matching green and red hippy outfits. Looked bloody ridiculous, like Hippy Dave crossed with Robin Hood. We got really drunk in Freak Street, and Gavin said something to a waiter and the staff all started shouting and throwing chairs at us. He reckons he only asked for some more cream for his chocolate cake. They chased us up Freak Street in our hippy gear - it was hilarious!"

"Well," I managed, smiling, "he does like cream."

He sat by the bed. I couldn't really speak, and I needed to rest. I dozed off and on until my dad turned up and gave Sean a lift home.

"I'll come back soon. Hang in there, tiger."

"Grrrrrrr."

It was good to see him, as ever. I fell asleep again.

The arrogant surgeon returned to see me that afternoon. He'd decided it was time for me to try and sit in a chair for a while.

"No! No, no," I pleaded, "Can't sit up."

"Nonsense!" he said. "Up you get." Then he powered off out of the ward.

Mum and my younger sister Alison were there when they finally convinced me to try and move. The bed head was slowly raised, folding my chest up, contracting my guts, and I screamed as best I could.

"Please... not yet."

"We have to get you moving, up you come." The nurses had been given their orders.

Everyone - Mum and Alison included - grabbed a couple of bags each, hooked pipes over their arms, and tried to lift me up and out the bed.

Ooooooooohhhhhhhh.

My head was light and spinning, and I could feel my blood pressure drop. They somehow lifted me up and out, and eased me onto the big brown armchair beside my bed, rearranging my bags and tubes in a circle around me as my guts did somersaults and dragged my organs around inside. Waves of pain rose from my bowels up to my chest. Mum and Alison were sitting in front of me, watching me writhe and silently scream, trying desperately to catch a breath. My face was contorting with the pain, and there was nothing I could do to stop the cycle. It was the most horrible feeling - like my organs were swapping places with each other.

Maybe five long minutes later, Alison ran off to fetch the nurses, unable to bear it any longer. I lifted my head from my chest and looked at Mum between twisted gurns, and I saw the anguish on her face. She had tears in her eyes and her mouth was trembling, and as the nurses gathered round me I saw her run out of the ward, covering her face.

I was put back into bed, very slowly and with a lot of very disturbed screams. I felt worse than before, like I'd unsettled something that was just about working out where to settle.

The doctors were never far away, with their anal probes and prodding fingers, checking for any signs of fresh blood in my bowel, which would have meant big trouble. There was no way I could have survived even the most minor of operations at that stage.

And not long after I was put back in bed, there it was for all to see: blood on my gown.

I can't describe the pain that followed as my stomach cramped up. The morphine, or pethidine, no longer touched the sides. The cramps were coming every few minutes, pulling me inwards and twisting on themselves until my whole abdomen felt like it was attacking me.

After one of many conferring huddles at the foot of my bed, the doctors decided I was to be taken for a barium enema. They had to know where the blood was coming from before working out what the hell to do about it, and their options were limited.

I was told I'd be taken in half an hour. Though my guts were knotting and twisting, in my addled thinking I thought that if I'd be having an enema shortly, I'd try to hang onto whatever was trying to force its way out of me. Lifting myself even the tiniest amount to slide over a bedpan would've been hell.

So I hung on to whatever was in there.

What the hell is inside me anyway? I haven't eaten yet...

The orderlies came and I was again wheeled away. I was actually relieved because by now I was busting to let go of what was inside me. I was taken to another far-flung outpost of St Peter's, and my favourite nurse from intensive care came along, holding my hand as we bumped down the corridors. I learned that the supervising doctor - the Queen of Barium Enemas - was a Scottish woman.

Ah good.

That made me feel a lot more comfortable. I had no idea what a barium enema was - as should be the case for all sentient beings. But I did know that an enema was a short fused bowel-emptying grenade rolled in through the back door.

The barium enema lounge was a room with an impressive machine decked with gauges, dials, hoses and pipes - if humans had tyres that needed changing, this was the kind of room they'd end up in. I was told rather bluntly to roll onto my side. I tried to explain how this was virtually impossible – the pain, my tubes, the bags... But the Scottish doctor cut me off.

"Och nonsense. Come on, get to it now, son."

She took hold of my skinny shoulder and bony hip and rolled me over, forcing me to reassess my belief that all Scottish women were perfect.

I lay gasping on the cold, plastic bed. An hour had passed since I'd taken the executive decision to hang onto the payload inside, and the pressure was mounting.

"Doctor... I have to go to..."

She lifted my gown and gelled me up. Brave lady.

"So - first thing we do is put this big pipe up you, and then we'll pump air up it to inflate your bowels and intestine..."

You're gonna do what? Put a bagpipe up me?

My eyes widened in horror. Was this the special equipment that you couldn't get hold of in Nepal?

"When you're nice and inflated we pump the barium in. You'll feel that as a wee bit cold. Then we'll ask you to hold it in for a few minutes whilst we take some X-rays."

I'd made a terrible miscalculation. This was no ordinary evacuate-the-building enema; no procedure designed to lighten the load within. This was top of the range, anally induced torture. No wonder they couldn't get it past customs in Nepal.

Through gritted teeth, I tried to salvage the situation.

"Ahhhh... Doctor - I... really need to go... to the toilet before..."

"Shhh now boy. We need to get on. You're not the only sick person in this hospital you know!"

"No... you don't understand-"

Whumph!

In went the tube. My eyes shot out of my head, hit the far wall and returned to their widened sockets.

"Aaaaarrrrgghhhhh! NO stop, I *have* t-"

Hissssssssss. The air pump began. I clawed at the bed as I felt the creeping inflation of my bowel, like one of those long, thin, stubborn kids' balloons inflating inch by inch as the wall of high-pressure air creeps along, expanding the rubber as it goes.

"Doctor - no, I can't! Stop! You... HAVE to stop!"

I have been tortured by a bagpipe. Of that, there is no doubt.

Again, I thought I was going to die from the pain. Except that this time, the pain was being directly inflicted on me by a Scottish warrior woman.

My nurse began to look increasingly agitated as my features ran around my face looking for help.

She tried to intervene.

"Doctor, I think this might be too much for-"

"Och rubbish - I do these all day."

"NOOOOOOO!" I scream-gasped, "STOP!"

When the air seemed to be inflating my ribcage from below, and my acid-seared liver was pushing up onto my chopped lungs, and my fresh wound felt it was ripping apart at the seams, the hissing stopped. The room fell silent. I lay there like a stuck pig; eyes locked onto my nurse as I tried to comprehend this foolhardy madness.

No one giggled.

Those sheep on windy-grass! No wonder they bloody kill themselves.

"Now - here comes the barium!" the doctor said jollily, as if she were introducing Coco the Clown to a kid's party, and not shoving radioactive porridge through a bagpipe stuck up my anus.

The thick, cold fluid was delivered to my cavernous digestive tract as my facial features rewrote the book of gurning. I clutched, clawed and grabbed at the table, shrieking and moaning like a persecuted donkey.

On and on it came, forcing its way up through me like oozing cold larva.

"NOOOOOOO! STOP! YOU'RE... KILLING ME!"

"Och shut up now, it's not that bad."

This is it. Here I go.

I whimpered and made some odd squeaking noises down below.

"Doctor, NO! *Please,* I'm going t- "

POP!

My bowel fought back. With one huge, violent cramp I expelled the pipe from my arse. The doctor leapt back in surprise, but she wasn't anywhere near quick enough.

First the barium shot out of me, under huge pressure, splattering her. This was followed by a bowel load of blood and other such foulness, and a cubic hectare of high pressure wind that had turned decidedly odorous from being inside my gut for too long. I looked over my shoulder at her, and she gaped back at me, with a splattering of my revolting gut debris sprayed over her white coat.

"Told you... I needed... to go."

I'm sure I saw my nurse smile.

Trouble was, I hadn't made it to the X-ray stage yet. So I had to go through the whole procedure again. It was awful, but nowhere near as bad as undertaking the process with an already full bowel.

So I had the double-barium-enema experience. Lucky boy. Not a great morning, for me or the doctor. I hope she's since enjoyed telling the story as much as I have.

"And then, silly me - I should've listened to the poor wee thing, the pipe shot right out of his arse – remember my face was only inches away – and I was covered in blooded shite and barium and almost had my hair blown off by his foul wind! Och, Roger, you should've seen the look on my face! Ho ho ho."

My nurse put a complaint in against her. I'd already made my feelings pretty clear.

36

Back and Forth

A couple of hours later, after I'd been inflated, deflated and mapped in glorious X-rays, the news wasn't good: the barium enema failed to show where the bleeding was coming from. Could have been my liver, or the spot where my gall bladder had previously occupied, or anywhere else in my ripped apart gut. Take your pick.

As the day wore on my fever returned and I felt the weakest I'd ever felt, with the unsettled feeling inside me intensifying; like something sharp was twisting or pulling. The barium enema news was a blow for all of us, and my family huddled around my bed. All the doctors could say was that they'd have to just wait and hope for the best. Then evening came, and my family had to go home again. No one was saying much.

That night, I began to feel like I wasn't really there anymore. Faces, shapes and voices seemed to come and go, drifting around my bed. The horses and the hand were back again, and the ward grew dark and menacing. Even the ever-smiling, ever-present nurses now seemed sinister to me. I was convinced that something untoward was going on just beyond my reach of vision, but I couldn't settle on what. This had been a constant theme since up in the hills, but it never grew any less scary. I heard strange whisperings behind me, and I was sure I could see the other patients being taken away somewhere in the dark. There was always a kind of commotion going on somewhere over to my right, but if I glanced that way everything would look normal.

My parents were in bed asleep, exhausted from the constant worrying, when the phone beside their bed rang, jolting them awake in an instant. The last time it had rung at night was after my operation, when I was in the corridor.

My dad answered the phone to the Sister from the intensive care unit. "Hello, Mr Giblin. I'm sorry, but you'd better come in - Mark is very distressed. He's shouting for you both - we don't think he has long left. The doctor doesn't think he'll make it to the morning."

They threw on some clothes, jumped in the car again and drove the five miles through the empty streets, back to St Peter's.

And then - suddenly, my parents appeared again in the half-light, their tearful faces lit up by the green and red lights on my monitoring machines. I was very confused.

"Why are you here? It's night-time, isn't it?"

"We just wanted to see you, son," my mum whispered, as she gripped my hand. "Just relax, we're here."

"Something's going on. There's people over there - I don't trust them..."

"It's just the nurses, they're here to help you, Mark."

But why are they scurrying about, whispering and dragging things around..?

I drifted further away, holding on to Mum and Dad. I had a horrible feeling that the world had sort of receded, like it was just beyond my reach; a dream I couldn't quite remember. But I knew it was still there. Everything became very still and very silent. Even the horses. They stood in the corner of wherever I was, which in a way was even more frightening than them hoofing around. I don't know where the hand was - maybe it was wrapped around me. Or gone to open a door...

I woke to the morning sounds of the nurses doing their rounds. My parents must have stepped out for some air. The cheery breakfast lady came past and smiled, as she always did. On her way back up the ward she stopped at the end of my bed.

"Still here then? That's good. I heard you were a gonner last night!"

What? 'Gonner'? What's she on about?

I don't know what shocked me more - finding out I was almost "a gonner" during the night, or that I'd found this out from the breakfast lady.

Hang on, was that why Mum and Dad were here during the night? Oh shit...

Mum and Dad returned, with Amanda and Alison. They all huddled around my bed.

"… Did I nearly die last night?"

"You weren't very good, son," Dad said, trying to talk through the break in his voice. "But you're still here, kid."

Mum and the girls smiled weakly, fighting off more tears.

The ward didn't look ominous anymore, but I wasn't any better than the previous day. Weak, feverish, freezing, bleeding from behind, and writhing with the never-ending contortions of my abdomen. That afternoon Maria came to visit, though I was far too weak for any real interaction. My family sat with me all morning, but they made themselves scarce when Maria arrived. She sat beside my bed and I lay, exhausted, watching her.

I still had all ten tubes and pipes attached to me. The thick, clear tube to my lung was the biggest, and along with the one in my neck, the most uncomfortable. Its unenviable task was to drain the fluids out of my lung - the mess left behind from the abscess and the surgery. The pipe snuck out between my ribs, out the gap in my gown and down the side of the bed to the collection jar, which was a big plastic bottle incorporating an S bend, like in a toilet.

This worked to keep the vacuum to my lungs intact, for obvious reasons. You can't just have the air from your lung hissing down a pipe straight out to the outside world, otherwise we'd all be doing it - and some of us would be fitting whistles and colourful balloons over the end. The fluid dribbled endlessly from my damaged lung, down the pipe, into the bottle. Every few hours a nurse would come and empty the bottle.

Once she'd recovered from the shock of my external plumbing system, Maria was fascinated by my multiple tube drainage setup. She gazed at all the pipes snaking around my bed. After a while, she began to fiddle with my lung juice bottle, tipping it this way and that, swirling it around. God knows why, because the stuff that was coming out of me was visibly disgusting. The jar had a big screw top, which is where the pipe went in.

"It looks full, don't you think, Mark?"

I watched as Maria began to unscrew the lid, seemingly in slow motion. We looked at one another, and she twisted her hand again… The lid raised higher on its thread. Even though the drugs I was on were pretty strong, I knew that as soon as she popped that lid off, the vacuum to my lung would be broken. I could only presume what would then happen – the air from my lung would wheeze out of the dangling tube, my lung would rapidly collapse, and in my weakened state, that would almost definitely be curtains.

I couldn't even motion to Maria to stop; I felt like I was in a dream. All I could do was stare, transfixed, as her delicate hand slowly twisted away. I pictured myself whizzing round the ward like a deflating balloon with a shrivelled face, and ending up flattened out behind a cabinet.

But just before the pop and the hiss could whisk me off, my dad appeared round the corner. It took him a few seconds to understand what he was seeing before he made a hasty grab for my lung juice bottle.

"What the hell are you doing?! You'll kill him, you fool!"

Maria jumped up.

"The nurses told me to keep the fluids level – I... I was just tipping the bottle. Promise."

Dad was horrified. I'd never seen him look so confused. He called a nurse over.

"Nurse, have you ever asked Maria to mess aboot with this bawttle?"

It was the Australian nurse - the one who'd caught Maria trying to give me a pleasuring a couple of days before.

She snorted and turned on Maria. "Those bottles should NEVER be touched by ANYONE other than the trained nurses! What do you think this is, a playground? If you can't leave Mark alone, you should NOT be in here."

Now that was an awkward few minutes. Maria sat by the bed, looking at the floor, biting her red nails down to the quick; foot-tapping like crazy. I lay there not knowing what the hell was real and what wasn't, and Dad stood over us both, on guard, trying to fathom the unfathomable.

Unsurprisingly, Maria went home not long afterwards. I couldn't get my head round the lung-tube incident - I knew it was real, because Dad had walked in on it. But what was she doing? Was she going to empty it onto the floor? Why? What was I doing? I could've called out to her, though talking still wasn't easy. The whole spell theory was really messing with me, and adding to the dark fears and visions I already had floating around my head.

If it was a reality check I was in need of, I didn't have long to wait. Soon after Maria went home, a nurse came to change the big dressing that ran from my chest to my groin. I'd been eyeing the thing off for a few days now, but hadn't really tried to imagine what carnage was under there. I peeked down as she slowly peeled the white dressing and gauze away, revealing - inch by horrible inch - a thick, livid red line that ran down from my sternum, stopping just past my belly button. Horrible black stitches zig-zagged down either side. It seemed to go on and on, like a huge, fat, ugly centipede. Eight thick plastic tubes, about four inches long, cushioned the deep stomach stitches that crossed the line of normal stitching. The drain pipes ran out of little red slices to the right of the wound.

My head hit the pillow. Until I saw that, I don't think I'd been able to comprehend the true devastation that had been unfolding in my guts as I stumbled around Nepal. It's all very well being told that you've been operated on, but a huge scar running the length of your belly is a sobering sight, especially on such an emaciated body. It was so vicious and fresh.

I lay very quietly for hours. I knew I had some thinking to do. I was still Mark in my head, but all I had to do was tilt my chin down - and there, stretched out beneath me, was a body I didn't recognise any more. It made me feel sort of nauseous. Though I already had quite a tasty scar where the bike speedo had ripped into my sides, this new scar was an inflamed monster in comparison.

I drifted the remainder of the day away, not even sure who was around the bed. Night-time must've happened, because it always did. Then morning came again - and I didn't know much about it.

My younger sister Alison had only just returned from Crete, and was still in shock at the state of my sickness. Mum, Dad, Amanda and Alison were constantly phoning each other - "Who's at the hospital? Who's going in next?"

That morning, whilst at work, Alison had a sudden, strong feeling that something terrible had happened. Oddly, no-one was beside my bed at the time. Maybe Mum had spent all night there and gone home for a few hours. So Alison drove to the hospital in a panic, and rushed into intensive care to discover a commotion around my bed. A nurse stopped her on the way in.

"I think you should sit down... I'm sorry, you can't see Mark at the moment. We've called your parents - they're on their way. There was no real warning... but Mark died a few moments ago."

Alison staggered back, the pink glow from the Cretan sun quickly disappearing as the blood drained from her face.

"We got to him very quickly..."

The curtains remained drawn around my bed, and she watched helplessly from the end of the room as doctors and nurses ran in and out.

After all that, he died on his own. Oh, Mark...

37

Slight Pop

I woke up with doctors and nurses all surrounding me, equipment being moved and orders barked. I thought I'd had another operation, as the pain was back in full force and I couldn't breathe again. Everything was really slow, like it was all happening elsewhere - possibly to me, but I wasn't sure.

"Mark - can you hear me?"

Yes. I could. But there was no air or energy to respond.

Blink Blink Blink.

I'm here. I'm alive, I think.

Then my parents were beside me, and Alison and Amanda. And I could feel the morphine again. *Thank god.*

"Did I have another operation?" I whispered.

Mum just shook her head, gripping hold of my hand, unable to speak.

Oh shit. Did I nearly die again...?

Late afternoon, I lay beside my beeping, flashing machines, holding Mum's hand.

"If I ever get out of here Mum... I'm going to settle down, buy a car... and live like everyone else does."

She looked at me and smiled a familiar, knowing smile.

"Aye, son. We'll see." The tears rolled down her face again.

It was a resigned and loving smile. She'd watched her little boy climb the rusty garden fence and escape into the fields to roam the countryside - first on foot, and then pushbike - she'd seen him swept up by music and friends and motorbikes, and then run from England as soon as a fresh passport and a fistful of travellers cheques would allow. Maybe, in a way, she thought she'd lost me years before this had all happened.

But she never had. She'd even saved my life on the glacier when I screamed out for her.

Most of my travelling mates were well on their way to Australia by this point. I was getting hilarious letters from all over the place, once the word had spread that I wasn't well – Tibet, China, Thailand, Singapore, Hong Kong, the Philippines, Bali, Sydney. That was the glorious free life I was missing out on. I could taste the beaches, the parties and the mountains pouring out of the letters. The one thing missing from those ludicrous adventures was me.

But that centipede scar on my belly really rammed home all that had happened. I was done with travelling. Travelling, I'd discovered, could kill you.

I was still passing blood and severely doubted my chances of getting out of there alive. I was so weakened by all I'd had to do to get to this point: the physical trauma of my ridiculous journey from Nepal, the weeks of drugs, the operation and its emotional aftermath, the ongoing guilt and sadness that I felt whenever I looked my mum in the eye. Not to mention all the dying. And the hexing. And the confusion over the lung-juice incident.

There wasn't much more anyone could do for me; if the bleeding continued then that'd be it - goodnight all. And quickly, by the look of things.

One more night maybe?

A doctor came round for another examination with his pipe-of-pain. A team of nurses helped roll me over. The first thing he said was "Well, there's no blood on your gown, Mark. Let's have a look inside." *Close your eyes, knees up, wahey!*

He fiddled around whilst I grimaced and tried not to wriggle away from the pressure as his pipe inched along its well-travelled path.

"Well, I can't see any fresh blood," he said, re-emerging from my interiors. "That, young man, is a very good sign."

I looked at Mum, and saw the hope in her tired, brown eyes. That was the first real good news I'd had in weeks. I dared to think that I'd been wrong to start doubting a recovery was possible.

"Och son, that's fantastic news. Ohhhhhhh." She clutched hold of my hand, which looked so weak and boney and ugly against hers, and tried to control herself from screaming with joy.

"Wait 'till we tell your dad, son, he's been so worried."

We had to wait a couple more hours for the next test, and I lay as still as I could, willing my insides to remain sealed. This is it. Make or break time. One more lot of blood, and I knew I'd be done. How could I come back from that? Mum knew it too.

The nurses rolled me over. The doctor wielded his divining rod. Up it went. Out it came.

The doctor looked at me, and once again the lips signalled the news before they'd said a word - he smiled.

"No blood."

"But," he cautioned, "we really need a good twenty four hours of this - but it's very encouraging. Then we'll start you on some food, and hopefully your system will kick into action again."

Dad turned up with my sisters, and Mum beamed with delight as she told them the news. As she spoke she hardly ever took her eyes off me - like it was fragile news, easily reversible - which I suppose it was. But it was a fantastic moment after a long line of incredible setbacks - and not one of those setbacks had yet managed to finish me off. Well, they had, but the skills of the doctors and nurses had brought me back. It was almost official - I was one incredibly lucky young man.

After a couple more days in intensive care, with no more blood and no more incidents, I was released back into a normal post-op ward, and greeted warmly by the ward Sister.

"Hello Mr. Giblin! We've heard all about you and your merry dance back from Mount Everest."

"Well it wasn't quite Mount Everest, it was…"

"Shhh shhh… Don't go ruining a good story, now!" she laughed.

I felt so much better. My breathing was growing stronger and slightly deeper, and the pain from my liver and surrounding damage zone was dropping down several levels to merely 'extremely painful' - which the morphine could easily deal with. My fevers had subsided, though I was still finding it very difficult to relax enough to get a good sleep. My mum beamed with pride as I was wheeled over to my new bed. Doctors and nurses from the various stages of my recovery frequently dropped in for a chat. There was a great bunch of men in the ward, and they drilled me over and over about my story.

"What? So you were how many days away from the nearest town? And you couldn't get a bus? That's bloody insane! Call that a holiday? What the 'ell were you doing there in the first place?"

"So they kicked you out of the 'ospital 'cos you never 'ad insurance! That's criminal. Bloody Yanks. Why didn't you just go to an English clinic then?"

Shit, never thought of that. Not for one moment.

Maria popped by a few times during the week, but was still visibly sheepish after the lung bottle incident. The middle-aged bricky in the next bed would put his paper down, fold his arms over his chest and take in the show as she click-clacked around my bed, fussing over me, or she'd perch on the chair, skirt riding high, her stockinged thigh flexing as her foot tap-tapped away.

"How the hell did you get a bird like that, mate? I mean, no offence, but you look like John McEnroe's sick brother. She must be like one of them scar perverts. You wanna watch her! She'll talk you into chopping a limb off next."

Maria still had a kind of hold over me. Now the life and death situation was seemingly over, my spell notion had receded to just an occasional doubt about her odd behaviour. I put the lung-juice incident in the too-hard-to-understand corner, and thought it best to leave it there. We even talked about the possibility of me going to visit her in Spain - when I'd recovered enough to actually move. She was leaving with her family in a few weeks. At least it gave me something to think about - something outside of hospital.

After a couple of days in the ward, I felt that I wanted to try to walk. I'd managed a few sitting sessions on the bedside chairs - thankfully none as awful as the first attempt that preceded the bleeding. But now Mum and a nurse slowly helped me from my bed, gathered my tubes and bags and hooked them onto two drip stands. Red, black, green, yellow, clear – unbelievable. Mum took hold of one stand and put one arm around me. I lay heavy against her shoulder, still nowhere near able to stand upright - anything less than a thirty degree tilt forward felt like I was ripping my wound apart. Grabbing hold of the other drip stands for more support, I took a step.

I grimaced, wobbled, contorted and nearly fainted.

But after a few moments, we carried on. Mum and I, step by slow, shuffling step, made our way up the ward, past all the other beds. The other patients, the ward sister and the nurses cheered and clapped me along, and I thought Mum would explode with joy. Her face was glowing. We turned around and slowly walked back.

Taking those steps, there in St Peter's Hospital, was one of the best moments of my life. We'd made it: me and Mum together. The trip now had a highlight - one I would never have expected three long months previously, and one I would never forget.

I still couldn't sleep very well though. Nights were particularly bad - they seemed to last forever, but by now - thankfully - the devil's hand and the horses had vanished. I liked to think that I'd beaten them - but I was careful not to feel too cocky about it. They still knew where I lived.

The next best thing that happened that week was eating food again. My brother Eric had returned from cycling around France, and he brought in a kiwi fruit. I'd never seen one before.

"Here you go, Mark, get that into you - no, you nutter, peel it first."

My boney fingers ripped the hairy skin off, and the green, juicy flesh hit my taste buds like a tropical bomb going off in my mouth. If ever a taste was like travelling to the equator, this was it.

"Ooohhh, Eric, I like that. Where do they come from?"

"Tesco," he laughed. "Three for a quid."

"Where's the other two?"

"I ate 'em."

"Pig."

"So, young man - what's it like? Dying?"

"Well… it's a lot quicker than living."

"That's all you've got?" Eric grinned at me, brown as a nut from his rambling cycle through Southern France, his short-sleeved T-shirt showing off the massive panther's head tattoo on his arm. I'd noticed that one or two of the nurses tended to hang around my bed more when Eric was around.

"I ain't telling you," I said. "It'll make me more interesting. I'm saving this one for myself."

"Well, you're gonna need all the help you can get looking like that." We laughed. "'Interesting' might be your best bet for a while."

I'd been on clear soups for a couple of days, and still hadn't tested out my new plumbing. I lay back, nervously awaiting some kind of explosive response from inside me.

A few gurgles bubbled around my empty chambers, which the nurses assured me was a good sign. Bubbles mean movement; movement is good.

I was incredibly excited to have my movements back again. That was the first real food I'd eaten for weeks. Every time I eat a kiwi fruit now, I think of that moment.

I'd lie awake for hours at night awaiting the breakfast cart. In the dark I'd imagine a full tray of Weetabix, milk, toast, even a cup of tea. I couldn't wait to get my knife into that butter.

The tube into my neck was the first of ten pipes to be removed. One by one, over the next few days the others followed. It felt like a massive personal achievement every time a pipe was detached from a different part of me. The lung pipe in particular was a huge relief when it popped out from between my ribs. A couple of stitches criss-crossed the hole to keep it together. It looked like a bullet entry point.

The last pipe out was the one that had been stuck into the place where my gall bladder once sat. The nurse came with her drain-removing paraphernalia - scissors, bowl, dressing - and she undid the little holding stitch and gently pulled. This usually did the trick - the pipe would normally slide out with a little sucking noise that gave me a slightly peculiar feeling - nothing too bad though. Slightly peculiar was a welcome upgrade from all that had come before. But this last pipe was going nowhere.

She went off to find the ward sister, and then she had a go at pulling the pipe.

"OK Mark," she said, "I'm going to give it a harder pull this time."

I braced myself as she yanked. Again, no movement. My side began to hurt. Once it was out, there would be no need for me to stay in hospital. I'd be free to go! I could walk - slowly, I was off all the drugs, and I could eat and drink again. Most importantly, I was having regular bowel movements.

But the pipe would not budge.

"This is very strange, Mark. I'm going to have to call a doctor."

The doctor on duty, who'd had the pleasure of affirming that my first bowel movement was free of blood, turned up.

"Right Mark, I'm really going to give this a pull now. Hang tight."

Man, did he pull. The plastic tube was stretched tight in his hands and my body was lifting off the bed, the side of my stomach pulling out towards him.

"STOP! YOU'RE KILLING ME!"

There was still no way the pipe was moving. My insides were aching like hell. I was starting to worry.

That tube HAS to be attached to something inside - what if they burst it? Oh God...

"OK," the doctor said, "I'll get you some Valium and we'll try again."

The Valium injection turned me into a grinning fool within moments, and I watched, laughing madly, as the doctor wrestled with the pipe. He had his knee against the bed as he heaved on the pipe, looking ridiculously flustered in his neat, white coat and stripy collared shirt. I couldn't feel a thing.

He carried on pulling on it, cartoon style, as a huge mound of my abdomen was pulled towards him. Still no use.

He gave up, and took a long look at my notes as I grinned stupidly up at him. He bent down to inspect the pipe at the entry wound - and then he found it: another tiny stitch. He cut the stitch with a scalpel, and with a slight POP - the pipe slid effortlessly and painlessly out of my abdomen.

That was it: my medical procedures were over. For the first time in over a month, I wasn't connected to a bag, a jar or a machine.

I was a free man again, with a lovely big shot of Valium inside me. I had Mum laughing at my antics for all of that hazy, floaty afternoon. It was the first time I'd made her laugh for a long time. We even walked down to the hospital cafe together to celebrate my new freedom - the exact same cafe we'd sat in fifteen years before, when I was a wee lad with asthma.

We had a lovely afternoon.

38
Adrift off Africa

The doctors decided to keep me in for one more night, though I was begging to be released. But that night I slept soundly right through. I awoke at seven, ready to eat my way through a field of converted wheat and an acre of buttered toast once the breakfast lady arrived. But she never showed. I'd also noticed the night staff hadn't said their goodbyes and handed over to the daytime nurses. One of them stopped by the end of my bed.

"You're awake! How on earth did you sleep through that?!"

"What? Have I missed breakfast?" I asked in a panic, eyeing up the packet of Rolos in her top pocket.

"Nooo! The storm! It was unbelievable. We thought the roof was going to come off."

16th October, 1987: a massive storm had ploughed through the south of England. Winds of over a hundred miles an hour brought down fifteen million trees, the national grid failed, and I didn't get my Weetabix because the breakfast lady couldn't get past all the blocked roads. The wind had raged and howled and battered all night long, and I'd had my first night of real sleep since before the trek - like it had blown all the demons away.

Dad was supposed to be arriving early to take me home. I sat on my bed, dressed in some skinny man's clothes that he'd had brought in for me the day before, staring at the clock at the end of the ward. I tried phoning home but all the lines were dead. About two in the afternoon, Dad turned up.

"Hiya kid. I couldnee get past the M25 rooondaboot. What a night! Come on, let's get you home."

I was leaving. A week in an isolation ward, a week in a general ward, a week in intensive care, a week in a post-op ward. And a night in a cold corridor. I walked slowly up the ward, still bent forward to alleviate the pressure on my wound, shaking hands with all the patients - they were sorry to see me leave, as it meant no more visits from Maria. The nurses all wished me luck and waved me off as Dad helped me through the doors, down a long corridor and out into the wet car park; past the plastic door flaps to A&E that I'd fallen through, filthy and stinking, with my note from Nepal.

That note had done its job - they had all helped this man.

We drove the twenty minutes back home, gawping at the ripped up trees that scattered the fields and footpaths. Everything looked the same, but different, like a big hand had reached down and grabbed and clawed at the green English countryside.

"How you feeling, son? Good to be out?" Dad smiled, his skinny hands gripping the wheel of his Peugeot.

I went to speak, but felt a big knot of emotion closing my throat. I just nodded, all my energy going into stopping my wobbling lips. Seeing the familiar countryside again, from the inside of Dad's car as we drove closer to home, had a similar effect on me as when Sean turned up in Kathmandu - it made the whole trip more real. I realised how close I'd been to the edge - well, I'd been over the edge, at least three times, and now I was back in the world again, with a rip up my guts that could never be ignored. But all from what?

The sky was grey with heavy rain clouds as we crawled home.

Look where I am, back where I left off...

We pulled into the drive at home and Mum was standing by the back door, looking as relieved as a mum could be. Dad had to help me out of the car and I gave her the biggest hug.

"Och son, it's sooo good to have you home." She hugged me back, very tightly, and Crispin the fat cat rubbed up against my ankles, purring away at my feet. Again, I was so choked up I couldn't speak. All I could manage to do was to drag myself up the stairs to the back bedroom and collapse onto the bed.

Bloody hell, Mark, what's happened? You could hardly speak to Mum and Dad.

What's going on?

I spent most of the next week in bed, eating and sleeping. I was forty two kilos when I arrived home, so Mum did her best to fatten me up. Huge breakfasts of Weetabix and toast, thick, creamy yoghurt and donuts for morning tea, cheese sandwiches with tomato soup for lunch and huge pasta or roasts with sponge puddings for dinner. I couldn't get enough in me - it was like I'd turned back into a ravenous teenage boy.

Maria came to visit me a few times over the next couple of weeks. I'd pretty much put the hexing out of my mind - or at least I thought it didn't matter any more. I was alive and recovering, and that's what mattered. Signs of normality were returning. I was more interested in her wiggling bum than her waving wand, though still very sore around my stomach, and still very skinny and weak looking, but that never stopped her jumping all over me. Maybe the builder was right about the scar fetish, because you wouldn't put me in the 'attractive' box - interesting, maybe, but not attractive. I still couldn't resist her, though Mum and Dad found it very difficult to have her around - especially Dad, after what he'd witnessed in intensive care.

One night she phoned me up.

"I'm leaving for Gran Canaria next week, my darling."

She always said "My darling," never just "Darling." It works a treat in a Spanish accent. If she'd said months ago, "I'm going to put a spell on you, my darling, that will leave you just this side of dead," I would have just smiled and felt all warm - and then left for India.

"Why don't you come over in a few weeks? I can show you all the special places on the island. Maybe you'll like it over there - you could play guitar in bars! Wouldn't that be funny!"

Didn't sound too bad actually - secluded beaches, no one around, just Maria in her little red bikini. And me in my Lord Canary suit. Sounded like the kind of place that a lucky man should be recovering in, though I didn't have the strength in my hands to hold a guitar string down. My fingers looked like Nosferatu's long lost English cousins, and were too weak to even play Silent Night, never mind twanging the Transylvanian Blues.

I agreed to come over, so long as my upcoming check-up at the hospital was satisfactory. It gave me something to think about, other than eating fattening stuff.

Four weeks after leaving hospital I had my post-op appointment, which I was looking forward to - hoping for some answers maybe, or at least a thorough check over from a knowing mind. I saw a doctor whom I'd never seen before, who looked over my notes, inspected my wound - healing nicely - and showed me the door barely ten minutes after I'd arrived. Shit, I thought I was still a St Peters celebrity, but this bloke couldn't wait to see the back of me. I thought I needed at least some advise though.

"Are there things I shouldn't eat? Or anything else I need to know?"

"No, no - do whatever you want, but just avoid alcohol for six weeks. Bye, Mr. Giblin."

"So, no news on whatever it could've been?"

"Liver abscesses. We can't say what caused them though. But you seem fine."

Though slightly bemused, I was so happy when I left the hospital that I walked the four miles home in the cold November air. Through the fields and footpaths, past the sheep grazing at the vet lab fields not far from our house; past the dried out blackberry bushes lining the pathways. Early that year I'd walked through those fields in the snow, playing loud music in my Walkman, dreaming of going back to India, to Kashmir; back up to Nepal.

And whatever was inside me was sitting there, waiting to blow. And I had absolutely no idea. Well, I've been back to India, and here I am in this field again. Shit, Mark, what a trip.

I hadn't felt so alive for ages. I sang an old Led Zep song about how long it'd been since I'd rock 'n' rolled. *Dun un, Dun un, Dun un…*

Mum was in the kitchen making scones when I burst through the back door, exhausted, happy and starving.

"All clear, Mum. Doctor said I should be ready for the Olympics."

She brushed the flour off her hands and gave me a hug.

"Och, shush yourself," she laughed. "That's fantastic news, son. I knew you'd be fine - you're looking that well, so you are."

"Mum, I'm going to visit Maria."

She plunged her hands back into the mixing bowl, and didn't answer for a moment.

"Uh huh. Aye, well… If you think you're strong enough…"

"Well I won't be doing much - no swimming, don't wanna pop me tum, Mum. Just a couple of weeks. Never been to that part of the world…"

I could almost see the words floating above her head: *Och Mark… I thought you were done with her… But I cannee say anything, you're not a wee boy…*

"I'm just going for a holiday, Mum. It'll do me good. Don't worry - I'm not going to marry her," I laughed.

Och, heaven help us, don't even joke about that…

I bought an open return ticket for the week after, cutting heavily into my remaining funds, and thought I'd surprise Maria by calling her up the night before the flight.

"Ola, buenos noches."

"Maria, it's me! I'm coming over!"

"Oh! Erm, great. When?" She sounded surprised.

"Tomorrow! I arrive at... Hang on, I'll just check the time... OH, SHIT!!!"

"Ohhh, not the middle of the night, I hope?"

"No. According to this I arrived four hours ago! BOLLOCKS!"

"Well you should have told me, silly boy. We haven't got time travel here. Ha! That's funny - do you like that joke, Mark?"

"Maria - I missed the fuckin' flight!"

"Oh... Does that mean you won't be coming?"

I wasn't really concentrating on what she said, so I don't know if she sounded disappointed or not.

I was furious at myself - I'd even lost the ability to read a bloody airline ticket properly. An airline ticket! The most precious collection of carbon copies ever invented.

Does this still count as part of the shit trip? How will I know when it's over?

I told my parents. Dad lowered his paper for a second.

"There's a sign forrr yee, son."

"Dad, I'm not going to marry her, I just want a holiday."

But the paper was back up. Not much ever came out from behind there.

Next day, I had to dip into the last of my money to buy the cheapest ticket I could - a two week return, leaving in a couple of days.

I arrived at Gran Canaria airport early evening, and Maria was there waiting for me - tanned and gorgeous in a white summer frock. I moved towards her; arms out for a hug, but she sort of deflected me with a shimmy to the left, instead offering me her cheek for a graze of a kiss, her dark eyes flitting everywhere but at me. Then I noticed all the young men around her, and Maria started chatting in Spanish to them, and I stood there like a tool, feeling extremely uncomfortable.

"Oh, these are my cousins, Mark, they wanted to come and meet you."

Well why the fuck aren't they even saying hello then?

"Hello, Ola," I thought it best to say, because I always thought that's what you did when you met people. The only thing I got back was a wall of Spanish sniggers.

Then the entourage, with Queen Maria firmly protected in the centre, scrummed its way out the airport and piled into three cars, with Maria in the front seat of one and me in the back, squeezed between two good-looking male relatives who talked to Maria the whole drive back to her village in the dark. Not a word was aimed my way as we whizzed down a busy dual carriageway, before heading off down some smaller dark roads through the rocky island.

Her parents were lovely to me, in Spanish; I was very appreciative, in English, and I was given my own bedroom with a single bed that practically screamed "NO SEX" out at me.

Course you'd be in a single bed, you bloody idiot, what did you think? A love nest, next to their parents' bedroom?

I still hadn't managed to chat with Maria. I sat at the table in the white walled kitchen behind a mountain of olives, caught in a crossfire of awkward smiles from her parents, whilst we waited for Maria to stop jabbering on the phone in the tiled hallway.

"Beautiful house... errr, tu casa es muy, err, beautiful." I nodded, throwing my arms open in a "Your house is beautiful" kind of way.

"Gracias, gracias. How... is... tu mother?"

"Ahhh. Él es muy... grande..."

Oh shit, I think I just said "He is very large."

"She said to say 'OLA!'"

"Ohhhhhhh!"

Maria eventually finished her ten thousand word conversation.

"Come on Mark, we'll go down to the bars on the beach."

Great, I was getting worried for a minute. Not that I could have a beer, but at least we could chat and I could cast my eyes out to the night-time sea again and taste some salty Atlantic air.

But we really meant we. Myself, Maria, and the airport gang. And the 'chat' was the gang jumping around trying to impress Maria. She was laughing and throwing her head back, giggling, scrunching her nose up - all the things I used to make her do, on my own. Now she needed a gang of tanned, muscle-skinny, fast-talking relatives to do it. I had about as much chance as a Windsor fox on a bank holiday Monday of getting away from this lot. I felt like her laughing was a shield to exclude me from whatever was going on. If I tried to talk to Maria, everyone would just stop and stare, making things very uncomfortable, until one of the hombres said something so hilarious that they'd all have to literally jump about laughing to get over it. I checked, and made sure I wasn't wearing all yellow, so it couldn't be that.

In bed that night I still sort of hoped there'd be a tapping on my door in the early hours, but it never came. Morning time was just as peculiar. I woke early, starving hungry, and ate a mountain of fruit and yoghurts and eggs with the smiling parents, waiting for Maria to awake. Which was late. Then she sauntered through with barely an "Ola" thrown my way. I cannot remember ever feeling more uncomfortable.

Early afternoon, I went to the beach with Maria and her mostly male entourage, and sat by watching them all jump around in the sparkling sea or playing beach volleyball - long dark hair flying around, leather necklaces and bracelets bouncing against dark brown skin. It seemed like a pretty good kind of life. Reggae pumped out from their boom box, and they kept sneaking off to the rocks for joints. But having had part of my lung recently chopped away had sort of put me off smoking. I was still hunched forward, still super skinny and weak; still slightly banana-faced. I kept my shirt on, hiding the livid red gash up my belly. I was in no condition to go in the sea, scared that one good wave would spill me open and turn me into shark burley - which would really ruin the beach party. My legs had no muscles, and they hung out of my shorts like a pair of knotted white ropes.

The awkward beach parties continued for a couple of days, until I heard Maria's mum having loud words with her in her bedroom, after which Maria allowed me to accompany her down to the harbour, alone. It was a warm afternoon, and the red, white and blue fishing boats were tightly moored along the harbour walls. We sat in the local bar, nibbling on some grilled fish, watching the sea birds swoop around the blue bay. It could have been so idyllic.

"How far are we from Africa, Maria?"

"I don't bloody know, Mark," she snapped. "What do you think I am? A bloody pirate? Sailing to Africa with a measuring stick dangling from the back of my stoopid boat?"

Well that started well. You bloody witch.

"No. I don't think you're a pirate." I rubbed my tired eyes. "Maria, what is going on? You invited me over here - you never said it was going to be like this. This is bloody awful - what am I supposed to do with myself?"

She was looking out to sea, her foot tapping faster than a flamenco metronome.

"You don't understand this country, Mark - it's not like England."

"Well I have been abroad before, in case you hadn't noticed."

"But you've never lived with a single girl," she shouted, "under her parents' roof, in a tiny Catholic village, on a small island in the middle of the bloody sea! Have you? Where everyone gossips about everyone else!"

She had me there.

"But you invited me here!" I reminded her, banging my hand down on the table, giving the fried fish a final jump into the air.

"Stop bloody saying that!" she yelled, turning on me.

"I've only said it once!" I shrieked, in a stupidly high-pitched attempt at defending myself.

She picked up her bag. "Twice. I'm going home."

We walked through the old streets in silence, between the white houses with their terracotta roofs, well away from any tourist routes. Old ladies in black robes peered at us as we walked by. A group of youths cycled past, shouting out unwelcoming sounding phrases at me in Spanish.

"God, this is terrible Mark," Maria said, burying her face in her hands.

"Why? What are they saying?"

"It is hard to translate, but it's like 'Fuck off, you weird foreign freak.' Only not quite as nice as that. It's OK for you - I have to live here after you leave! You should never have come here."

Well, that's that taken care of then.

We walked back up the hill without another word. Next day I phoned the travel agent, only to be reminded that my flight could not be changed. If I'd had any money left, I would've bought a new ticket and hightailed it out of there. But I was stuck for ten more very long days. That was twice in only a few months that I'd desperately needed to be helicoptered out of somewhere.

So I started walking. I'd eat breakfast with her parents in the morning, and then head off out of the village on the main road - not even waiting for Maria to wake up - and wander down tiny roads until I'd find some other little village, where I'd sit for as long as it would take to get the energy to walk back again. The longer I walked, the more chance I had of sleeping at night. Each day seemed to last a week. I'd sit under trees on the side of hills, overlooking the Atlantic Ocean, which Maria would be cavorting in back at the village with her protective ring of black-haired male friends and family. I'd sit for an hour in the shade of a village taverna, eating fish and chicken. Then I'd walk again. It was like a really bad version of a Laurie Lee book.

Finally, the time came to leave. Everyone must've been so relieved - I know I was. Maria's parents waved me off from their home, as Maria, myself and about ten male cousins and friends drove to the airport. No one spoke to me. At the check in gate I turned to say goodbye to Maria, and just for a moment, the entourage scattered, leaving us alone.

"Well, Maria, that's that then."

"I am sorry, Mark. You will never understand this place."

"No, Maria. I'll never understand anything about any of this, even if I live to be a hundred."

She looked me in the eye - possibly the only time she had done since I'd been there - reached up on tiptoes and gave me the merest hint of a kiss on my lips, whispered "Goodbye," turned on her heel and walked away.

I watched her wiggle her way back to her clan; long black hair swaying in time with her hips, her tanned calves flashing under her beach dress. She'd traded the high heel shoes in for canvas trainers. She never looked back, and I never heard from her again.

I was so happy to be flying home, as it'd been such a lonely time. I wasn't strong enough for that yet. The hospital experience had left me stripped of my natural defences to the world, and when I saw Dad at the airport, I came over all weepy.

Damn, here it comes again! What's wrong with me?

"Dad... it was terrible."

He saw it all welling up in me, and sort of turned away, deflecting any chance of an emotional outpouring.

"Uh-huh, well, that's that then, eh?" he mumbled, as he walked towards the exit, with me trying to calm my quivering lip a step or two behind him.

He'd been there for me when I was in crisis - a crisis that he could understand. But he definitely wasn't going to start opening up to me about relationships and emotions, now that I was upright and almost functioning again. Normal service had been resumed.

Mind you, he had seen the crazy witch undoing my lung tube pipe.

39

Speed Bump Himalayas

I was back at home sitting on my bed, just about strumming my guitar, feeling a bit depressed. Christmas was over, and all my good mates were off travelling, arriving in varying states of disarray in Australia. Sean had moved back to London and was sniffing around the open mic comedy scene. Everyone seemed to be doing something exciting. I was recuperating at Mum and Dad's, with virtually nothing left from my year in Tesco.

Mum tapped on my door.

"Mark, can I have a word?"

"Yes, 'course Mum. Come in."

"It's nice to hear you playing guitar again." She sat on the bed. "Look, why don't you go to Australia, son. All your friends are there. You don't want to be trapped here."

I'd been thinking the same during the past few weeks - I must've been passing smoke signals.

"I probably will, Mum. But I need to get a job first to pay for the flight."

"Just get a job when you get there. I'll pay for your flight on credit card - and you can pay some back when you get working." She was smiling. "Like you were ever going to settle doon here!"

"I can't take your money, Mum."

"Shhhh. I don't want to see you miserable. Come on, let's walk to the shops. See how much flights are."

Ten weeks after I left hospital, I flew to Sydney. Mum and Dad took me to the airport, and we talked about the long flight ahead; warm weather, English winters. I felt a growing nervousness as we drove up the M3. None of us wanted to talk about me actually leaving again, or what we'd all just been through. My brain felt like it was trembling with emotion inside my skull, driving my lips into hyper wobble mode and pooling water behind my eyes ready for a burst dam of tears.

We parked the car and walked into departures, all my energies going into keeping my brain tent pegs from flying off and letting loose the gibbering boy that was fighting to leap out and have a public emotional breakdown. The poor boy had every reason to be scared; to not trust what mess the grown up version of himself was going to lead him into next.

This man should not be steering this ship - he's incapable. I need a new pilot. Isn't it obvious?

"Now - you be careful, Mark. Make sure you write, and please, look after yourself. If you ever need anything, well…" Mum smiled that smile, the one that said "Whatever nonsense you get up to, you're still my wee boy."

"Yes, Mum, I will. And thanks… for everything."

Oh god, here we go again! I can't bloody say what I feel. I want to say that without you both I would've died. I want to say that I was terrified of not seeing you again, and that's how I managed to climb back on the bus to Kathmandu. I want to say that I felt myself die during my first ultrasound, and I left you all behind. And I want to say I'm sorry for putting you through all that. And I feel like a little boy inside again, and I'm bloody scared.

"Bye, Mum. Bye, Dad."

"Bye, Mark. Take care, my love."

The plane flew across India and over the Himalayas. I knelt on the floor by the emergency door at the back, peering down, watching the white peaks below.

Only four months ago I was down there, about to explode…

The Speed Bump Himalayas. They slowed me right down. Maybe that's what they really are. They slow us all down, anyone that goes near them.

I had a beer as the mountains slipped away, and promised the young boy inside - who I'd not given a thought about since I was fourteen - the young boy who still had a Derbyshire accent and a birds' egg collection, and big Airfix models of Spitfires, hovercrafts and Richard the Lionheart; who would almost wet himself with excitement on FA Cup Final day; who wanted to bring home a stick of rock from Lhasa for his mum - I promised him that I'd try and be a better pilot of the ship we were both in. God knows, he needed some reassuring. Since he'd handed over control to me

I'd given him a hellish ride - I should've died on the motorbike, I could easily have been buried under a glacier, and how I'd made it out of the last scrape I don't think I'll ever know.

Then I forgot all about him for the next twenty years.

We flew over the snaking waterways of Bangladesh and then down over the equator; the islands of Indonesia splattered across the incredible blue of the Indian and Pacific oceans. It felt like a long, long way from home. I was going to meet all my mates, but I was nervous. Everything still felt very raw - even the scar - and I tried to push away the thoughts that I might not be the same carefree nutter that I used to be, like my mates obviously still would be. Maybe I'd be ruining the party, like on the beach in Gran Canaria.

I landed early morning in Sydney, in late January, 1988. I had none of the excitement I used to have at being somewhere different. I'd carried the bag of nerves that had appeared in the car park at Heathrow Airport all the way to Australia with me.

I jumped into a cab under the blue Sydney sky, swatting away the early morning flies.

"Kings Cross, please." Backpacker territory, red light territory. Gareth had a flat there with Leigh, my old guitar partner from back home.

Leaving Sydney Airport, the driver provided me with some advice that did nothing to boost my confidence.

"Up the Cross, eh? Fuck me, mate, I hope you can handle yourself. Mate, if you get in a fight with an Aborigine, don't try and punch him in the head, cos you'll break your hand. Kick him in the shins - that's where they're weakest. And they're bloody brilliant boxers."

What? Why is he telling me this? Why would I get in a fight with an Aborigine?

I don't wanna get in a fight with anyone. I'd burst open - instantly.

I was still only sixty odd kilos. Mind you, my knuckles stuck out like sharp weapons. Maybe I could wave them about in front of me, like Sean with his boxing boot.

The driver dropped me outside a modern block of flats. An Aboriginal man - completely out of it - was lying face down on a mattress on the grass outside, a four litre cask of port beside him. Presumably empty. I rung the intercom bell beside the security gate.

"Hello?"

"It's Mark. I'm here."

"Who?"

"Mark - Gareth and Leigh's mate."

"Oh, yeah, come up." *Christ, don't sound too excited, pal!*

Some English bloke let me in the flat, looking like he'd just woken up. "They're at work. I'm Andy - I live here too."

I didn't want to talk to Andy, and he didn't look like he could be arsed to talk to me, so I dumped my bag and guitar and went for a wander. The flat was a twenty metre walk to the heart of Kings Cross - a busy street lined with strip joints, dodgy looking bars, bikers, spruikers, Bureau de Change windows and hostels. A few working girls in stretchy black skirts hung outside the strip joints, buckling at the knees as their morning hit rolled their eyes back; cigarettes burned down to the yellow filter hanging from their red painted mouths. Drunks from the night before were crashed out in shop doorways, puddles of piss spreading out from their filthy shorts. Police strolled along carrying bags of McDonalds; guns clearly on show in their black holsters; eyes hidden behind mirrored sunglasses. A greasy-haired man with a seventies moustache and a terrible suit stepped out from a strip joint and tried to steer me down some dark stairs.

"You looking for girls, mate?" he sleazed from the corner of his moustachioed mouth, "You're in the right place... Show starting in five minutes. Fuckin' top quality, mate."

At ten in the morning?

I ducked around him into the staggering path of a filthy, drunk, one-legged man on a knackered old crutch, who screamed through his matted long grey hair at me to "Git out me farckin' way, ya farckin' two legged caaaaaant."

Then he laughed his head off at the shocked look on my face.

"Ya skinny farckin' wanka. Git farcked!" Then he did the most disgusting spit I think I've ever seen - it seemed to go on for about a minute.

What am I doing here? What was I thinking?! I'm not ready for this...

A poster in a travel agent advertised cheap flights to the UK. I desperately wanted to run in and buy a ticket, grab my things and leg it back to the airport. But I had no money, of course, and no return ticket.

I didn't want to be there. I didn't want to be anywhere. I wasn't even sure that I wanted to see my mates - they'd all been away for over a year, looking after themselves, having a laugh, getting in and out of trouble. And I'd just been hanging onto my mum's hand...

I felt like I'd been dumped in the school playground again. All I needed was the one-legged foul-mouth to pivot up on his crutches, swing his good leg out and kick me in the balls, and the picture would be complete.

It was time to grow up. Again.

Gareth and Leigh came home from work late afternoon, both deeply suntanned, both fighting fit, obviously revelling in their life in Sydney.

"Giblin, you dirty dog! Christ - look at you! Show us yer belly, you ugly swine. Whooaaaaa! You... poor... sod."

Within an hour we were in the pub round the corner for a five dollar steak and a night of storytelling, lies and admiring bronzed, drunken Swedish girls. I felt better already. A couple of days later, whilst Leigh was at work on the railways, I bought a car battery, which we rigged up to an amp and took to the streets of Kings Cross at night-time, where we belted out twelve bar blues until our guitar case was full; then we'd convert all the heavy coinage into beer before morning came.

Over the rest of the summer we got to know the working girls and the bouncers, the foul-mouthed one-legged man - who's swearing tirades were legendary - the derelicts and bums, the Swedish girls and the police, as we twanged the guitars as loud as we could; the drunks crawling around the amp, swigging on their precious bottles of meths and milk.

"Best farkin' drink in the world, mate - the White Lady. Wanna try some - yer Pommie fuckin' baaaaastards."

I let Leigh take care of the fights.

I didn't return home for almost two and a half years. A year in Sydney, where I worked as a cab driver and a busker, then on up to Bali, Malaysia and Thailand before heading to Tokyo for an arduous six month busking binge. Then I spent six months on Thai islands, steadily working through my hefty wedge of travellers cheques I'd earned in Tokyo. It took me a long time to really feel confident again, but I hid it well. Apart from the occasional crippling bouts of wind, which would leave me bent double and immobile for up to an hour, I was perfectly healthy, if a little underweight. I was like any other young lad careering around the globe at that time, except with an electric guitar, an amp in my backpack, and a huge fresh scar up my belly. My lung pipe hole looked like a bullet wound, and my stomach looked like I'd been gargled by a shark.

When I returned to England, I went to London to stay with Sean for a few days. He'd been hard at work on the comedy scene, and was playing at Jongleurs in Camden. I was strangely nervous when the compère for the night hollered into the microphone, "Ladies and Gentlemen, please welcome to the stage... Sean Lock!"

I didn't know what to expect when he stepped from behind the curtain, but what I got was twenty minutes of hilarious, surreal rantings which had me and the audience in hysterics. He spun his endless crazy notions like a comedic plate-spinner, until he had eight or nine ideas whirling around the stage - and he'd jump back to the first idea and give that a spin as the audience were still laughing themselves mad over the other ideas. Then he stuck his hand in his pocket and jangled his coins, holding the microphone against his pocket, the amplified jangling of the hidden coins louder than the hysterical laughing from the crowd. He put on a face of ridiculous concentration, his lips moving silently.

"Two pound eighty seven," he announced, with absolute perfect timing, smiling happily like a modern day Tommy Cooper. He ranted about cooking bacon with no shirt on, being so bored he couldn't even be bothered to move his own head - now that one had to come from India - his dad catching him trying a bra on - on and on until people were in tears. I thought the girl beside me was going to have a stroke.

I went backstage when he finished.

"Sean, that was brilliant!"

"Did you like it? Ah, thanks, Mark. Went well, I thought."

"Sean, I don't think you'll ever need the 'There, that was fun, wasn't it?' line."

"No? Well that's good to hear."

40

Sheep Eye Pie

Only a year or so after I returned from my big Australia and Asia trip, my mum was diagnosed with lung cancer, and was told straight away that she had no hope of beating it. By the time she was diagnosed I'd returned once again to Australia, but flew home immediately when I learned of her illness. She and Dad met me at Heathrow. I was a gibbering wreck when I hugged her in the arrivals lounge.

"It's OK son - we'll fight it together shall we?"

I nodded and nodded and nodded, and at the very most managed a tiny "Yes."

We drove back home through the most beautiful autumn sunset; the fields surrounding the M25 looked like they were on fire against the orange sky. I spent the next eighteen months looking after her, along with Dad and Amanda, Alison and Eric. She almost died in St Peter's Hospital after the cancer reached her brain. I remember sitting with her as she raved about the strange happenings in the ward at night-time.

"There's something going on - I can hear people moving around at night."

"I bloody told you that years ago - remember?"

"Oh, son," she said, looking at me with perfect clarity, which was getting pretty rare by that stage, "I remember everything about that time. You wee bugger."

I smiled at her, propped up on her pillows.

"You know, son, if you'd died back then - and believe you me, we thought you were going to for sure - I would've followed you over."

"Oh Mum, don't be silly.."

"I'm not being silly, Mark. There's no way I would have let you go on your own - you were terrified. I've never seen anything like it. You were always such a happy boy, son."

Oh shit.

My lip wobble started again, and the feeling of unfathomable emotion gobbled me up. I lay my head on the bed by her feet and fell asleep, slumped forward like I'd been shot from behind, as my dying mum spilled the beans on how she'd felt as she'd nearly shepherded me over to the other side.

She suffered terribly before she died at home. She was only fifty seven. There was a half-read book about travelling through South America on her bedside table.

Dad's drinking had increased heavily - I'm not sure if the stress I'd put them both through had added to this. It certainly can't have helped. When I flew back to Australia after Mum died, Dad took me to the airport. He hung around whilst I checked in, right up to the point when I was going through to customs.

I still found it very hard to say goodbye to people I cared for. Something must've broken inside during my illness.

"Look after yourself, Dad" was about all I could manage.

"Aye, kid, don't be worrying aboot me. You just look after yerrrself."

He looked so old, with pure white hair and shaking, alcoholic nerves. He reached up and gave me a kiss on the forehead, just like he had done in the corridor of the hospital after my operation, and told me he loved me. That was very unlike Dad.

He turned and walked out of the airport, and I knew then I would never see him again. Everything about him was retreating from the world. He drank himself into an almost lonely death, by himself in the house not too far from Woking, but he managed to cry out to the neighbours, who called for an ambulance. He died in St. Peter's Hospital, a year and a day after Mum had passed away. No one could have stopped him. Amanda and Alison just made it to the hospital in time. He was fifty-nine.

The year Dad died, I noticed I was feeling a bit sick in the stomach after meals, and more worryingly, I had a sharp feeling around my liver. I went to see a doctor in Sydney, but he wasn't too concerned, though he was very impressed by my scar, which hadn't really faded that much in the five years since the slice.

"So, what did you have wrong with you?" The doctor asked, inspecting my scars and holes.

"They never found out. Liver and lung abscesses, and they took my gallbladder out."

I was living fairly well, not drinking too much, but my liver readings weren't the best. He advised me to look after myself a bit better. Damn - I thought I was! Certainly in comparison to the time I'd spent in Asia - that Thai whiskey was almost as bad as the Israeli vodka. Plus a few months busking in Oslo drinking potato Moonshine. That stuff could give the Scorpion a fair fight.

My girlfriend at the time told me to go and see an iridologist.

"What, to get glasses?"

"No, you berk, they look in your eyes and can tell what's going on in your body."

"More than a doctor can? This should be good," I snorted. But I was still feeling sick, so I found a number in the local Bondi paper, where such alternative therapy minded people tended to advertise.

A girl in her early twenties - obviously just finished her iridology course - invited me into her flat near Bondi Beach, armed only with a pen light and a magnifying glass, which she peered through as she shone the light into my eyes. She could've done with one of those Kashmiri mirror hippy tunics to deflect my cynicism.

She got to work, inspecting.

"Hmmm... Ahaa... Yep... Oooohhh."

"What is it," I asked, trying not to blink. "You can't see a giant hand in there, can you?"

"Err, no... But I know why you're feeling sick. It's your gallbladder. It's in a terrible state."

"That's amazing! You're absolutely right, it is! It's buried beneath tonnes of landfill about twelve thousand miles away from what's left of me."

She leaned in for another look around the back of my eye ball.

"Well your eye is showing me that you have a gallbladder, and it's blocked - which is why you feel sick. I'd advise seeing another doctor."

I left, cursing at the waste of twenty five dollars - about two hours' pay in the warehouse I'd been working in, labelling bras. The supervisor always gave me a funny look when I repeatedly refused a supervisor's job - "No thanks, I'd rather be using my hands."

But I was still feeling sick and sore around the liver, so I booked an appointment with a specialist. I was starting to feel the fear growing that maybe whatever it was had returned. And I didn't fancy my chances of fighting it off a second time, even if it hit me within a hundred metres of a liver specialists' convention.

I explained my medical history to the doctor, who dug his fingers around my liver area, bringing back painful memories of reset buttons, Pokhara hospital, Kathmandu, St Peter's Hospital. Not that this was anywhere near as bad - but there was definitely a sharp pain under his fingers.

He had no answers on the day, but sent me for an ultrasound. And there, dangling under my heavily scarred liver like a greedy fat prawn, was my gallbladder, packed full of stones.

A classic "What? You carry pigs?" moment.

The doctors had definitely told me they'd taken my gallbladder out. But then they also told me they'd had to abandon the operation because the horses had taken me. Not that they used that phrase, of course. Maybe there'd been such a mad panic that they weren't sure what they'd done:

"Did you take his gallbladder out?"

"No - I was on lung duties. You were on liver and gallbladder."

"No - I was on resuscitation and pipe insertion."

"Oh - I thought Phil was doing that. He must've been on acid dribbling and scooping."

"Hmm. OK, mark it down as 'removed'."

Within a week I was whisked in to Royal Randwick Hospital, Sydney, to be cut open again, and this time they actually did pull my cheeky little gallbladder out. When I woke up - under perfectly controlled conditions and nicely plugged into the morphine pipe - the impressed nurse was excitedly waving a jar of jade coloured stones in my face.

"Look at this! It must be a record - three hundred and thirty five gall stones! No wonder you felt sick, mate!"

A couple of days later I got to see my new scar across my poor belly, almost joining up my vertical slice with my angled and mangled motorbike scar. I seem to collect them like others collect tattoos. Before I was released from hospital later that week, the surgeon came to see me. He was a cheerful, bearded country Aussie man.

"G'day, Mark, I had a good look around, and your liver has certainly taken a beating. There's some serious scarring down there. You told me the doctors had no idea what happened to you, correct?"

"Yes - just that there were abscesses."

"Well, they should've called me. Those abscesses were caused by hydatid disease. I've seen them before. Very nasty. It's a tapeworm that starts in a sheep."

I did one of those "What? It starts in a sheep?!" faces, which is a cross between extremely surprised and very nauseated.

"A tapeworm? From sheep? That's disgusting…"

"Not as disgusting as the next bit. The tapeworm causes abscesses to form in the gut of the sheep. The sheep dies, a dog sticks its nose in the carcass to get to the offal, eats the tapeworm abscess, then the swallowed cyst bursts and the eggs get passed on to humans through the dog's faeces."

"What?! I never ate dog shi-"

"No, you don't look like you're that kind of bloke," he laughed, which was good to know. "You can pick it up from patting an infected dog. You know how dogs can lick wherever they want…"

What?!

Shouldn't EVERYONE know this??

We should be told that as soon we learn to talk! The first sentence ALL humans should hear is "DON'T PAT DOGS." It should be blared out of speakers in shopping malls, stamped across your passport, on the news every night; in little warning cards that tumble out of your cornflakes box.

But of course, it's not that bad. The dogs have to have eaten the offal of infected animals - and the chances are that Fluffy the pet poodle hasn't done - unless he's been sneaking out at night and breaking into the abattoir again.

I still think it's worth a mention though.

"Those abscesses inside you would've had millions of tapeworm heads in them."

"Christ, you're making me feel ill, Doctor."

"It's pretty rare in Europe, which is probably why it went undiagnosed in you, though I thought that was what the Hospital for Tropical Diseases was there for. It's more common in Asia, and over here in the sheep farming communities."

He stood up to leave.

"You have no idea how lucky you were to survive that."

Yes. I bloody well do.

"When the abscess eventually bursts, the toxic shock would probably kill you. But the tapeworm heads get shot around the body, forming more and more abscesses. Very, very nasty."

Oh my God - the bus journey. How did I survive that battering…

I've never been a big patter of dogs - certainly not the mangy mutts I'd encountered on my travels, and definitely not the Kathmandu street brutes. I tried to think back. I was in a village in central Turkey once during the Sacrifice Feast, which you want to steer clear of, if you're a sheep. It's a religious festival involving the slaughter of our tasty wooly friends to commemorate the story of the Prophet Ibrahim, who demonstrated an incredible obedience to God by agreeing to sacrifice his son. God must've thought even he'd gone too far by requesting such an extreme show of loyalty, so he sent a relieved Ibrahim a ram to be slaughtered instead.

During the festival, the village streets were running with sheep blood, and I presume the dogs were dancing with orgiastic joy in the red rivers that flowed over the cobbles. And maybe they would've risked a kick in the sides just to bury their greedy snouts in the freshly slaughtered carcasses. And maybe I brushed my hands against a delirious dog a few days after it'd got lucky. So there was a possibility - but that was only a couple of years before I went to India. Probably not enough time to grow my abscesses.

Then I remembered something else. Cairo, 1982: I was nineteen - five years before I became ill. I was there with Alan, a boy from Stockport. We'd been kicked off a kibbutz in Israel for vodka related incidents, and had taken a bus across to Egypt. I got to see the pyramids at last, and Tutankhamun's tomb in the Valley of the Kings - my boyhood dream. But the next bit could've been the start of my nightmare. We were in Cairo during Ramadan, sitting with some men in a dirty backstreet as they ate sheep eyes from a bowl. They laughed at our scrunched up faces as they dropped the round balls into their mouths and munched them to a pulp. A pack of friendly dogs were roaming around with them, which I'm sure I can remember pushing away with my hands.

With their "Mmm, these are delicious" faces, the happy Egyptians convinced me to eat a sheep's eye. It was disgusting - like eating a warm, firm, animal-tasting jelly. I thought I felt the aqueous humour squirt out, and I was nearly ill there and then. Alan never had one.

That night stuck in my mind. Could one of the dogs have been around when those sheep were slaughtered? It fit, time-wise, with when I got ill...

I knew it was a bad idea at the time.

So I wasn't hexed after all, and would've exploded even if I hadn't returned to India with Sean, possibly in the dog food aisle in the Tesco warehouse as Phil Collins was singing 'One More Night' on the local radio, which would've completely ruined my story.

Apart from the case of the missing gallbladder, I've been consistently healthy in the thirty years since it all happened. I've never been back to

India or Nepal, though I do quite fancy it lately.

I used to wonder where the horses and the giant hand had disappeared to. Were they just for me? Or do they scour the globe looking for extremely deranged, terrified, almost dead souls to taunt on their way out? Or were they there to stop me from dying? Because I would've gone for sure, if they'd have been more welcoming. Either way, I've since travelled many miles to put them off my trail. And I used to wonder where all that pain disappeared to. Does it leave a memory behind in the body - surely it can't just vanish into nothing?

These days my only lasting hangover from the whole experience is the occasional nightmare. When it happens, I'm suddenly in that hut up on the trek again where I crawled around in the dark after climbing the stairs up from the rope bridge, with something hideously evil present in the room. I'll feel something ominous coming on even before I fall asleep - something just outside my vision, and I've no way of stopping it.

My wife Therese has to shake me awake, if I can manage to make a sound, and the horror lasts for a couple of hours, as I sit there with the light on, thinking of horses and hands and kiwi fruit. And my mum and dad.

But I can live with that.

* * * * * *

Sean Lock went on to become one of the UK's top comedians and TV personalities. We've had a few great trips together since India, but nothing nearly as dramatic. We travelled across America to celebrate him winning the Perrier Comedy Award in 2000; through central Australia when he played at the Adelaide Festival in the late nineties, and more recently, along the Great Ocean Road of Victoria and South Australia. I had a superb night out with him at the QI club in Oxford, drinking whiskies and ale under the giant pictures on the wall of all the comedy stars from the show - Sean, Stephen Fry, Alan Davies - whilst some American student was belting out Scott Joplin rags on the honky tonk piano in the corner. The following week he was best man at my wedding to my Australian wife, Therese.

When we see each other, we still remember moments that we'd completely forgotten from that particular trip to the Himalayas in 1986. Our unspoken goal is always to somehow reduce ourselves to the hysterical state of the two young lads on the donkey trek. We usually manage this, but it takes time.

Gareth married and settled in New Zealand, had three great kids, occasionally rides and crashes motorbikes and makes fantastic 3D models and sets for anyone that will cross his palm with silver.

Craig carried on travelling; eventually settling in Miami, and now has an American accent.

I settled in Sydney, where I live with my wife and our boy. I make cartoons and music, still twang away at the guitar, and have added the banjo to my noise making endeavours. I also make motorbike and car art for my T-shirts and clothing company Revs And Threads, and can sometimes be found on a Saturday morning at my market stall across the road from where I first lived here with Gareth and Leigh in Kings Cross. The one-legged man is long gone, as are most of the street girls and the mayhem that made the place so wild in the late eighties and nineties. It's now a very pleasant suburb. I think I prefer it the way it was.

Acknowledgements

I'd like to thank the many people that have helped steer me to finally get this story out of my head and onto paper. My sisters, Amanda and Alison, helped fill in some gaps from the darker moments in the book. My brother Eric gave me a biro and told me to get on with it.

Edrie Cullen provided useful advice in the early stage of writing.

Sean encouraged me to make this book the best it could be (it's pretty daunting to be told by a top comedian: "You can make this a lot funnier, Mark. I know you can.")

Rose Lock, in the role of editor, has done much more than that. She pushed me to bring the episodes alive, and helped turn what was once just a great anecdote into what I hope is a great read.

My friend Hamish Gilbert offered (well, I asked) to design the cover, and I love what he came up with.

Lisa Petroff offered her design skills (I asked her, too) for help in typesetting the manuscript.

Stuart Spence provided his photography skills (yep, asked him too).

Jamie Sterckx has been most generous in helping to finance this book.

Myrna Van Pelt, my new friend - and now my publicist - has been invaluable in raising the bar, the finances and the wine glass.

But most of my thanks go to my gorgeous wife Therese, who has allowed me the time and space to struggle through the many stages of writing. We've moved house twice since I started. She has the patience, and the name, of a saint.

I would love to thank my mum and dad, but sadly, you can't have everything you want.

But I'm still going to do it: thanks Mum and Dad.

Sydney,
November 2016

About the Author

Mark Giblin is a guitar playing, song writing, banjo twanging, ale loving, cartoon making, motorbike riding Englishman living near a bay in Sydney, Australia, that is unswimmable due to a high shark population.

This is his first book. Some things take time...

Photo by Stuart Spence.

Thank you for reading

As this is a self-published work, any reviews at Amazon or the sites below will be most welcome.

www.speedbumphimalayas.com
www.goodreads.com
www.facebook/speedbumphimalayas

Made in the USA
Middletown, DE
09 December 2018